# THE
# AMERICAN PRESIDENCY
*Leadership, Partisanship, and*
*Popularity*

In the challenging, revolutionary Sixties, the American Presidency will demand more than ringing manifestoes issued from the rear of the battle. It will demand that the President place himself in the very thick of the fight, that he care passionately about the fate of the people he heads, that he be willing to serve them at the risk of incurring their momentary displeasure. . . .

No President, it seems to me, can escape politics. He has not only been chosen by the nation—he has been chosen by his Party. And if he insists that he is "President of all the people" and should, therefore, offend none of them—if he blurs the issues and differences between the parties—if he neglects the party machinery and avoids his party's leadership—then he has not only weakened the political party . . . he has dealt a blow to the democratic process itself.

—JOHN F. KENNEDY

# THE
# AMERICAN
# PRESIDENCY

*Leadership, Partisanship, and
Popularity*

## STUART GERRY BROWN

THE MACMILLAN COMPANY, *New York*
COLLIER-MACMILLAN LIMITED, London

*Second Printing 1966*

Designed by KAYUM SUKRY

*Library of Congress catalog card number: 66–16092*

THE MACMILLAN COMPANY, NEW YORK

COLLIER-MACMILLAN CANADA, LTD., TORONTO, ONTARIO

*Printed in the United States of America*

# Preface

So THAT there will be no misunderstanding, I should like to say at once that there is no attempt here at providing a rounded account of the Presidency of the United States. That task has been well performed by such writers as Harold Laski, Sidney Hyman, and Clinton Rossiter. Here there is no account either of the structure of the executive department over which the President presides nor of the functions he performs. There is a good deal of history, but it is incidental to the main purpose, not that purpose itself. What I have tried to do is simply to illuminate the process of presidential leadership from the perspective of presidential popularity. The method is to focus upon examples, or cases, in which popular Presidents have or have not made important decisions, have or have not conducted effective policies. But the instances are highly selective, and there is no pretense to political "science." In short, the book is an essay, or series of related essays, on the connections between presidential popularity and presidential leadership.

It has been a long time in the making, and I have incurred a good many obligations to friends, libraries, foundations, and universities. For yeoman labors in the various stages of research I am indebted to Donald G. Baker, Robert L. Piper, and Eugene Wise. For insights developed in my seminar on the Presidency over the years, I am indebted to many students but particularly to Fred Bartle, Russell Farnen, Frank Gibson, Paul Goodwin, and William A. Riley. Friends and colleagues who have been generous with their time and good advice, either in conversation or in reading portions of the manuscript (or both!), include John Allison, Stephen K. Bailey, Harlan Cleveland, Ralph Ketcham, Max Lerner, Seymour Lutzky, Roscoe C. Martin, V. K.

Menon, Clinton Rossiter, William Siffin, Gregg Sinclair, and the late T. V. Smith.

Like a host of other scholars, I have been impressed once again by the efficiency and courtesy of the people who staff our great libraries. My particular debts are to the New York Public Library, the Library of Congress, the libraries of the universities of Pennsylvania and Hawaii, the Syracuse and Princeton university libraries, and the Research Collections of the East-West Center. I am especially grateful to Mrs. Harriet C. Owsley of the Tennessee State Archives, who helped me to find several useful letters of Jackson, Polk, and Van Buren that seem not to have been previously noticed.

The early stages of the research for this book were assisted by a grant from the Rockefeller Foundation to Syracuse University and resulted in the publication of *The Autobiography of James Monroe* (1959); the research was completed with the aid of a generous grant to Syracuse University by the Alfred P. Sloan Jr. Foundation. The time to write was made possible by a research leave from Syracuse University and an appointment as Senior Scholar at the East-West Center of the University of Hawaii. I am deeply grateful to my friends Chancellor William P. Tolley of Syracuse, President Everett N. Case of the Sloan Foundation, and Ambassador John Allison of the East-West Center. And I should like here to express my appreciation of the privilege of association with my colleagues, both Asian and American, among the scholars of the East-West Center and my gratitude to the staff of the Institute of Advanced Projects for many courtesies.

Finally, I wish to thank my wife, for being a wise counsellor and a tough editor on all my books, but never more than on this one. This book is for her—with love.

*East-West Center*                                    S. G. B.
*Honolulu*
*December 1965*

# Contents

# I

## *Introduction*

If the American Presidency has been more often studied than most of the important leadership positions in the history of the world, there are good reasons for this scrutiny. The President of the United States heads a nation that has been consistently growing in wealth and power for nearly two hundred years, and the office he holds is unique in scope and power. Every aspect of it is interesting; most are of immediate consequence to Americans; some are crucially important to everyone on earth. Both Presidents and private citizens have often pointed out that the powers of the President are probably greater in their span of effectiveness than those of any other man. What he does or does not do with his powers makes up a goodly portion of the history of the modern era. And what he does or does not do is frequently closely related to his popularity.

In this era of widespread and instantaneous communication presidential popularity has taken on immense importance. It was not always so. Presidents John Adams, John Quincy Adams, and Hayes, to name three who were at least moderately effective, were not popular. Nor were Presidents Pierce, Tyler, or Arthur, who were adequate if not distinguished. And, of course, there were others. But in the twentieth century popularity has become increasingly important. Theodore Roosevelt and William Jennings Bryan ran a kind of continuous popularity contest. Taft was regarded with affection. Wilson won fervent admirers, as well as implacable haters, but never commanded a solid majority. Harding and Coolidge were certainly not exciting figures, but in a sense they were throwbacks to the nineteenth century who could reach the Presidency only in the tired aftermath of the Great War. Franklin Roosevelt, Eisenhower, Kennedy, and Lyndon Johnson have all, for one reason or another, been supported by tremendous popular majorities. And the depths of unpopularity to which President Truman descended in the last years of his administration must not obscure the fact that he was the "plucky little guy" so many people honored and loved in 1948.

The personality of the President is, and probably will continue to be, a familiar part of daily American life. In 1964, in fact, there was some feeling that the President and his opponent were too well known, that people were growing cynical about their President because it had become impossible for him to keep a dignified distance from the mass of the people. In the future, it seems safe to guess, the personality and personal lives of Presidents and presidential candidates will be more, not less, closely scrutinized. A man who cannot build and hold personal popularity of one sort or another seems unlikely to have a serious chance to win a major party nomination. And the polls are always available to tell us how his efforts are faring, just as they keep us up to date, like a fever chart, on the President's rating with the public.

It is an interesting question whether his popularity has always been a device available to a popular President to support his leadership. Some have used it consistently, others sparingly. And sometimes it seems not to have been useful at all. The inference must be that as there are different kinds of popularity, so there are different degrees to which it may be useful. In the 1950's liberal journals like the *New Republic* were sharply critical of Eisenhower because he "refused" to invest some of his great "political capital"—his popularity—in pressing for certain of his programs. Federal aid to education was a case in point. But on examination, as we shall see, it does not appear that Eisenhower did in fact have the kind of popularity that could be cashed to bring about federal aid to public schools.

In a perceptive chapter on the President's public prestige, Richard Neustadt observes that there is "rarely . . . any one-to-one relationship between appraisals of a President's popularity in general and responses to his wishes in particular." He cites Eisenhower's failure in 1957 to persuade the governor of Arkansas to let Central High School in Little Rock be peacefully integrated and Truman's inability to persuade the steelworkers' union to return to work in 1952. But are these examples, on examination, really persuasive? In the Eisenhower case, there was reason to suppose that the President's popularity in the South rested in part on the belief that he would *not* press for civil rights, whereas in the Truman instance the devotion of the union to the President was predicated on the belief that he would support them against the companies, not ask them to break a strike. When, that is to say, a one-to-one relationship between popularity and effective leadership does occur, it will have to be in accord with the President's image, not contrary to it. Popular Presidents cannot be expected to use their popularity to achieve objectives contrary to what they are popular for. By the same token, a President may find his popularity not only useful but indispensable when he needs, say, to get Congress to take action that its leadership does not like but the President's majority clearly wishes. Lyndon Johnson's insistence on federal aid to education, in the wake of his election on a platform calling for it, is a case at least as much in point as Eisenhower's failure to press on the same issue.[1]

Careful examination of instances throughout American history in which popular Presidents have or have not relied upon their popularity to make their leadership effective leads to the conclusion that, with some important exceptions, popular *unpartisan* Presidents have been either unable or unwilling to make use of their popularity as a means to leadership, while *partisan* Presidents, again with some important exceptions, have been not only willing but anxious to cash their popularity with their constituents. Unpartisan popularity has often seemed to depend upon inaction; partisan popularity seems to require vigorous action to sustain it.

Thus the practical usefulness of a President's popularity as a means to leadership seems to vary in proportion to its relevance to the purposes for which it might be used. The more divisive the purpose, the more partisan the popularity needed to achieve it; the more widely approved the purpose, the less partisan the kind of popularity that is likely to be effective. But because Presidents cannot have both partisan and unpartisan popularity at once, and because controversial issues and purposes must, among free men, be far more common than shared objectives, the areas of discretion available to popular partisan Presidents—and their potentials for effective leadership—proportionally exceed those of popular unpartisan Presidents.

The instances examined in these studies are drawn, first, to display the two principal kinds of popularity as such and then to see how these fare in matters of constitutional controversy and crisis, in domestic policy, and in foreign affairs. The emphasis throughout is on *what* was done, or not done, and *how* and *why*, not on *whether* it should or should not have been done. If the partisan Presidents come out, on the whole, much better than the unpartisan in such studies, this is because most of the outstanding achievements of the American Presidency have in fact been owing to the leadership of partisan, even highly partisan Presidents. But some important instances display equally that unpartisan leadership may be essential on matters affecting the durability of the Union and that effective presidential leadership is not, in any case, a satisfactory end in itself. It is a process which, depending on the manner and purposes of its use, may be wise or not, courageous or not, firm or not. There is no attempt here to avoid judgments on such things. But the focus of attention is on the process itself, on the intricate relationship between a President's popularity and his power to lead.

# II

# The Politics of
# Presidential Popularity

1. *The dimensions of popularity. Eliminating such Presidents as Harding and Coolidge from consideration* ટ≈ It is probably safe—and not very useful—to say that in some sense every American President is popular or at least *was* popular at the time of his election. In the excitement of a national campaign the opposing candidates have excited followers, one more than the other. Upon the outcome seems to hinge the whole critical future of the country. Under these tense and abnormal conditions both candidates seem both better and worse than they are. Their virtues, as their supporters see them, are of heroic quality; their defects, as their opponents see them, are a genuine danger to the future of the republic. Popularity is thus an immensely important influence upon the public choice on election day, sometimes, no doubt, a decisive influence. But not always; many elections have been decided on issues, or by habit, or even by inertia. Only *after* the election does presidential popularity become central and decisive. As Adlai Stevenson told the Democratic convention of 1952,

More important than winning the election is governing the nation. That is the test of a political party—the acid, final test. When the tumult and the shouting die, when the bands are gone and the lights are dimmed, there is the stark reality of responsibility. . . .

What matters to the republic is what the President can do with the popularity that got him elected—or what he is *willing* to do with it, which may be something quite different.[1]

5

It ought to be easy to say what presidential popularity is, since everyone is familiar with it. Yet it is, upon analysis, anything but easy to judge from such evidence as statistics. The late Charles A. Beard once stated categorically that Warren G. Harding was the most popular of American Presidents. It is hard to see how Beard could have been serious. Harding was elected by an immense margin but surely not because of any personal qualities of Senator Harding. The fact is that he was almost unknown to the general public, which is why he was nominated at the Republican convention. The leading candidates for the Republican nomination, men like Governor Frank Lowden of Illinois and General Leonard Wood, were well known, and, at least in the case of Lowden, their views on the issues well defined. In 1920 it seemed as certain as anything ever can be in politics that the Republican nominee would be elected. The men who controlled the delegates, therefore, wished to make sure that they would also control the nominee and thereafter the President. Thus they rejected the proven leaders and selected Harding precisely because the country did not know him and had, of course, formed no fixed image of him as a public person. His distinguished appearance did the rest.

The outcome, it seems clear enough, had little to do with Harding—or even his opponent, Governor James M. Cox of Ohio; it had everything to do with the abyss of unpopularity into which President Wilson had fallen, and with the postwar settlement. The reaction against Wilsonian idealism, to which Cox and Franklin D. Roosevelt were committed, was overwhelming, and so the boss-picked and boss-shaped candidate became President. But Harding as President made little impression. In foreign affairs, he hid behind the eminent stature—and the distinguished beard—of Charles Evans Hughes; on the domestic side, he dodged behind the unconscionable set of trimmers who nearly brought down his administration. That his successor, Calvin Coolidge, was elected in 1924 by the largest percentage of the two-party vote ever recorded is no measure of either Harding's popularity or Coolidge's. It is the measure of the nation's first, and last, economic wild party. The rejection in 1932 of Herbert Hoover, better known and far more highly respected than Harding or Coolidge, bares the moral of the tale.

At the opposite end of the spectrum is the case of John F. Kennedy. Elected by the closest popular margin in history and carrying what was thought to be the political onus of his Catholicism, Kennedy, in a few short months, achieved higher Gallup Poll ratings than had either Franklin D. Roosevelt or Dwight Eisenhower. And there was no doubt that his popularity was personal: the difference, as measured by Gallup, between Kennedy's personal popularity and the popularity of his program was always substantial. The national grief over Kennedy's tragic death, no doubt much augmented by the circumstances of assassination, was bitter and deep and personal. Harding's death, at about the same stage in his administration, occasioned no more than formal mourning. Lincoln, one of the most hated presidents, was also more deeply mourned than perhaps any other, suggesting that the popularity he had generated was more than a match for the animosity he was unable to dissipate. Garfield and McKinley, two other victims of assassination, do not appear to have been mourned more than perfunctorily, though both were well known and well respected. Americans who were old enough to understand what happened in April, 1945, will never forget the emotional experience of Franklin Roosevelt's death. Many a dedicated Roosevelt hater was heard in those days to lament the passing of a great man, and the tears were seldom of the crocodile variety.

**2.** *The political career of James Monroe from bitter partisan to national father* ৡৈ৶  In earlier times, James Monroe was elected (1816) by an immense margin, but popular participation was limited, and his victory seems to have had little of the personal about it. Yet after his tours of New England in 1817 and of the South and West two years later, he became so much the beloved and even revered figure of the "last of the Founding Fathers" that in 1820 no one could be found to challenge his election to a second term. If feelings were not in fact good during the "Era of Good Feelings," no one thought of blaming the President.

Monroe's effort to win the support of the people (1817, 1819) is worth recalling in some detail, as it was the first such effort

made by an American President. Washington had toured all of
the thirteen original states as a gesture of national unity, but his
effort was on a small scale compared with Monroe's. Monroe
wrote to Jefferson from Plattsburg, New York, that he had expected to make his tour as a "private citizen." But by the time
he reached Baltimore he found that this would be impossible.
"I had," he said, "the alternative, of either returning home, or
complying with the opinion of the public, and immediately I
took the latter course, relying on them to put me forward as fast
as possible, which has been done." At every stop on the journey
through the Middle Atlantic and New England States and then
New York and Ohio, Monroe was swept up by immense crowds.
"In principal towns," he told Jefferson, "the whole population
has been in motion, and in a manner to produce the greatest
degree of excitement possible." "So heavy has been the pressure
on me, that I often feared it would overwhelm me," he told
Madison, underlining, no doubt unintentionally, the contrast
between his own new found popularity and the public disappointment with his predecessor.[2]

Lacking the "advance men" who prepare the way down to the
minutest detail for a modern President or presidential candidate,
Monroe had to guard against delays in one place in the sure
knowledge that they would mean delays further on. "It has been
my constant effort to press forward, well knowing that delay at
any place would produce it elsewhere, & thus retard, far beyond
my wish, my movement, and even beyond what would be proper."

To Richard Rush, Monroe suggested that the newspaper coverage of the tour was inadequate. "You can hardly form a correct
judgment from the papers," he wrote, "tho' they give many details of the obstacles I have had to encounter and surmount in
my tour. They have been very great." When he wrote this, Monroe was probably thinking less of the political character of the
news reporting of his trip than of sheer physical inconvenience.
The day of the professional coverage of news had not, of course,
yet arrived. But it is worth noting, from the vantage point of
historical perspective, that the opportunity to make political
capital was what frankly appealed to the press. The *National
Intelligencer*, the only national paper at the time, quoted the
*Boston Chronicle and Patriot* as follows:

The introduction of the President of the United States into the town of Boston, was a spectacle truly magnificent. It was a triumph of Republican principles and feelings over all opposing sentiments, and softened political asperity is indeed wonderful. It was not a little astonishing to see the most determined opposers of the late administration vieing with each other, as well as its firm and steadfast supporters, in exhibitions of respect and attention, while with apparent united affections, the first officer of the nation was made welcome to the capital of New England.

This might have been fair enough crowing for an organ of the President's party, if it had been an editorial. But it was not an editorial; it was a "news" column, and it did not stop there:

This spontaneous effusion of joy, and in a particular manner the pacific overtures of the opposition to republican principles, let us accept as the sincere peace offerings of men who have long led their followers through mazes of error and delusion. This homage, paid at the shrine of liberty, let us receive as an honest pledge, that hostility to our constituted authorities and laws will in future cease. If, in the present instance, the opposition have become politically virtuous from necessity, this display of virtue will still be productive of great good. It will evince to our southern and western brethren, that republicanism is not extinct in Massachusetts. This exhibition of free men will also convince those who have been blind followers of the blind, that error is unstable, and that truth will eventually prevail.[3]

If it is hard to believe that Federalists who only a few years before had been prepared to break up the Union were suddenly swayed to pledge allegiance not only to the flag but to the Republican Party and President Monroe, it is nevertheless certain that these demonstrative outpourings did take place. Monroe himself saw in what was happening the surrender of the Federalists. "The most distinguished in the opposition in private life," he wrote Madison, "seemed to seize the opportunity which my journey afforded them . . . to get back with the great family of the Union, & most of the leaders have held language of the same kind." The reason for this, he thought, was "a conviction, that they had suffer'd in their character, by their conduct in the late war, and a desire to show that unfavorable opinions and as they thought, unjust, had been form'd in regard to their views and principles."[4]

The demonstrations had a soothing effect on Monroe's own partisanship. From the beginnings of government under the Constitution he had been in the thick of the party battles. From the time of his ill-fated mission to France in 1794, when he was exploited by the Washington Administration in an effort to forestall French annoyance with the Jay Treaty, Monroe had, in fact, been among the most bitterly partisan of all the Republican followers of Jefferson. But at the first signs of disengagement he seemed willing to forgive and to forget. As his triumphal tour progressed, he was at every stop presented with an address of welcome and patriotic sentiment. He reciprocated with words of appropriate sentiment. His remarks were the first itinerant political speeches in American presidential history. It was not surprising that their tone should be conciliatory. But as he rang the changes on national unity and patriotism, he seemed to generate a nonpartisan enthusiasm of his own. At Kennebunk in Maine, for example, he told the audience, "the further I advance in my progress in the country, the more I perceive that we are all Americans—that we compose but one family—that our republican institutions will be supported and perpetuated by the united zeal and patriotism of all." Carried away by his new vision, the old political infighter went on, "nothing could give me greater satisfaction than to behold a perfect union among ourselves—an union, . . . which . . . is all we can ever want to make us powerful and respected."5

Monroe was approaching sixty, after a lifetime of almost continuous public service, beginning with heroic fighting in the Revolution and close association with Washington. His career in public affairs had been launched under the joint auspices of Jefferson and Washington. But as the two great men came to political parting in the 1790's, Monroe had gone with Jefferson. Washington, indeed, was still President when Monroe had been recalled "in disgrace" from Paris in 1796, and in his righteous anger the young diplomat had not feared to denounce the President for listening to unscrupulous advisers. The Republican Party, he then thought, must organize to save the inheritance of the Revolution and, indeed, the nation itself. Now, twenty years later, he was pleading for precisely the patriotism and disinterested dedication to national unity that had animated Washington and led him to plead, almost desperately, with Jefferson and Hamilton to work together. Monroe was effectively emulating the idol of his youth in playing down political partisanship. And there is no doubt that he was conjuring up once more in the minds of the people of New England the mystique of the Revolution and the first dawn of nationhood. In this new dawning Monroe himself had become the father of his country.

In 1819 he toured the South and West with similar acclaim and similar demonstrations of national unity. Again he received formal addresses of respect, welcome, and even veneration. His replies, however, were more personal on this second tour. It was as though, having established himself as the patriarchal voice of the heroic days, as the father image of the nation, he wished to make his own personality more directly felt. At Louisville, for example, his speech contained these sentiments:

> The generous review, which you have taken, and the approbation you have expressed, of my conduct in the various stations with which I have been honored by my country is particularly gratifying to me. Knowing well that the trust which I now hold, the hightest recognized by the Constitution—was conferred on me in consequence of the favorable opinion entertained of my conduct in other stations, I should consider myself among the most unworthy of men if I did not meet by a like conduct, in this office, the just expectation of my fellow citizens. Professions count for nothing. The evidence before you will I trust inspire you with confidence that my life will be consistent; that the principles for which I contended in my earliest youth, with many who are now present, and the jealous attachment which I have shown to the rights and interests of my country in every transaction in which I have been engaged, will never cease to gender and animate my conduct.

Thus the President reviewed his career, not failing to stress his part in the Revolution nor his devotion to its principles. The national symbol whom the people had assembled to venerate was also a living human being with a past of which he was proud as well as a present in "the highest station." There was no hint of bad taste. The appropriate tone of humility was there, but so was the careful reminder that the speaker deserved well of his fellow citizens.[6]

Despite his unprecedented opportunity to talk directly with

the people, Monroe never referred, even in passing, to the issues of the day. There was nothing in these speeches to suggest that the President had a program for the nation, that he was interested in bills before the Congress, or even that he wanted popular support for his foreign policy. Always he stressed unexceptionable "republican principles" and the revolutionary inheritance. The message was unity, not action. Thus the President underlined his symbolic role in the nation's era of nascent nationalism without risking the disapproval of any interest group or faction. He made himself personally known, thereby touching new generations with something of the glamor of the revolutionary age. They had seen and heard one of the Founding Fathers, not the less affecting because he was the last to hold the Presidency. No President thereafter could hope to be approved and revered by so nearly unanimous a constituency.

But this was a kind of popularity others were to emulate. Grant, for a brief moment in the wake of the Civil War and the confusion and disillusionment of Johnson's impeachment, and Eisenhower, for nearly two terms, sought with considerable success to act as the symbol of national unity and hold the respect and affection of the whole country by avoiding the divisive issues.

An essential step to presidential popularity of this nonpartisan sort is that the President, as candidate, appear to be reluctant; the honor must be thrust upon him. If he seem anxious, he immediately risks a division of opinion and an outcropping of the common prejudice against ambitious men and, above all, against "politics." The politics of unpartisan popularity is thus transcendently a politics of antipolitics. For Monroe this was a peculiarly difficult kind of politics to practice because he had for so long been identified with the fortunes of one party. Doubtless he could not have succeeded at all had it not been for his effective and unique role in the War of 1812, when, at a time when American fortunes were lowest, he took over the War Department, in addition to State, and brought some order into administrative chaos. Nor could he have successfully filled the role of national father except in the wake of an unpopular war, when the people were anxious to get on with the business of developing the country and pursuing their individual happiness. It is perhaps not accidental that something of the same state of affairs prevailed at the moment when Ulysses Grant emerged as national hero and again at the critical moment of Dwight Eisenhower's dramatic decision to answer the call to larger duty in 1952.

**3.** *How Grant maintained his role of national hero while winning an intensely partisan nomination* ❧ Grant was notoriously reluctant and notoriously nonpolitical in the years just preceding his nomination in 1868. At least so he contrived to let it appear. For the fact is that Grant was ambitious for the Presidency even before the assassination of Lincoln. All through the Johnson Administration he conducted himself with primary attention to the politics of his unpartisan popularity. That he succeeded remarkably is attested by the repeated informal proffer of the Democratic nomination as well as the Republican. As early as November, 1867, astute Ohio Senator John Sherman was privately telling his brother, the general, that Grant "is inevitably the candidate." As he saw it, Grant's tactic was to "allow himself to drift into a position where he can't decline if he would." Sherman was "sure he don't want to decline." Prophetically Sherman observed that "Chase is better for the country and for Grant himself." But Grant did not think so.[7]

With the war over and Lincoln gone, President Andrew Johnson relied heavily on Grant to manage the military establishment and direct the military side of reconstruction in the South. It was a difficult position, certainly. Secretary Edwin M. Stanton was an open opponent of the President, who could not dismiss him because the Radical Republican majority in Congress had put through the Tenure of Office Act requiring Senate consent to dismissals. The General of the Army was thus thrust between his civilian boss and the commander-in-chief. Grant was, on the broader stage, placed also between the Radicals, who were pushing harsh reconstruction policies, and the moderates, led by the President, who were for binding up the nation's wounds.

For Grant there was the additional complication that as early as 1864 there had been talk of him for the Presidency. The adulation that had begun in that year increased with the Union victory and remained at an unprecedented peak throughout the whole of Johnson's term. Showered with gifts and public addresses of praise as no American had ever been before, pressed on every side to give his voice or his support to particular groups and interests, Grant concluded that silence was the wise course. He would do his duty, with formal obedience to the commander-in-chief and official respect for the Secretary of War, and he would "keep out of politics."

It was a fortunate choice for his ambitions; it was also an honest one, for there is no reason to believe that Grant had, by 1865, developed any strong political convictions. For him the politics of popularity was a politics of silence. But he took care to cultivate socially anyone and everyone of any influence in Washington. Gideon Welles, the pungent diarist who was Secretary of the Navy, frequently noted the receptions Grant gave to his admirers. At first these were by invitation, but there were so many gate-crashers that Grant simply adopted the practice of announcing in the newspapers that he and Mrs. Grant would be at home to their friends on such-and-such an evening. Welles gives this account of the Grants' last reception of the season in 1866:

. . . there was present not only a numerous but a miscellaneous company of contradictions. There had been some pre-understanding on the part of the Radicals, or a portion of them, to attend and to appropriate General Grant, or at least his name and influence, to themselves. But most unexpectedly to them, as I confess it was to me, the President and his two daughters appeared early, and Montgomery Blair and some of his ladies were also on hand. There came also Alexander H. Stephens, Vice President of the late Confederacy, so called. When, therefore, Thad Stevens, Trumbull, and others, not exactly homogeneous though now acting together, came in, they were evidently astonished and amazed.

Ben Perley Poore, the inveterate Washington observer, recollected that Grant's "receptions at his home on Minnesota Row were the social features of Washington. Cabinet officers, diplomatists, Judges, Congressmen, officers of the Army and Navy, residents, and the strangers within their gates made up the throng." Thus almost everyone of any consequence was socially indebted to General Grant. And no one was offended by being excluded.[8]

That Grant's feelings about the South, about reconstruction, and even about slavery were moderate cannot be doubted. At the outset of the war he was much less anxious to return to service to fight the Confederacy than he was to obtain what he thought would be suitable rank and assignment. There is little evidence that his feelings ever became deeply engaged in the issues being fought over. His magnanimous treatment of Lee at Appomattox was appropriate not only to the tone that Lincoln, his commander-in-chief, wished to adopt, but to Grant's own predisposition. In the summer of 1865 President Johnson sent him on a tour of the South to see what should be done to hasten the rebuilding of the war-torn areas and to gauge the attitude of the people and their leaders. His report was conciliatory. He was for a light touch on the reins of power and early rehabilitation of the leading men, both military and civilian. Indeed, at the time the report was submitted, the "moderate" President was himself for a degree of punishment beyond anything suggested by Grant.

But soon enough Grant saw that the President was not master in his house. The General of the Army would have to go to Congress, rather than the President, for authority and money if he were to carry on a program that was, in his estimate, good for the Army and adequate to carry out the new laws. Because the Radicals in Congress had maneuvered themselves into the positions of power, Grant resolved to make no enemies among them if he could help it. Thus when Johnson almost literally dragooned him into going on a political junket into the West, as a prize exhibit in the President's party, Grant was bitter. He went, but he took every opportunity to underline his nonpolitical military status; on the pretext that he was needed at the War Department, he left the train before the tour was completed. If, as was widely rumored, he more than once drank too much during that ill-fated tour, his political misery makes his reliance upon whiskey at least understandable.

When Johnson was impeached, Grant was caught directly between the Congressional and the Executive fires. Johnson, having finally defied Congress by dismissing Stanton, had persuaded Grant, as a matter of patriotic duty, to become Secretary of War *ad interim.* Thus Grant was technically a member of the Administration. But he disassociated himself as much as he could by refusing to use the War Department offices and by repeatedly announcing his impartiality. He was not, in fact, impartial. His testimony in the impeachment proceedings could quite possibly have vindicated the President. But he did not take the opportunity; instead, he confined himself to perfunctory answers to unavoidable questions. He continued to give the appearance of nonpartisanship, but he did the work of the Radicals.

By the spring of 1868, Grant had seen that he could not obtain the Republican nomination unless the Radicals wanted him. Reconstruction, under his own direction, had made the Democratic nomination practically useless by disfranchising almost all the Southern Democrats. To be President it was necessary to be nominated by the Republicans; to be nominated by the Republicans it was necessary to please the Radicals; to please the Radicals one could not go to the defense of Andrew Johnson. In this negative way Grant managed to ingratiate himself with the Radicals without losing his public reputation for nonpartisanship. As the clamor for his nomination grew, reluctance remained his constant posture. When public endorsements were followed by the action of the Republican Convention itself, the General could go before the people as their best hope of rising out of the welter created by the "battle of Washington."

James G. Blaine, battle-scarred veteran of Washington and Republican politics, looking back on the moment of Grant's elevation to the Presidency, had this to say about the General's popularity:

The enthusiasm for General Grant was due to something more than the mere fact that he was the chief hero of the war. It rested upon broader ground than popular gratitude for his military services—great as that sentiment was. During the conflict between Congress and the President, General Grant had been placed in a trying position, and he had borne himself with a discretion and dignity which deepened the popular confidence in his sound judgment and his tact. The people felt that besides the great qualities he had displayed in war, he was peculiarly fitted to lead in restoring peace and the reign of law.

Blaine was right. That Grant had in fact no such ability and, indeed, no such character, was for the moment irrelevant. The people thought he had—except for dyspeptic young Henry Adams—and popular favor was what was needed to make him

President. Popularity he had earned in the war. His skill in the politics of nonpartisanship had placed him on the loftiest eminence.⁹

**4.** *The parallel between Grant and Eisenhower, its extent and its limits. Eisenhower reflects the hopes of his country-men ౭౿* A Bill Mauldin cartoon of the 1950's suggests the remarkable, if limited, parallel between Grant and Dwight D. Eisenhower. It shows "Ike" seated at his desk looking, utterly disconsolate, at papers labeled with all the insoluble problems of the Cold War. Behind him stands the ghostly figure of Grant, in uniform, with a benign smile upon his lips and a hand on Eisenhower's shoulder. The caption is "A Tough Job, Eh, Soldier?" It was indeed a tough job, and Eisenhower went into it reluctantly. But like Grant, he had an immense popular backing.

The parallel between Grant and Eisenhower is a parallel of personal quality and conception of the Presidency, not a parallel of political issues faced. It is a parallel of prominence, not of leadership. It was fashionable among some Democrats of the 1950's to compare the two West Point presidents in very direct terms, to the belittling of both. But this was partisan polemics, not sober historical judgment. On any showing, Eisenhower's achievement, disappointing though it may have been, was far more substantial than Grant's. But the similarities in popularity, in approach to the Presidency, in the "nonpolitical" tactics of politics, and in the circumstances that made their emergence as national leaders possible, are all striking.

Like Grant, Eisenhower came from a long career in the Army; like Grant, he was a bona fide hero of a great war; like Grant, he was approached by Democrats as well as Republicans; like Grant, he firmly declined on the first approach; like Grant, he overcame his reluctance when a military man seemed to many to be needed; like Grant, he turned out to be drawn to the men of wealth and influence who controlled the Republican Party. Like Grant, again, he was careful to offend as few molders of opinion as possible, while ingratiating himself with those who actually controlled the apparatus of nomination. Finally, like Grant,

Eisenhower was seldom if ever blamed by the public for the untoward events of his administration.[10]

But, transcending Grant's achievement, Dwight Eisenhower succeeded remarkably in maintaining over the years the image of unpartisanship. He conveyed to the people the sense of an alliance with them against the "politicians," a notion the people themselves had conjured out of his great war record, his habitual appeal to moral principles, and his nearly irresistible geniality.

When Eisenhower was first mentioned for the Presidency, he was basking in the glow of the victory in Europe. Whether, in 1945, President Harry S. Truman in fact offered "Ike" the nomination for 1948, as Eisenhower insists, or whether he was simply using hyperbolic language to express the nation's appreciation of the General's contribution to victory, as Truman insists, will never, of course, be known. But regardless of what was actually said in that mysterious conversation between the President and the Supreme Commander for Europe, there is no doubt at all that Eisenhower's name was presently in the forefront of political speculation and remained there until he became a candidate seven years later. "Ike" was a "natural" for party leaders in search of a candidate who could win. He had no political record, hence no personal political enemies, and no group of citizens had been alienated by his views. The whole nation, indeed the whole world, looked upon him with admiration and gratitude for his performance in leading the Allied forces to victory over Mussolini and Hitler. His visit to Moscow and his friendship with Soviet Marshal Zhukov seemed to herald an era of cooperation and hope between the West and the once-hated Soviet Communists of Joseph Stalin. By 1948, when Eisenhower had retired from the Army to become president of Columbia University, a number of leading Republicans were prepared to discard Governor Thomas E. Dewey of New York, defeated in 1944, if they could replace him with Eisenhower. Their campaign reached such proportions that Eisenhower was forced to make a solemn declaration that he was not available. This, with the leverage Dewey still commanded in the Party, was sufficient.[11]

But on the Democratic side a similar movement was presently launched. Liberals and one-time New Dealers, comparing Harry S. Truman with Franklin Roosevelt, found the President wanting. For his part, Truman had dropped enough liberals and New Dealers from the government and brought in enough conservatives and anomalous cronies to show clearly his intention to be independent of the old Roosevelt coterie. The liberal Democrats prepared to "draft" Eisenhower. Leaders in the movement, like Franklin D. Roosevelt Jr. and Adolf A. Berle Jr., went about the country asserting that Eisenhower had been trusted by F.D.R. and must therefore be a liberal, even though there was no record to prove it. As the movement grew, it was presently joined by Democratic conservatives who were just as sure that Eisenhower was a conservative. Southerners like Senators Lister Hill and John Sparkman of Alabama and Northerners like Mayor Frank Hague of Jersey City formed an uneasy coalition with their traditional intraparty enemies of Americans for Democratic Action. When hard news indicated that there would be solid blocs of delegates for Eisenhower at the Democratic Convention and even that he might just possibly nose out Truman, the General decided that it was time to speak out. He was careful not to make a "Sherman statement" ("If nominated I will not run; if elected I will not serve."), but he stated his unavailability categorically. He was convinced, he said, that a lifelong military man ought not to offer himself for political office in the absence of "overriding" considerations. The needs of dissident Democrats for a stick with which to beat Harry Truman did not constitute such an overriding consideration. Thus ended the Eisenhower boom of 1948.

But the General, recalled after the formation of NATO to serve in Paris as Commander of Allied Forces in Europe, kept his eye on developments at home. Republican leaders kept their eyes on him—and kept his name in the paper as a possible candidate in 1952. Approaches by various Republican leaders, however, only determined the fact that he was serious about refusing a nomination unless there were "overriding" considerations.

What such considerations might be began to appear after the outbreak of the Korean War in 1950. Although Eisenhower deplored the war as a failure of the great powers to accommodate their differences, he had no doubt that President Truman was right in giving all support to South Korea once the North Korean Communists had invaded. Senator Robert A. Taft of Ohio, the leading candidate for the Republican nomination in 1952 and certainly the best-loved member of the party, was an outspoken critic of the war and of Truman's policy. Indeed, Taft was cautiously reviving the characteristic prewar isolationism of rural middle-western Republicans. He spoke caustically of the United Nations and deplored American involvement in Europe. To the General in Paris these were disturbing views. Ineptness on the part of the Administration was one thing, and not, of course, a good thing, he thought. But a return to isolationism was quite another thing, and a worse thing. By 1951 Eisenhower was confiding to intimate personal friends a considerable anxiety about the future. If Taft were nominated, he might well be defeated; thus the worn-out and overconfident Democrats would be given a new charter to continue on what he considered their stumbling course. But things would be even worse if Taft were elected, because there would then be the danger of a utopian attempt to repeal the past instead of making every effort to secure the peace through international cooperation and collective security. Eisenhower had reluctantly answered President Truman's summons to head the NATO forces because he believed in NATO and in the United Nations. How could he now stand by to see these structures endangered, not so much by attacks from the natural enemy as from mistaken policies in his own country?

In the winter of 1951–52 these considerations, pressed upon him by distinguished internationalists of the Republican Party— Henry Cabot Lodge, Governor Dewey, Paul Hoffman, John J. McCloy, John Foster Dulles—at last appeared to him "overriding." Senator Lodge, as emissary for the Eisenhower group, went to Paris to obtain an affirmative answer. The Gallup polls, he told the General, showed conclusively that he would not only be the popular candidate in a contest with Taft, but that he would win the election. The opportunity was his, and the duty, to take over the government and set the nation on its proper course. He accepted the "summons," as he called it, and Lodge announced that Eisenhower would resign from NATO and return to campaign against Taft.

In retrospect it appears that 1952 was really "no contest." Eisenhower's confrontation with Taft at the polls in Minnesota, where he won by a write-in vote, was decisive. Once he began to appear before the people, "Ike" was unbeatable. The Republican organization men, devoted to Taft as a leader who had stuck with his party and fought for it through all the lean years, were frustrated and angry. They determined to fight it out at the convention. And when they went down, it was with bitter prophecies of disaster for traditional Republicanism.

But such was not the case with the rank and file. Eisenhower charmed them, and he charmed the "independents," too. As for the Democrats, they were badly split over civil rights; many were disillusioned by the revelation of corruption in the Administration; others were dismayed by charges of infiltration of Communists. Most Americans, regardless of party, were sick of the stalemate that had come about in Korea, where, it seemed, Americans were dying only to hold a mythical line in a faraway and little-known corner of the world. The General, by promising to replace corruption with "woodshed honesty," and inflation with a "sound dollar," to root out the Communists, and to bring an end to "bumbling and stumbling" in Korea, appealed to all segments of American life. He was careful never to attack Democrats as such but only the Administration. He spoke not at all of civil rights and thus persuaded many Southerners that he was a better hope for the Southern Democracy than was the Democratic Party itself. If trade union leaders expressed their doubts of a man who had done nothing and said nothing for labor, rank and file unionists, and especially their wives, were no less attracted by Eisenhower's campaign for peace and a sound dollar than were farmers and businessmen.

That the Democratic candidate, Governor Adlai E. Stevenson of Illinois, was a man of remarkable cultivation, rich experience in administration and international affairs, and one of the most effective and appealing orators in American history, roused millions of people to a new sense of democratic discipline and responsibility. But the record of the Truman Administration, not then to be seen in perspective, was a handicap perhaps no one could have overcome in the face of the General's nonpartisan popularity. When, in mid-October, Eisenhower climaxed his campaign with his pledge to "forego the diversions of politics" and go instead to Korea, the contest was all over. Stevenson received the largest vote that had ever been accorded a losing candidate, but he was swamped by the largest vote that had ever been accorded a winner.

Dwight Eisenhower came to the Presidency with the good will, even the affection, of a great majority of Americans. He had vigorously attacked the "Administration" for an assortment of sins, some heinous, some merely venal. But all of them, he suggested, arose from the infection of politics. He treated politics as a kind of disease from which he hoped to immunize the country. Instead he would take the people on a "crusade." As he had promised the Republican Convention, he had swept "from office an Administration which has fastened on every one of us the wastefulness, the arrogance and corruption in high places, the heavy burdens and anxieties which are the bitter fruit of a party too long in power." If elected, he had said, he would "give to our country a program of progressive policies drawn from our finest Republican traditions"; he would "unite us wherever we had been divided," and he "would build a sure foundation for sound prosperity for all here at home and for a just and sure peace throughout the world." With such a program no one would be alienated. With such a President, everyone would be hopeful.[12]

Four years later, despite a record mainly noteworthy for inertia, except that the war in Korea had been brought to armistice, and in the midst of a warlike crisis in the Middle East, a great majority was still hopeful. Indeed, many more were hopeful enough to vote for "Ike" than had been in 1952. In both elections Eisenhower carried traditionally Democratic Southern states. If this was to be expected because of his sidestepping of civil rights, the Democrats could find no similar excuse for Eisenhower's margins in many large cities and for the great inroads he made in such Democratic strongholds as New York and Chicago. In 1952, as the follow-up studies of scholars showed, Eisenhower had significant if not majority support in every section of the country and in every social group except Northern big-city Negroes; in 1956, his margin among all groups increased, and he won a larger share of the Negro vote.[13]

In modern times there has been no parallel to such breadth of popularity. Nor has any public figure so consistently sustained a favorable image. Political psychologists concluded that the nation was looking for a "father," and "Ike" filled the role. Like

Monroe, in an earlier era, he lived on a plane of eminence un-
challengeable by any "politician." He could not be, and was not,
held responsible for the errors or failures of his administration.
Though Theodore Roosevelt had presumably established fifty
years before the principle of presidential responsibility for the
national welfare, Eisenhower was hardly more blamed for the
repeated economic recessions that tainted American prosperity
during his administration than Monroe was blamed for the Panic
of 1819. To most Americans the President seemed somehow unrelated to such things. The Secretary of the Treasury, or of
Agriculture, or of the Interior, or even the attractive lady who
had charge of Health, Education, and Welfare, were proper tar-
gets for criticism when things went wrong at home. The Secretary
of State, John Foster Dulles, willingly took upon his broad
shoulders the responsibility for foreign policy, including the
crushing burden of blame that goes with "cold war" frustration.
But the President not only remained unscathed; he seemed to be
more successful and better liked and trusted with every failure of
omission or commission. His heart attack and his dangerous bout
with ileitis might have been expected to testify that the President
could not any longer give full time to his job—that, indeed, he
should retire. But, on the contrary, these handicaps seemed only
to endear him the more to a people who felt better when he was
in the White House—or even on the golf course!

If Eisenhower's popularity rose when he met with Khrushchev
at Geneva or when he sponsored the internationalization of
atomic energy for peaceful purposes, there were few corresponding drops. His ratings were little affected by the Dixon-Yates
scandal, for example, or by repeated recessions, or by the collapse
of American policy at Suez. The disillusionment of the Southern
segregationists in 1957, when Eisenhower sent troops into Little
Rock to restore order and maintain law, was soon followed by
the realization that, in explaining his action to the nation, the
President had been careful not to endorse desegregation. He had
only upheld the law as his constitutional duty. Gallup polls presently showed the President's popularity once more on the rise in
the South.

In the late stages of his administration, Eisenhower's popularity ratings did indeed fall somewhat. But this may well be

accounted for by his entrance into partisan politics to support the intensely partisan Richard Nixon to be his successor. Nixon's popularity, such as it was, had nothing of the quality of cutting across the lines of party and interest that always characterized Eisenhower's. Nor could he claim a place of affection in the national heart. Eisenhower may have jeopardized momentarily his own public standing by his espousal of Nixon. But not for long. The same Gallup polls that showed a nearly dead heat shaping up between Nixon and John Kennedy, showed that Eisenhower himself would have defeated any Democrat in 1960 by a great margin. And so he retired with the flag of his personal popularity as high as ever. The "great crusade" was over—perhaps had never taken place at all—but its leader went marching on in the abiding affection of his countrymen.

5. *The partisan Presidents. Mr. Jefferson, best loved and best hated, placates the opposition as he smothers it*   But by no means all of the most popular American Presidents have been nonpartisan. There is another, quite different sort of popularity—the popularity that may accompany intense partisan leadership; the popularity of a man identified with ideas that divide, not unite, the country; the popularity of a man who makes devoted friends of a majority but earns the sometimes irreconcilable animosity of a minority. Washington, striving to avoid the growth of parties and partisanship, was able to maintain his own popularity but not that of his government. The political realities of American life were revealed in the tense and unremittent struggle between Secretary of the Treasury Alexander Hamilton and Secretary of State Thomas Jefferson: the people were united in respect for the President, but for very good reasons they were partisans of either Hamilton or Jefferson.

That John Adams succeeded Washington in the election of 1796 was an accident of the early electoral process. If there had been a popular election, there is little doubt that Jefferson would have won. Adams was respected by many but disliked by more. Only an Electoral College composed mainly of Federalists appointed by their legislatures and a long step removed from the people, could have elevated Adams to the Presidency. Even under such conditions he defeated Jefferson by only three electoral votes. Jefferson's defeat, Monroe's recall from Paris, the undeclared naval war with France, and the Alien and Sedition Acts brought Jeffersonian Republicans together into something like a national party organization for the contest of 1800. That Jefferson nearly lost out a second time was another accident of the electoral system, which did not distinguish between candidates for President and Vice-President. But there was no doubt in anyone's mind that Jefferson had won the votes of the popular majority, and by a great margin.

Jefferson was a natural partisan, not because he was contentious by temperament—he was reserved and gracious—but because he held strong and clear convictions. As early as 1774, when he was just over thirty, he wrote a penetrating tract on the nature of political freedom and of government by contract that justified revolution and placed its author permanently on the side of liberalism and change. Although the Declaration of Independence was a public document, approved by men of varying political views, it nevertheless expressed the radicalism of the Revolution's moment of truth. Immediately after it was adopted, Jefferson set out to reform the laws of Virginia, hoping that the reforms would spread to the rest of the new nation. He called for the total separation of church and state, the abolition of primogeniture and entail, universal free manhood suffrage with property qualification guaranteed by the distribution of land to the landless, a system of universal free education and a state university, and humanization of the penal laws.[14]

In France in the 1780's Jefferson gave counsel to the revolutionists and approved Lafayette's draft of the "Declaration of the Rights of Man and the Citizen." He criticized the draft American Constitution for having no bill of rights and for removing the executive too far from the people. He advocated strong state governments as bulwarks against a national tyranny. When Hamilton's program assumed the state debts, levied taxes on whiskey, and created a national bank, Jefferson thought he saw the dangers of monarchy and tyranny arising. He sounded the alarm, and the Republican Party was born. Throughout the 1790's he led the fight for what he believed were the aims and purposes of the Revolution against the forces of consolidation and conservatism. When the voters and electors chose between him and Adams in 1800, there was no doubt in their minds as to what he stood for; they knew the meaning of their votes.

Jefferson could not and did not maintain such views without creating intense political and personal animosity. Of all American leaders, not even excepting Lincoln or Franklin D. Roosevelt, Jefferson was assuredly the most hated. In the day before newspaper editors and publishers had agreed to some measure of self-imposed restraint in their treatment of public men, Jefferson was reviled in a manner literally unbelievable by today's standards. The latrine rumor and the vicious whisper of which such men as Franklin Roosevelt were victims in the twentieth century were commonplaces in the public prints of Jefferson's day. It is not edifying to go over the old numbers of the *Connecticut Courant* or the *Columbian Centinel* and read about Jefferson's alleged escapades in the beds of Negro women or his intention to legalize adultery and to elevate murderers to public office. Yet Jefferson was, at the same time, probably more loved by the great majority of the people than any other American.

Once his popularity was converted into victory, President Jefferson was both gracious to his fallen and embittered predecessor and conciliatory to the Federalists. "We are all Republicans; we are all Federalists," he said in his inaugural address. But at the same time he spelled out his principles once more and pledged himself to extend individual liberty wherever he could. Before long, as was certainly predictable in so partisan a politician, his definition of conciliation with Federalists was revealed to be a willingness to retain in office those Federalists who would renounce their Federalism. Jefferson's personal victory clearly was also a party victory; if the party had not been the popular party, its leader could not have won. Although an Eisenhower could win, as in 1956, while his party was losing, Jefferson had to sink or swim with his Republican followers. The very different Republicans of Eisenhower's time often tried in vain to forget their label and attach themselves to the General. Jeffersonian Republicans, united with their leader in principle rather than attached to a symbol of victory, were proud of their partisanship. What Jefferson himself lacked in breadth of popularity he made up in the intensity of the devotion of his followers—devotion both to himself and to his principles, which were inseparable. When such Jeffersonians as John Randolph or Nathaniel Macon believed that Jefferson was too flexible and was deserting Jeffersonian Republicanism, they broke with him and formed their own group—the "Tertium Quids"—to fight against Jefferson for "Jeffersonian principles" as they saw them. One can scarcely imagine a group of dissident supporters of Grant, or Monroe, or Eisenhower forming to fight for the principles their leader had abandoned, and in the name of their leader!

Yet in the midst of political contention, both in and out of his party, Jefferson was triumphantly returned to the White House in 1804 by one of the great majorities in presidential history. And, significantly enough, more citizens could participate in that election than had taken part in any of the preceding contests. Jefferson's popularity was severely strained in his second administration by the unpopularity of his measures to forestall war with Britain, especially the embargo. There is no doubt that he lost friends, not only in the Northeast but in most sections of the country, because he was identified with worsening economic conditions. But he gladly took the responsibility. When circumstances—and public opinion—forced him to capitulate, his position in the party was still strong enough to allow him to dictate the terms of the capitulation. And when he retired, his partisan majority, both in Congress and in the nation, was sufficiently disciplined to enable him to name his successor and see him elected.

6. *Jackson and the fomenting of class antagonism* ᙣ᠉ It was a similar case with Andrew Jackson. A Republican partisan of Jefferson from the time of his entrance into national politics in the Congress of 1796, Jackson reached for a time after 1815, in the wake of his victory at New Orleans, a pinnacle of nonpartisan popularity that might have made him President in 1824 had he been willing to mute his principles and make the necessary arrangements with influential public men. His correspondence with Monroe, after the election of 1816, shows that he looked to that old Revolutionist for sound "nonpartisan" leadership. He ventured to offer advice on the new President's major appointments,

especially the Secretary of War, urging that party considerations be set aside:

> Everything depends upon the selecting of your ministry, both as to yourself and country. In every selection party and party feeling ought to be laid out of view (for now is the time to put them down) by selecting those the most honest, possessing capacity, virtue, and firmness. By this course you steer the national ship to honor and preferment; and yourself to the united plaudits of a happy country—consult no party or party feelings in your choice.

These were Monroe's sentiments exactly, but they seem startling from the man who is credited with developing the "spoils system." What is even more surprising is that in his first years at the national capital Jackson had been shocked by the manner in which President Adams filled public offices with his own supporters. He wrote bitterly to a friend during the debate on the Sedition Law in 1798:

> I have not time to give it [substance of the debate] in detail, but in the argument the policy of the Executive has been taken into view, relative to his removing all those from office who differ with him in politicks and filling those offices with men who subscribe tacitly to all his acts.

The issue, said Jackson, was between

> . . . those that wish to extend Executive influence by discarding from office every man who does not compell himself to think as the Executive does or those that oppose that execrable system.[15]

It is hard to imagine the Jackson of, say, 1832 expressing such sentiments—or tolerating in office anyone who opposed his Administration. But his criticism of Adams was made before parties were accepted as the normal if informal vehicles of government. When, in 1816, Jackson echoed these sentiments, putting the matter in positive rather than negative terms, we may take for granted that he proceeded upon the assumption that the Republican victory over the Federalists was permanent. Thus party differences, which he advised Monroe to ignore, were only differences between members of the Democratic-Republican Party or, at worst, differences between men who were agreed in principle.

Though Jackson managed to maintain good relations with Monroe, at least formally, and seems never to have held him responsible for decisions he disapproved, the General soon fell out with leading members of Monroe's Administration, notably John Quincy Adams and William H. Crawford. Whether what soured Jackson was the policy of national consolidation these men seemed to be pursuing in pressing Monroe for internal improvements and maintaining the Bank of the United States, or perhaps only the scarcely disguised impatience of the Administration with his cavalier march into Spanish Florida, there is no doubt that he was soured. The opposition led by Henry Clay was even more faithless to the Jeffersonian inheritance. By the early 1820's Jackson was crying out for a return to "true Republican principles in the party of Jefferson."

In the election of 1824, the last in which the popular vote was largely if not entirely irrelevant, Jackson was the leading candidate. The popular wing of the Democratic-Republican Party had failed in all pre-election maneuvering to obtain the nomination for Jackson. But its strength was such that the Congressional caucus nomination, which went to John Quincy Adams in a tight race with Crawford, entirely lost the value it had formerly had. A determined effort was made to obtain electoral votes for Jackson by open and vigorous campaigning. The General himself observed the traditional taboo against a candidate's appearing in his own behalf, but his temper had been so raised by the treatment he was receiving from the statesmen of the party that he gave full encouragement to his supporters. When their efforts brought him a plurality in the Electoral College only to be followed by defeat at the hands of Adams and Clay in the House of Representatives, Jackson and his advisers decided the time had come to abandon the old party and strike out for themselves. Or better, they concluded that Adams, Clay, and company had abandoned the Republican Party.

Throughout the unhappy administration of John Quincy Adams the Jacksonians worked to build their party, a Democratic Party on the base of old Jeffersonian Republicanism. Their success in 1828, bringing down Adams and with him the remnants of Federalism that had gathered around him under the National Republican banner, was a partisan success in every sense. The candidate, no less than his supporters, did not hesitate to take divisive positions on such matters as the Bank, internal improvements, patronage, and the moneyed interests. Thus, like Jefferson, Jackson was sent to the White House with a mandate. He wished, as he said, to be President of all the people, but he was and could be the leader only of some. They were a majority to begin with, and in the years of his administration their numbers grew until they were sufficiently numerous to give Jackson massive popular support against the Bank, against Southern sectionalists, and against the spokesmen for both in the Congress.

Washington and Monroe had made official ceremonial tours of the country hoping to encourage national unity, and Monroe's had turned into a political success. But Jackson, responding to urgent requests from Democratic leaders in the Northeast, made the first unofficial, politically partisan tour by a President. In the spring of 1833 he went from Washington to New Hampshire along a previously arranged route, meeting political supporters, receiving tributes, and boosting the Democratic Party and Vice-President Martin Van Buren, whom he had already chosen to succeed him. With "Old Hickory" and Jefferson and Jeffersonian principles as their constant rallying cries, the Jacksonians swept their leader along in triumph. Lewis Cass, then Secretary of War, who was in the Jackson party, reported that Democratic "mobs went wild in their jubilation, the popular enthusiasm was undoubted, but the aristocrats averted their faces." Jackson himself, as reported by the Washington *Globe*, "was gratified to see the warm welcome extended to him by the good and true of . . . the party." At the Philadelphia Navy Yard Jackson's boat was met by a crowd of thirty thousand. At New York more than one hundred thousand turned out for his arrival, and on the last day of his visit there he paraded before more than two hundred thousand in the streets of north Jersey and New York City. In New England, where he had carried only two states in the election of 1832, things were a good deal quieter; yet at New Haven and Boston the largest crowds in history greeted Jackson. Harvard gave him an honorary degree, despite the bitter protest of John Quincy Adams that the university would demean itself to honor "a barbarian who could not write a sentence of grammar and hardly could spell his own name."[16]

The opposition press was constantly critical of Jackson's tour. The Democrats, they said, marched the President "up and down the streets as if he were a wild beast to be exhibited gratis." They protested "in the name of *Liberty,* and of that Democratic simplicity which is now converted into Royalty and its trappings." They ridiculed Cass, Levi Woodbury, and Governor William Marcy of New York when a footbridge gave way and these members of the President's party, along with dozens of plain citizens, were given a ducking. The Democrats themselves at times wrestled with each other so strenuously for Jackson's favor that they disgusted the President. Overcome with sickness and fatigue, he abruptly ended the tour at Concord, New Hampshire, and went home virtually incognito to avoid the crowds. On the whole the tour was certainly a great political success for Jackson himself. There were no scientific polls of public opinion in those days to take precise measurements, but local successes of Democrats who had basked in the company of Jackson gave evidence that his endorsement was effective. Above all, the election in 1836 of the stuffy and rather unattractive Van Buren was certainly a climactic triumph for Andrew Jackson as partisan leader.

Jackson's own appreciation of the partisan image he had created and fostered and its effect upon his Presidency is revealed with remarkable clarity in a letter he wrote to his intimate associate Roger Brooke Taney toward the end of his administration. That Taney was Chief Justice of the Supreme Court and presumably removed from politics is not the least interesting aspect of the letter. He was considering, Jackson told Taney, the preparation and delivery of a kind of farewell address. "It strikes me," he said,

that in quitting public life, the motives of whatever I may suggest as the experience of a long life spent in the discharge of public duties will be more impartially considered than any communication made at a time when my anxiety for the success of my measures might be suspected of warping my opinions, and when the interests of an opposing party produced an inclination in all under its influence, to judge most uncharitably of my intentions.

He went on to ask Taney's advice as to when and where he should deliver such an address and, finally, suggested that Taney draft it for him. "I would also be gratified, if consistent with your convenience, that you would throw on paper your thoughts as to the topics which you would consider most appropriate for the address." All this is somewhat disarming. A partisan career is about to be concluded with a conciliatory address, explaining at a time when ambition has died the great principles of a presidential administration. With partisanship muted Jackson seemed to believe that his ideas would get a fair hearing by all parties. He would seek counsel for this effort not from men in the thick of political struggles but from the serene detachment of the Supreme Court. However, the illusion is quickly dispelled. If Taney was puzzled by the tone of the first part of the letter, he must have chuckled as he finished it. The old warhorse was still smelling gunsmoke. The principles he wished to explain to the people with appropriate detachment included "aversion to the sectional jealousies, the sectional parties . . . centering on mischievous and intriguing individuals," "the dangerous power of the United States Bank, and the dangerous tendency of privileged monopolies generally," the idea "that one of the greatest threateners of our admirable form of Government is . . . stockjobbing, land jobbing, and every species of speculation," and finally the dangers of "the *paper system,* which has introduced a thousand ways of robbing honest labor of its earnings to make knaves rich, powerful and dangerous." Thus would Jackson, the hero of the Democracy, go out of office with a blistering campaign speech. Anything less would have been out of character and would have left his immense following with a sense of betrayal. But neither Taney nor the rank and file Jacksonians had anything to fear; the General was loyal in his loves and in his hates.[17]

7. *Theodore Roosevelt's popularity helps him break a tradition and win an election—and then lose one* ويه So, in his way, was the Colonel. After Jackson no President attained a great partisan following until Theodore Roosevelt converted his hero's adulation into political capital after the Spanish-American War. Roosevelt, a conservative by conviction, dabbled in reform from his early beginnings in politics. In the New York legislature he was persuaded to support labor legislation after he saw the

sweatshops of the city. He tackled both Tammany and the Radicals when, in 1886, he tried for the New York mayoralty. His identification with reform put him in line for the U.S. Civil Service Commission when Benjamin Harrison won the Presidency in 1888. Back in New York in 1893, after Harrison's defeat, T.R. was an energetic and effective police commissioner. At each stage his flair for the dramatic, his vigorous oratory, and his flamboyant personality brought him increasing numbers of devoted followers.

But his reform inclinations were pragmatic, not deeply principled. Roosevelt was no political philosopher, like Jefferson or Woodrow Wilson, nor was he conscious, like Jackson, of a great inheritance of democratic tradition. His skills were political in the operational sense. His public posture was controversial and therefore partisan, and the causes he espoused were often divisive. But he knew how to yield a foot to gain an inch—or to stay in office! And he well understood the uses, and the evanescence, of popularity.

As Assistant Secretary of the Navy during McKinley's first term, Roosevelt was bored. When circumstances permitted, he acted to build up the strength of the Navy, but too often he found himself leading the sort of sedentary life of routine office work which he detested. The troubles that fell upon the Spanish in Cuba fell on T.R. like manna from heaven. He hoped for war and did what he could to start it. When it came, in the spring of 1898, he welcomed the opportunity for action, resigning from the Navy to help form the regiment that became famous as the Rough Riders. The first American politician who fully understood the potentials of newspaper publicity, T.R. cultivated the reporters and photographers and thereby placed himself in the center of the wartime news. However minor its actual effect on the outcome of the war, the battle of San Juan Hill seemed to the American public to be the climax and the symbol of victory. When his "splendid little war" was over and the hero of San Juan Hill returned to New York, his political fortunes were made.

Every school child already knew of Roosevelt's successful battle with ill health in his youth and of his days as a hard-riding rancher. The "Teddy Bear" was a popular toy. Now T.R.'s romantic image was touched with military glory. He was a natural candidate for Governor of New York—natural both for the stalwarts of the Republican organization seeking a winner and for the reformers, in and out of the Republican Party, who were looking for a man to lead the "forces of decency" to victory over the strong alliance of Richard Croker of Tammany and Tom Platt of the Republican old guard.

Roosevelt's pragmatism was tested as soon as the campaign got under way. He was offered and accepted both the Republican nomination and the nomination of a reform party calling themselves the Independents and based on the Good Government ("Goo-goo") clubs of New York City. To Roosevelt, the opportunity to appear twice on the ballot was an important advantage in what he knew would be a close election. To the Independents, a Roosevelt victory assisted by their votes meant a strong claim to influence over the Governor in both policy and appointments. To Senator Platt, however, the idea was intolerable. Showing Roosevelt who was indeed boss, Platt told the Colonel he could have either the Republican or the Independent nomination, not both. Roosevelt had no difficulty in choosing. His difficulty came, rather, in explaining his default to his old reform friends in the Independent Party. As John Jay Chapman reported his conversations with T.R., the future President never surmounted that difficulty. Instead, he lost the confidence of the Independent leaders permanently. Many years later, when they were reluctantly persuaded to rally to him once more under the Progressive banner, many predicted that Roosevelt would once more let them down. And so he did, after the 1912 defeat, when he allowed the Progressive Pary to collapse and himself returned to the Republican fold.[18]

But Roosevelt's pragmatism neither stunted his growth as a reform leader nor dulled his appetite for popular esteem. As Governor of New York he perfected his skill in the politics of partisan popularity. But the special quality of Roosevelt's notion of popularity was that it should be as broad as possible rather than as deep as possible. Unlike Monroe or Eisenhower he did not seek to please everyone. But unlike Jefferson and Jackson he was not bound by his convictions to follow a straight course when flexibility would win friends or hold old ones. In a frank letter to an English friend, after his term as Governor was well under way, Roosevelt reviewed his position:

Although my chief interest in our affairs is really in national matters, and especially in connection with the Philippines and Cuba, my work is almost exclusively in domestic politics. So far I think I can say I have made a pretty fair Governor. I have put my ideals into effect. I have tried to be practical yet decent. I have gotten along with Platt and the machine; but I have never taken one action concerning which I would be ashamed to put down to you in writing every reason which influenced me, though it might be that I should not want an unscrupulous enemy to get hold of the letter to you.

He ought almost to have punctuated the last clause with an exclamation mark. A year later he estimated that he had satisfied Platt about once out of five times, but twice out of the five he had taken action directly opposed by Platt. Presumably the remaining two of each five actions were not interesting to the machine. He told a friend that every "decent man" in the machine was for him, but that he had, in every branch of the State service, "been turning out political workers and putting in men, who though good Republicans, merely run the offices as offices and not as patronage machines." But at the same time his earlier friends of Independent days had become "pretended reformers." This went for Dr. Parkhurst and for Henry Villard ("our stockjobbing friend who now controls the *Evening Post*"). Roosevelt got results, both in reform and in placating the machine, he said, by serving only "what I believe to be the best interests of the State."[19]

Roosevelt's popularity was so strong and so broad that as early as October, 1899, he was being approached on the possibility that he try for the Republican presidential nomination against McKinley in 1900. His reply to one such overture shows how sophisticated was his sense for political reality and how honest he was with himself. "If I hadn't happened to return from the war in a year when we had a gubernatorial election in New York," he said, "I should probably not now be Governor." On the other hand, he speculated, "if I had returned at the end of the second instead of the first term of the existing President, I should have had a fair show for the nomination." Roosevelt refused to be coy. He was no more reluctant about the presidential nomination or the office itself than Jackson had been, but he knew when he had no chance. "I have no Hanna," he said, and "there is no person who could take hold of my canvass and put money in it and organize it." Further, his progressive and reform leanings alienated the moneyed interests. "The big corporations who supply most of the money," he observed, "vary in their feeling toward me from fear to tepid dislike." What he did not say, but what his behavior showed he was thinking, was that because the Republican Party leaders would not have him, and because his prejudice against the Democracy was deep and abiding, his only hope of holding the governorship and eventually moving from there to the White House was to build his own party within the Republican framework. If he had no Hanna, neither had McKinley nor anyone else led the charge up San Juan Hill or excited the imagination of millions of Americans. But he would need to move quickly, because, as he put it, he was "not in the least taken in by the present wave of enthusiasm for me." He knew, he said, "that such waves always mean that the crest is succeeded by the hollow."[20]

While he was still riding the crest, Platt and Mark Hanna, as well as President McKinley, saw in T.R. a formidable threat to their control of the Republican Party both in New York and in the nation. Business leaders were uneasy, which was bad for Republican business. And so it seemed wise to sidetrack the Colonel by placing him in the Vice-Presidency, where he would be noisy, perhaps, but harmless, and where, in accord with the unbroken tradition of both parties, he would reach the end of the political road. The dimensions of such an achievement, in the view of the Republican leaders, were to be seen in the fact that Roosevelt was not yet forty-one. If not politically disposed of then, he would probably be around a long time to dispose of them.

Roosevelt understood perfectly why the way was opened for him to the vice-presidential nomination. His letters to Henry Cabot Lodge, his closest political confidant, show him at first skeptical of his chances, despite the public acclaim he was receiving, but quite willing to accept if the nomination were tendered. "I am for it," he wrote, on the perfectly simple ground that I regard my position as utterly unstable and that I appreciate as well as any one how entirely ephemeral is the hold I have for a moment on the voters. I am not taken in by the crowds in the west or by anything else in the way of vociferous enthusiasm for the moment. It would be five years before it would materialize [a presidential nomination] and I have never known a hurrah to endure five years; so I should be inclined to accept any honorable position; that the Vice-Presidency is.

He went on to belittle his chances for the presidential nomination even in 1904. But, he said, if he were a "serious possibility" for that year, he would agree with Lodge, who had written to say that the Vice-Presidency might become a stepping stone. This was in the summer of 1899. Six months later Platt was pushing T.R. for the vice-presidential nomination, and it looked as though the party leaders were going to agree. Roosevelt took Platt's support in stride. He explained it to Lodge with his customary candor and lucidity:

I have found out one reason why Senator Platt wants me nominated for the Vice-Presidency. He is I am convinced, genuinely friendly, and indeed I think I may say really fond of me, and is personally satisfied with the way I have conducted politics; but the big-monied men with whom he is in close touch and whose campaign contributions have certainly been no inconsiderable factor in his strength, have been pressing him very strongly to get me put in the Vice-Presidency, so as to get me out of the State.

There is a note of pride in Roosevelt's statement that "big insurance companies . . . to a man want me out" and that the "great corporations affected by the franchise tax, . . . in fact all the big-monied interests that make campaign contributions of large size and feel that they should have favors in return, are extremely anxious to get me out of the State." The penalty for progressive leadership in New York State was, in short, to be kicked upstairs. But Roosevelt, for all his righteous hostility toward the "big-monied" interests, showed no sign of disapproval of Platt's arrangements with them. That big contributions should produce "favors in return" was, apparently, entirely proper. If one of the favors was the removal of the reforming Governor, so be it. The Governor was not disposed to fight. By yielding graciously to the pressure to accept the Vice-Presidency he could ingratiate himself with the party leadership and accommodate its financial backers. The public might understand the whole arrangement as a promotion for their favorite.[21]

And T.R. evidently decided that he would make it in fact a promotion. He campaigned hard for McKinley, always with the consciousness that it was he, Theodore Roosevelt, who was being exposed to the people, getting the chance to enhance his popularity, while the President was content with another "front porch" campaign. Once elected, Roosevelt continued to travel about the nation, meeting and conferring with party leaders and meeting and addressing crowds of people. When McKinley died from an assassin's bullet on September 14, 1901, there is no doubt that the country knew his successor far better than they had ever known the fallen President.

As President, Theodore Roosevelt almost immediately set about the unlikely task of reversing an American political custom. Since the founding of the Republic, no Vice-President, succeeding to the Presidency by the death of the President, had ever been nominated for a presidential term in his own right. The assumption had gone unchallenged that a Vice-President, upon becoming President, did not thereby also become leader of his party. He had, in most instances, been chosen Vice-President because he was *not* a leader of the party's majority. Thus when his term as President expired, the party leadership reverted to the organization. The organization had the right to select the presidential nominee and would not, almost in the nature of things, choose the President to succeed himself, for they had never intended him to be President in the first place. Roosevelt had known these facts of political life well enough when he accepted the vice-presidential nomination in 1900. But what had always been, he resolved, need not necessarily always be.

Taking up where he had left off as Governor of New York, T.R. practiced his special brand of the politics of partisan popularity with historic success. He took every suitable occasion to enhance his "public image" as the dynamic leader of progressive Republicanism and reform, working tirelessly to increase his following among the people. Like John F. Kennedy in a later era, the young, vigorous President—the youngest in history—surrounded by a young and attractive and vigorous family in the

White House, made skillful use of the press. The newly popular Sunday rotogravure sections soon became a focal point for Rooseveltiana. No other Republican and no Democrat, not even Bryan, could expect so much coverage, simply because nobody else was so interesting. With familiarity went the aura of action. Here was a President who was "telling them," who was getting things done—in Panama, in Venezuela, or in the coal fields.

The "private image," the Roosevelt who dealt on close and intimate terms with party leaders, was rather different. If he knew the powers of patronage and did not hesitate to use them, he nevertheless convinced the party men that he was a party man. If what he wanted was the nomination in 1904, this was an understandable political motive, the more readily understandable to a politician whose candidate for postmaster or judge was up for presidential approval. And the party men began to admire the perilous balance Roosevelt maintained between leading a popular attack on the "big-monied interests" and dealing privately in a friendly and even conciliatory fashion with those big-monied men whose campaign contributions, as he had learned from Platt, were indispensable to victory. Trust-busting was no doubt in the public interest, but it was also in the public interest that the trust-buster should stay in office. If this meant that there would have to be rather more talk about trust-busting than busting of trusts, who could deny the responsibility of the President to educate the people? If it meant that there had to be only a few bad trusts, and many more good ones, T.R. thought that the distinction was correct and that to make it was in the public interest. The managers of the "good trusts" agreed.

If there was a contradiction between the two Roosevelts, T.R. himself seems not to have been troubled by it. To one friend he wrote candidly:

Of course I should like to be re-elected President, and I shall be disappointed, although not very greatly disappointed, if I am not; and so far as I legitimately can I pay heed to considerations of political expedience—in fact I should be unfit for my position, or for any position of political leadership, if I did not do so.

Yet to an editor who had suggested in an editorial that this was precisely Roosevelt's line of thought, T.R. wrote in stuffy self-righteousness:

It is pleasant to think that one's countrymen believe well of one. But I shall not do anything whatever to secure my nomination or election save to try to carry on the public business in such shape that decent citizens will believe I have shown wisdom, integrity and courage.[22]

In combination, these public and private Roosevelts proved unbeatable. Long before the convention of 1904 it was a foregone conclusion that T.R. would be nominated without serious opposition. In the election compaign afterwards, he chafed with the inaction that in those days was still thought incumbent upon a President seeking re-election. His opponent, Judge Alton B. Parker, went about the country addressing meetings while Roosevelt sat in his White House office or vacationed with his family, issuing occasional statements but otherwise ignoring the campaign. His frame of mind as election day drew near, and his opinion of his first term and his standing in the nation, are well set forth in a letter to his son Kermit:

I have continually wished that I could be on the stump myself, and during the last week or ten days I have been fretted at my inability to hit back, and to take the offensive in person against Parker. He lays himself wide open and I could cut him into ribbons if I could get at him in the open. But of course a President can't go on the stump and can't indulge in personalities, and so I have to sit still and abide the result. I shall be heartily glad when the next two weeks are over and the election is decided one way or the other.

It was "no small triumph," he said, that he was the first Vice-President who became President by the death of his predecessor, "who has ever been nominated for the Presidential office." In winning the nomination, he had won "unquestioned headship" in his own party. That is, the Roosevelt Republican party had got control of the party as a whole. T.R. thought this was due in large measure to his achievements, as it certainly was. He reviews his record for his son:

. . . the Panama Canal, the creation of the Department of Commerce and Labor with the Bureau of Corporations, the settlement of the Alaska boundary, the settlement of the Venezuela trouble through the Hague Commission, the success of my policy in Cuba, the success of my policy in the Philippines, the Anthracite Coal Strike, the success of such suits as that against the Northern Securities Company which gave a guaranty in this country that rich man and poor man alike were held equal before the law, and my action in the so-called Miller case which gave to trade-unions a lesson that had been taught corporations—that I favored them while they did right and was not in the least afraid of them when they did wrong.

It was indeed an impressive list of achievements. Most of them bore the special stamp of T.R.—"my policy," as he said. The outcome of the election would depend upon how many partisans he had won to his partisanship as measured against the enemies he had made. It turned out that 60 per cent of the two-party voters were for the Colonel, and their numbers were greater than had ever voted for a President before. Roosevelt's conduct of the politics of partisanship, in his own peculiarly cautious fashion, had won an historic victory.[23]

In the flush of his victory, evidently feeling less partisan than merely triumphant, T.R. announced that he would not seek another term. Whether this was heartfelt at the moment or merely rhetoric that seemed appropriate, nevertheless few Presidents have ever more deeply regretted a categorical statement. In the years of his second term Roosevelt was more, rather than less, progressive and partisan than he had been in his first term, but his partisan popularity could lead nowhere except to a moment of satisfaction in naming his successor. Successful prosecutions of American Tobacco and Standard Oil, federal inspection of meats and drugs, the great drive for conservation of natural resources, and, in the foreign field, winning the Nobel Prize for peace and sending the White Fleet around the world to signal America's arrival as a great power—these were achievements scorned or deprecated by some but approved and applauded by the Rooseveltian majority. In all likelihood T.R. could have built an election victory in 1908 on that record. But he had eliminated himself and had to be satisfied with the choice and election of Taft.

If the genial but cautious Cincinnati lawyer seems, upon careful scrutiny, to have been a curious choice for Roosevelt to make, one explanation may be found in the nature of the politics of popularity. For a man who was accustomed to adulation and to the sense of power flowing into him from the multitude, for such a man to offer his status to another seems to require more in the

way of selflessness than Roosevelt commanded, even if he could
have done so. And so Taft may well have been chosen precisely
because he was no threat to the Colonel's popular status. At any
rate, hindsight shows clearly enough that T.R. could never have
sat through two terms of Taft without reasserting, or trying to
reassert, his hold over the progressive partisans whom Taft
seemed to be abandoning. Roosevelt's campaign against Taft for
the Republican nomination in 1912 and his fight for the Presidency as a Progressive after losing to Taft taught him a salutary
lesson that may be equally valuable for students of the Presidency. T.R.'s immense popularity was simply not enough to get
him elected. Either he was too partisan to win the necessary extra
votes from non-Republicans, or he was not partisan enough to
capture the Republican organization from an incumbent President. Not only could he not have it both ways: he could not have
it either way.

And so the historic parallel with Jackson breaks down. Jackson's devotion to principle and policy was as important a link
with the masses who supported him as was his shining reputation. A less attractive man like Van Buren could win with Jackson's blessing and be defeated only by a pseudo-Jacksonian candidate when the Whigs ran General Harrison in 1840. But Jacksonian democracy was not ended by the defeat of Van Buren.
Four years later another and nearer disciple of Jackson's, James
K. Polk, won the Presidency and carried on the Jackson program.
But Theodore Roosevelt cared less for principle than for power,
else he would not have chosen a Taft to succeed him. When he
rediscovered his principles in 1911 and set forth to head the
forces of progress once again, something had gone out of his political magic. His personal popularity was certainly still very
great, but it was more personal and less partisan. Some partisans,
indeed, even preferred Robert La Follette of Wisconsin as their
leader, and not a few had learned to be very skeptical of the
Colonel's pronouncements. Thus when he made the most radical
address in his life at Oppotowatamie in 1911, and when he told
the Progressives at Chicago in 1912, "we stand at Armageddon
and we battle for the Lord," there were a good many people who
concluded that the call was really to battle for T.R.—and that
was not enough.

Roosevelt quite unintentionally wrote his own political obituary in an incisive letter to Lodge during the summer of 1908 as he was preparing to yield place to Taft. At least it may serve as a political obituary, because in the years after he wrote it, Roosevelt's disillusioned prophecies as to what might have been turned out to be. His usefulness, he said, had "been predicated upon the belief of the plain people" that his service had been "sincere and distinterested." They believed "that when I had given my word, my word was good." This was the crux of the popularity question. Roosevelt saw it clearly enough:

The ordinary plain man, the man who has stood behind me in what I have done or have striven to do, and who has accepted me as his special representative, is not given to hair-splitting or to making fine distinctions. Even when he did not approve of my having said I would not run, and wisht that I could be nominated again, his final verdict was certain to be "Well, he said he would not run, and he never goes back on his word, and that is all there is to it." I should have damaged this man morally if I had made him feel that after all I was vacillating or insincere; and even tho he had voted for me, as I think he would have done, he would thereafter have put me on a lower plane, and his own character would thereby have been somewhat hurt, while my ability to do good work would have been immeasurably decreased.[24]

## 8. *Franklin D. Roosevelt unites, then divides, the nation* ❧

But split hairs was precisely what T.R. did after 1910, and his devoted partisans did indeed put him on a lower plane. Franklin Delano Roosevelt, who cast his only Republican vote for T.R. in 1904, profited by the unhappy example of his cousin and was careful not to make the same mistake. The second Roosevelt, no less pragmatic perhaps than the first, never confused his ambition, or his sense of the public interest, with the pronouncement of moral sentiments, and so never said he would not run for a third term, or even a fourth. And his partisans were numerous enough and devoted enough to elect him President four times.

Franklin Roosevelt was no hero when he first campaigned for the Presidency. He was an attractive Democratic politician with a great name and a special sort of appeal that came from the

courageous way in which, overcoming the handicap of paralysis
from polio, he had returned to the political wars to win the
governorship of New York. Roosevelt was, no doubt, more attractive than the other possible candidates, Democratic or Republican, in 1932. But there was no special aura about him. He was
not identified with a positive and challenging program; neither
had he been a particularly distinguished governor. If ever the
times made a President, the depression of 1929–1933 made F.D.R.
Politically he was ready; intellectually he hurried to catch up.
That he succeeded is attested by the way in which his leadership
satisfied the great mass of Americans, while it alienated permanently a bitter minority. Not since Jefferson and Jackson had a
President built such an immense following at the expense of so
much animosity.

Politically, Franklin Roosevelt had begun to prepare himself
in his youth. As early as 1912, after gaining public attention by
a sensational fight against Tammany over a U.S. senatorial election, young state senator Roosevelt cast his lot, contrary to the
wishes of the New York Democracy, with Woodrow Wilson.
When William Jennings Bryan, that least intellectual of national
Democratic leaders, decided to support the most intellectual, Wilson was in, and with him went Roosevelt. After Wilson's accidental victory in the three-cornered race with Theodore Roosevelt and Taft, Franklin Roosevelt was rewarded with the Assistant Secretaryship of the Navy. The World War lifted that post
out of the rut of routine and gave Roosevelt his chance for
national prominence. His youth, his vitality, his winning manner, and his name were priceless advantages that he skillfully
exploited.

Born into the Hudson River aristocracy, F.D.R. had learned in
Albany and saw again in Washington that the day of the
country squire's automatic assumption of political power was
gone, or nearly gone. His democratic inclinations fitted much
better the expectations of the Democratic politicians he was meeting all over the country, and he was constantly encouraged to
indulge these inclinations by his friend and devoted promoter,
Louis Howe.

The Roosevelt who was to become in later years the greatest of
all champions of the "common man" may be seen emerging in

the alarmed eyes of his mother in those World War I years. One night in October, 1917, when Sara Roosevelt retired after what was apparently a deadlocked argument with son Franklin and daughter-in-law Eleanor in which the old order was challenged finally by the new, she wrote her children a poignant letter. "I am sorry," she said, "to feel that Franklin *is* tired and that my views are not his, but perhaps dear Franklin you may on second thoughts or *third* thoughts see that I am not so far wrong." What Sara Roosevelt's ideas were, and Franklin's, flow out of the sentences that followed:

The foolish old saying "noblesse oblige" is good and "honneur oblige" possibly expresses it better for most of us. One can be as democratic as one likes, but if we love our own, and if we love our neighbor, we owe a great example . . . for with the *trend* to "shirt sleeves," and the ideas of what men should do in always being all things to all men and striving to give up the old fashioned traditions of family life . . . of what use is it to *keep up* things, to hold on to dignity and all I stood up for this evening. Do not say that I *misunderstood.* I understand perfectly, but I cannot believe that my precious Franklin really feels as he expressed himself.[25]

But Franklin nevertheless did believe what he was saying to his mother. If he never ceased to *be* an aristocrat in voice, in devotion to his family estate, and in the unconscious flair of his manner, public and private, he nevertheless ceased altogether to *practice* aristocracy. And when, twenty years later, he bore down upon the "economic royalists" and was denounced for his pains as a "traitor to his class," he had well earned the denunciation and reveled in it. The men in "shirt sleeves" had adopted *him* as sure as he, in his fledgling days as a politician, had adopted *them.* As President he had converted his inclinations and his sense for the political into a philosophy that could be applied in any walk of life. He told the graduating midshipmen in 1933 at Annapolis, for example, "When you make a close examination of any profession, you will find very few successful men, or for that matter women, who do not take into consideration the effect of their individual efforts on humanity as a whole." As for himself, he was proud to say, by way of illustration, that "a columnist complained the other day that I had overestimated the importance of understanding of, and sympathy with, the point of view and the general well-being of what might be called the average citizen." F.D.R. was very sure that it just was not possible to make that kind of overestimate.[26]

His talents and the special circumstances of his career, including his exuberant though unsuccessful run as the vice-presidential nominee under Cox in 1920 and his massive correspondence through the years of his illness with party leaders everywhere, had prepared him politically to be a successful candidate for a state governorship and even the Presidency. But neither his education nor his career had prepared Franklin Roosevelt intellectually for the immense responsibility he undertook in 1932. He was a good conversationalist on general subjects and a real expert on such hobbies as the Navy, forest development, and political psychology. But he was neither a philosopher, like Jefferson, nor a student of government, like Wilson, the two Presidents he most admired. In college he had been inspired by Josiah Royce to take a worldwide rather than a parochial view of the human condition, but otherwise his teachers made little impression on him. He was an indifferent law student and thoroughly bored by the practice of law. The only large subject that seriously engaged his mind was the politics of power in a democratic society. Thus he had observed carefully the political behavior of leaders like Theodore Roosevelt, Bryan, and Wilson, and he had read a good deal in American political history and biography, as well as the biographies of European statesmen. He had been close enough to Wilson between 1913 and 1921 to learn a good deal about the potentialities and limitations of the presidential office. He was well schooled in what political mistakes *not* to make. But he had no strong convictions in matters of public policy, leaning only toward progressivism, and no program such as other partisan Presidents had had.

If F.D.R.'s place in American history had rested on his campaign of 1932, it would have been undistinguished. Though he had invited Raymond Moley, Rexford Tugwell, and Adolf Berle to assemble a "brains trust" more than six months before the nominating convention, and though Berle had prepared a long memorandum that reads in retrospect like a detailed forecast of both the first and the second "New Deal," most often Roosevelt's campaign speeches failed to contain expressions of the new ideas.

Years afterward Tugwell still could not reconcile himself to Roosevelt's campaign practice of asking for speech drafts both from the brain trusters and from political advisers, expressing delight with the brain trust product and assuring its authors of his agreement and then discarding their work when the moment of delivery came. One reason, of course, was that F.D.R. had a better sense for what would win votes than did his scholarly advisers. But another reason was that Roosevelt was honestly confused by the conflict between the planning and spending measures the brain trusters were advocating to bring the nation out of depression and the old shibboleths he had been brought up to respect: sound money, economy in goverment, and balanced budgets. His sense for the urgency of the situation told him that old remedies were no longer adequate, or perhaps not even remedies at all; but his sense for politics told him to be wary and to attack the Republicans not for doing bad things, but for doing badly what everyone thought ought to be done. When the votes were counted, Roosevelt's margin over Hoover was only slightly greater than Hoover's had been over Smith in 1928. Any Democrat who could have commanded the nomination in 1932 probably would have been elected; thus there was nothing distinguished or dramatic in Roosevelt's triumph.[27]

But it was characteristic of Roosevelt's political astuteness that once having been elected by skillful use of traditional means, he at once set out to break with tradition and establish new rules that would give him the advantage for years to come. If the campaign had produced only a somewhat vague image of a well-intentioned, attractive new President, it was the historic Roosevelt who spoke the Inaugural Address of March 4, 1933. And the historic Roosevelt was no longer simply an attractive man obscured by his own obscurantist expressions of hackneyed political generalizations. Henceforward F.D.R. meant ideas, meant biases, meant joyous but sharp-edged partisanship. The ideas might from time to time be inconsistent, but the leaning was always in the same direction, and the partisans were never much worried by changes of plans and programs.

The first New Deal appealed to businessmen to cooperate with labor and government in the interests of national recovery, and for two years a good many Republicans were inclined to favor

Roosevelt's emergency program. But even while NRA was catching the headlines and engrossing the attention of industry, TVA was shaking the foundations of private power, trade unions were being encouraged to grow and to demand the right to bargain, and the bases for a social security system were being worked out. Relief jobs and a new attitude of optimism and, above all, renewed confidence born of energetic leadership brought Roosevelt the endorsement he wanted in the Congressional elections of 1934. With bigger majorities in both houses—indeed, with immense majorities—Roosevelt and his brain trusters went to work to build the Second New Deal. With the Wagner Act, the Social Security law, the regulation of security exchanges, permanent public works programs, and government entrance into cultural activities through WPA, the characteristic Roosevelt policies and issues were laid out for all to see and for conservatives to reject. Now Roosevelt became the symbol of love or hate. No one, thereafter, was indifferent.

The chorus of criticism, in fact, swelled so loud that some of the Roosevelt circle thought he might be defeated for re-election in 1936. Harold Ickes, among others, a one-time Bull Moose Progressive and Republican who was F. D. R.'s Secretary of the Interior, confided to his diary that the Republican nomination might be worth having and suggested that he might himself be a good man for the job. The *Literary Digest,* leading weekly magazine of news and views, found in its famous quadrennial straw poll that Alf M. Landon, the Kansas governor who had won the Republican nomination, would be an easy victor. With near unanimity the columnists and other self-appointed political prophets announced that the outcome was in doubt, because Roosevelt had failed to create prosperity and had blasphemed against traditional American economic philosophy. Only Democratic National Chairman James A. Farley and the President himself seemed to agree with the findings of an obscure prognosticator named George Gallup, who was saying that an accurate forecast of a national election could be made with only some 5,000 sample ballots, provided the sample was truly representative of the significant voting groups in the nation. Gallup concluded, after studying his sample, that Roosevelt would win in a landslide.

With several minor parties in the field, including a jerry-built organization called the Union Party backed by rightwing demagogues—Father Coughlin and Gerald L. K. Smith—and based on the pitiful belief of thousands of old people in the crackpot pension plan of Dr. Townsend, the campaign was colorful and sometimes tense. But Roosevelt dominated it from beginning to end. The crowds that turned out to see and hear him exceeded anything in previous political history. So did their enthusiasm. And so, in the end, did the numbers of their votes. Not since Monroe's unanimous re-election in 1820 had a President won by so decisive a margin. Roosevelt won by more than 11 million votes and carried all but two states. "As Maine goes, so goes Vermont," chortled James A. Farley.

Franklin Roosevelt's victory in 1936 marks perhaps the high tide of partisanship in modern presidential history. The opposition, which tallied better than 17 million votes, ranged from the millions who simply voted the Republican ticket because of party loyalty to disaffected businessmen who, though they were better off than they had been four years before, were not willing to acknowledge a debt to the champion of labor; from left-wingers who still hoped that the depression could be converted into a communist revolution and saw F.D.R. as the chief obstacle, to Liberty League financiers, lawyers, and out-of-office statesmen who saw in F.D.R. the betrayal of the "American Way." For the latter the United States had fallen upon evil days from which, fearfully, it might never recover. For the President with greater or lesser devotion—mostly greater—were the "common men" of the farms and factories, the shops and shipyards, and the educators, students, and intellectual men who saw in Roosevelt and his New Deal an historic resurgence of democracy. For them "happy days" were "here again."

Roosevelt's popularity was, after 1934, no accidental phenomenon. If the times had made the man at the outset, the man had a good deal to do with making the times afterwards—and increasing his personal popularity. His use of radio, unprecedented at that time as much as campaign tours had been in earlier years, was both frequent and unforgettably effective. F.D.R. "visited," as he liked to put it, with his constituents in their living rooms. Even though fireplaces probably did not grace the homes of a great many of his supporters, the idea of the "fire-side chat" was appealing. And he tried to make such talks as chatty as he could.

Roosevelt strove to reinvigorate the national spirit as much as the national body, but he was highly sensitive to the fact that moral exhortation, however uplifting and proper in times of crisis, is indigestible as a regular diet. Ray Stannard Baker, a skilled writer and biographer of Wilson, once urged Roosevelt to give more effort to expressing his "vision" of the future. The President's reply explains a good deal about his hold on people:

> You are so absolutely right about the response that this country gives to vision and profound moral purposes that I can only assure you of my hearty concurrence and of my constant desire to make the appeal.
>
> I know at the same time that you will be sympathetic to the point of view that the public psychology and, for that matter, the individual psychology, cannot, because of human weakness, be attuned for long periods of time to a constant repetition of the highest note in the scale.

The "one third of a nation" that was living in poverty, F.D.R. rightly judged, was less interested in moral exhortation than in groceries. This was what Wilson had not quite understood, and Hoover, if he understood, had failed to act upon it. Roosevelt knew just how to mix up appeals to what Walter Reuther in later years called the "gut issues" with statements of renewed faith in democracy and individual liberty. Putting the matter in terms of his predecessors, he observed that "Theodore Roosevelt lacked Woodrow Wilson's appeal to the fundamental and failed to stir, as Wilson did, the truly profound moral and social convictions." But, on the other hand, he went on, "Wilson failed where Theodore Roosevelt succeeded in stirring people to enthusiasm over specific individual events, even though these specific events may have been superficial in comparison with the fundamentals." Franklin Roosevelt strove always for the nice balance of both.

And whether on radio or in personal appearances he was wary of overexposure. "There is another thought," he told Baker, "which is involved in continuous leadership—whereas in this country there is a free and sensational press, people tire of seeing the same name day after day in the important headlines of the papers, and the same voice night after night over the radio." Writing in the spring of 1935, he said he thought that he would have been unwise to keep up the pace of the early New Deal days. "The histrionics of the new actors, Long and Coughlin and Johnson," he said, "would have turned the eyes of the audience away from the main drama itself."[28]

From the moment of his First Inaugural until the moment of his death more than twelve years later, Franklin Roosevelt was always the "main drama." His vehement and often joyous partisanship characterized his leadership, and his popularity, in the days of peace. That partisanship, transmuted into leadership of the forces of freedom against totalitarian tyrants in war, put him in the end at the head of a united country. Along the way, especially perhaps in 1940 when he was elected to an unprecedented third term, he presided over a divided nation. The issue was himself and the ideas forever identified with his name and his leadership. Thus he cannot be compared with such men as Washington or Monroe or Eisenhower despite the comparable dimensions of their victories. Roosevelt stands rather with Jefferson, Jackson, and Theodore Roosevelt as a sign of turbulent years, whose turbulence he in no small part himself promoted. He, like his cousin, once inadvertently wrote his own political epitaph, but with happier results: "Judge me by the enemies I have made," he told a campaign audience in his first try for the Presidency. At the end, thirteen years later, he would not have wished to change a syllable.

**9.** *John F. Kennedy, gaining popularity AFTER his election, cautiously practices what he has preached* ৪৯ It is something of a paradox, at least on the surface, that John F. Kennedy, who was outspoken in his wish to emulate Franklin Roosevelt, might have preferred, in the first years of his administration, to be judged by the friends he had made. The fact of Kennedy's tragically shortened administration makes it all but impossible to estimate the breadth and depth of his popularity or the uses he made of it. But the shift in his approach to the people between

his first years and his last months in the White House is sharp
and instructive.

Although Kennedy did not live to try for a second term that
would have documented the issue of his popularity with an historic record, the barometer of his standing with the public was
meticulously kept by students of public opinion and by himself
and his assistants. As a Senator, Kennedy had shown an acute
awareness of the importance of the "public image" in a public
man. As a candidate, first for the Democratic nomination and
then for the Presidency, he relied heavily on the findings of polls,
both those published in the press and those he commissioned for
his own use. The wafer-thin margin of his victory over Richard
Nixon no doubt increased, rather than diminished, his concern
over his popularity rating. As a candidate he had built a more
liberal program and leaned more strongly toward the liberal side
of the political equilibrium than he had done as a Senator. His
Catholicism, the polls showed, had cost him heavily; the effect
of his liberalism was harder to measure. Faced, as President, with
so little apparent popular backing, Kennedy proceeded to build
by an astute combination of word and deed the popular majority
he had failed to attain as a candidate. The words he spoke were
calculated to tell the people what he meant by his aim to "get
the country moving again." The measures he proposed were
calculated to move it. But the cautious manner in which he
treated the leaders of Congress—often amounting to curiously
inappropriate deference—assured that controversial measures
would not pass unless in the diluted form Congressional pride
required.

As the President spoke and the Congress dallied, the President's
popularity rose. His youthful appearance and winning manner,
his lovely wife and children, and the exuberance of his whole
family, like that of Theodore Roosevelt sixty years before, won
the American heart.[29] The words, carefully accented in speeches
and flowing with quick brilliance in press conferences, won the
American mind. Within six months the Gallup poll showed Kennedy's popularity apparently at a higher point than any of his
predecessors had reached. As his popularity rose, he seemed to
take greater care not to offend. Somewhat ostentatiously he consulted Eisenhower and even Herbert Hoover, as well as Harry

Truman, on matters of foreign policy. He spoke kind words for his most inflexible opponents in the Congress. More like a Senator, indeed, than a President, he praised the Congress and paid deference to its leaders on both sides of the aisles. When civil strife followed in the wake of the denial of civil rights, it was the President's brother, Attorney-General Robert Kennedy, who took the leadership and seemed to take the responsibility for bringing to bear the power of the federal government on behalf of equality before the law.

In the spring of 1962 Kennedy gingerly tested out the popularity the polls showed him to have. When United States Steel announced that the price of steel would be increased, the President reacted quickly, vigorously, and with a public display of indignation. There had been an understanding, he said, that the strike settlement reached only a short time before would not affect the price of steel, thus breaking to the public benefit the wage-price spiral that had played so prominent a part in postwar inflation. Steel, the President said, had deceived the country— and the President. Instead of deploring only, Kennedy acted. He instructed government agencies to review their steel requirements and contracts with a view to cutting off the flow of orders to companies that followed the lead of U.S. Steel, and the Secretary of Defense announced that procurement of steel would be limited thereafter to companies that honored the agreement by holding prices steady. In short order the steel companies capitulated to the overwhelming power brought to bear by the President. The stock market plunged downward. But the President's popularity did not; he lost a few points, but Gallup and other experts asserted that the drop was not significant. Feeling was divided on the President's action. Some thought he had not played fair, but more thought he had given the kind of aggressive leadership the issue called for.

But Kennedy was not prepared to rest his popularity on partisanship—not yet. In the following weeks he took several opportunities to assert his sympathy with business and to reassure industry that his Administration would maintain close cooperation with the business community. A year later, when steel prices crept up one at a time, Kennedy told his press conferences that though he would watch carefully to see that the main portions of the line were held, "selective" increases need not be inflationary.

By the spring of 1963 Kennedy had sustained continuously high popularity ratings longer than Eisenhower had done. If little of his program had become law, his re-election by an immense margin seemed assured. The only shadow across the sunlit highway ahead was persistent unrest both South and North over the Negro demand for equality. In 1960 Kennedy had rightly asserted that much could be done to foster civil rights by vigorous enforcement of existing statutes. As Attorney-General, his brother Robert had made a distinguished record of enforcement. John Kennedy had also pledged in 1960 to bring an end, by executive order, to discrimination in public housing built with federal funds. He had delayed nearly two years in issuing the order. Now, in the early months of 1963, it had become apparent that executive orders and strict law enforcement would not, in the long run, be enough. Congress would sooner or later have to act. The President would have to stimulate such action, either before he ran for a second term or after. If after, he could perhaps maintain a semblance of national unity behind himself and a moderate policy. His re-election in that event would be as certain as anything can be among the uncertainties of free politics. If he acted before, on the other hand, there was every prospect that the only immediate result would be loss of popularity and perhaps the election, and Congressional action might well be delayed beyond the election anyway. The author of *Profiles in Courage* considered his own future as against the public interest and found that his courage would not allow him to confuse the two. To the Congress he sent a special message, calling for the fullest implementation of the fourteenth amendment and the recent decisions of the Supreme Court ending segregation. "I am proposing," said the President, "that the Congress stay in session this year until it has enacted—preferably as a single omnibus bill—the most responsible, reasonable, and urgently needed solutions which should be acceptable to all fair-minded men." Overnight the popularity of the President dropped to the level of partisanship. Thereafter, like Franklin Roosevelt, he would be judged by the enemies he made.

After the civil rights message, in the few short months before he was cut down by an assassin's bullet, Kennedy seemed older and somehow more mature. But his energies were better concentrated and his drive for other measures, such as his far-reaching proposal to cut taxes, was more buoyant and vigorous. If he had divided the country, it was only because the division was there anyway. This is the point about true partisanship. The partisan leader takes sides in a real issue; the partisan President leads a faction because he believes it is best for the nation. The unpartisan leader avoids the issue if he can; the unpartisan President plays down factions because he fears their divisive influence upon public order and morale. A President cannot have it both ways, as John Kennedy discovered. Whether he would have gone on to build partisan popularity as skillfully as he had built his unpartisan following after the election of 1960 will never be known. The politics of partisan popularity, as practiced by a Jackson or a Franklin Roosevelt, is a different art from the image-making sort of unpartisan politics Kennedy had been practicing. But his place in history already seems likely to rest upon such words as these in his Inaugural Address: "Ask not what your country can do for you; ask what you can do for your country." To find the courage to place his own ambition behind him and, instead, take the leadership in the bitter struggle for civil freedom was what *he* could do for *his* country.[30]

10. *The popularity of partisan Presidents* 𝕆𝕎 An examination of the popularity of Presidents thus underlines a rough but useful distinction between two main kinds of public approbation. One sort of appeal is to a faction, or combination of factions, having a common interest or interests that are by no means unanimously shared by the whole people. Such interests are, of course, shared by a majority, else the man who speaks for them would not be President at all. But a minority, of varying size and degree of feeling, vigorously opposes both the President and his policies and program. The President, for his part, must, of course, speak for the whole nation as its responsible chief executive. But in speaking *for* the nation a partisan President decidedly does not speak what is approved *by* the whole nation. He finds the public interest in the majority interest; he

is and must be a partisan. His hold upon his office and his power to act arise from his being the leader of the stronger side in a divided country. He retains his leadership by satisfying his partisans, so long as his partisans, together with those who are merely loyal to the party, form a majority. Conspicuously successful partisan Presidents have been Jefferson, Jackson, both Roosevelts, John Kennedy, and, perhaps, Lyndon Johnson. In their different ways, and to different degrees, these Presidents practiced the politics of partisanship.

The other sort of popularity belongs to Presidents who appeal broadly to all or most segments of opinion by virtue of a successful effort to find least common denominators of agreement among them. Such a President symbolizes the unity of the nation, such as may exist, rather than its divisions. His ability to hold his office arises from the sense of the people that he is not a partisan, that he places something called the "national interest" above any particular interests. In short, he convinces the people that he is above politics.

In parliamentary systems, no doubt, there is really nothing other than partisan politics. The party takes the responsibility; the leader is understood to be the leader of the party. National unity is expressed not by the prime minister but by the chief of state, who is not an executive officer and who is either elected by the whole people or holds his position by inheritance. In the American presidential system, however, there are alternative possibilities for presidential politics. Because the President is both chief of state and chief of government, he may elect to practice a politics appropriate to either of his roles, or he may strive to walk a political tightrope between them. Emphasis upon his role as chief of state will necessarily emphasize nonpartisanship; emphasis upon his role as chief executive will necessarily emphasize partisanship.

To straddle is, as the history of the Presidency shows, all but impossible. Washington, presiding over the birth of the republic, had more success than any other in his heroic attempt both to unite the country as its first chief of state and to govern the country as its first chief executive. But he fought a losing battle against parties and in effect succeeded in carrying out a program of action only by siding with Hamilton and the Federalist faction. If he did not in fact alienate the Republicans, this was not because of his handling of the Presidency so much as the sense of gratitude the whole people felt to him. After Washington no President has succeeded in at once appealing to the whole people as a revered symbol of national unity and winning the devotion of a partisan majority, although Monroe, Grant, and Eisenhower at least were accepted by the whole nation as its honored chief.

But the critical test is the use a President makes of his popularity. Or, indeed, whether he *can* use it or *does* use it at all. If there is a politics of popularity that a President must practice in order to become or to remain popular, there is also a politics of power he must practice in order to conduct his office as he understands it.

# III

## Presidential Popularity and Constitutional Issues

1. *Washington's unpartisan prestige and Hamilton's partisan bank* ૐ All of the more vigorous Presidents of the United States have had problems of applying or interpreting the Constitution. Some of them, Jefferson, Lincoln, or Franklin Roosevelt, have wished to interpret the Constitution liberally in order to find warrant for policies or programs that would break with established practices; others, Jackson, Monroe, or Eisenhower, have hidden behind the document as a device for avoiding action; still others, like Eisenhower again, have been pressed, by new interpretations of the Constitution, to advance or at least defend policies of which they did not approve.

Because of the very constitutional provisions that establish his office and confer upon him his powers, the President cannot escape constitutional questions. As chief of state he must perform ceremonial duties; as commander-in-chief he is responsible for the safety of the nation; as chief executive he must carry out the laws. If, in addition to these inescapable responsibilities, he is also a vigorous chief of party, he may be vitally concerned with the meaning of particular phrases or clauses in the Constitution. Washington, the first President, had to deal frequently with matters of constitutional interpretation, since there were no precedents. One hundred and seventy years later there was a massive body of constitutional law and innumerable precedents; but the most recent President, John F. Kennedy, had nevertheless to reach crucial new decisions on matters of interpreting and upholding the Constitution. The ways in which the popular Presidents have committed, or failed to commit, their popular standing on constitutional issues provide a valuable index to the politics of presidential leadership.

Washington, anxious to conduct the government in strict accord with the newly adopted organic law and fearful lest any act of his Administration should undermine the public confidence in the document, proceeded with meticulous care on every question involving the Constitution. As presiding officer at the Constitutional Convention he had played a major part in conciliating the various factions; he had staked his reputation in the campaign to get the Constitution adopted. He believed deeply that if there was ever to grow up a nation out of the thirteen little republics spawned by the Revolution, that nation would have to depend upon popular adherence to the Constitution.

Almost immediately upon taking office, Washington was faced with the kind of problem that, although it could never be solved, had to be resolved—and resolved again and again for generations. Secretary of the Treasury Hamilton wanted a national bank as a means of building a national financial system. There was no provision in the Constitution that would authorize Congress to create such a bank. In Hamilton's view, however, because a bank was necessary for the sovereign to function, Congress could establish a bank under its power to make all laws necessary to carry out the powers expressly given to it, such as borrowing money or levying taxes. According to Hamilton, the power to incorporate a bank was a reasonable inference by construction. The Secretary of State, Mr. Jefferson, for his part was suspicious of all banks whatever, and of a national bank in particular. In his view one of the aims of the Revolution had been to get out from under the financial domination of Great Britain, centered in the Bank of England. Now it was proposed to copy that hated institution in the brand-new republic. Jefferson looked into the Constitution and saw nothing resembling a power to create a bank or to charter any other sort of corporation. If, said he, a power was not expressly granted to Congress, Congress did not have it, and that was all there was to it. The point was not to have as much government as possible, but as little.

The President, knowing that the idea of a bank was in dispute, asked the members of his Cabinet to give their views in writing

on the question of constitutionality. The responses of Hamilton
and Jefferson both became classic political papers. The Hamilton
paper set the pattern, once and for all, for "loose" construction;
the Jefferson paper provided the prototype for all later "strict"
construction. As for the President, he could, of course, find no
middle ground and so had to take sides. He agreed with Jefferson's interpretation as a matter of principle, but as a matter of
practice he agreed with Hamilton that the bank was necessary.
Thus he threw his support to broad construction and became, in
effect, a partisan of federalism.

Unfortunately for the student looking back on this decision
from the vantage point of a later day, there could be no referendum on Washington's choice. The new republican system was
representative but not yet popular. In the election of 1792 Washington himself was re-elected with all but three of the electoral
votes, and those three merely abstained. But the opponents of
Hamilton's fiscal policy, choosing to make a principled fight on
the Vice-Presidency, rallied 50 votes for "republican" George
Clinton of New York against "federalist" John Adams. In the
Congressional elections there was little but confusion. Both the
federalist and the republican factions claimed victory; but there
were no organized parties, and many contests were decided without reference to the national issues at all. What is certain is that
the third Congress contained at least as many opponents of
Hamilton as friends. Only the prestige of the President kept
Hamiltonian legislation flowing.

If any judgment can safely be made on the President's role in
this first great constitutional struggle, it must be that Washington's personal standing with the whole country allayed the fears
of those who were against a loose construction. Though he made
no appeal to the people, the nonpartisan image of the "father of
his country" held their confidence, while the President was
in fact making a highly partisan decision. This kind of leadership so disturbed the forthright partisan, Jefferson, that he eventually resigned from the government.

But despite his intimate knowledge of the way the decision
had been reached, Jefferson was unwilling to say openly that
Washington had gone over to the Federalists. Though his confidence in the President's judgment and in his selection of ad-

visers was destroyed, he thought it both patriotic and politic to keep silence. In his retirement he wrote to his old friend Philip Mazzei in Italy a frank account of his feelings. To Jefferson's dismay, and the permanent rupture of his relations with Washington, Mazzei made the letter public. It contained such things as this:

It would give you a fever were I to name to you the apostates who have gone over to these heresies [Hamilton's bank and fiscal program] men who were Samsons in the field and Solomons in the council, but who have had their heads shorn by the harlot England.

This kind of expression ensured that its author would, upon becoming President, have to stand or fall by his convictions. He could not and did not hope to hold the esteem of his opponents while he took action of which they strongly disapproved. Such an action was the purchase of Louisiana in 1803.[1]

2. *Jefferson purchases Louisiana and avoids a real constitutional crisis by creating a false one* ⧸≈⧹ Even in the circumstances of the beginning of the nineteenth century, with painfully slow communication, worse transportation, and wholly inadequate maps, it is difficult to understand how any important segment of American opinion could have opposed the acquisition of Louisiana. Yet many substantial citizens in the Northeast feared the westward expansion they saw as inevitably following the purchase, and assumed that their position would be so weakened economically and politically that there might be no other solution for their interest than to split the union into separate confederacies. It was the old argument of Atlantic fisheries against Mississippi navigation, which had divided American leaders since the Revolution. Louisiana brought the controversy to a climax.

Jefferson, who sent Lewis and Clark to explore the whole West from the Mississippi to the Pacific, mapping as they went, was perhaps the one American who fully understood the immense significance of the bargain James Monroe and Robert R. Livingston had made with Napoleon. Livingston, who afterward wished all the credit for the great stroke, saw at first no point at all to buying more than New Orleans and the land east of the Mississippi and was persuaded by Monroe only with great resistance to sign the conventions. Monroe himself, though he immediately saw the political advantage in ridding the trans-Mississippi area of French and Spanish influence, was very doubtful about the possible economic consequences of the purchase. But to Jefferson, Louisiana meant an immense extension of the "empire of liberty." He was ready to take any action, pay any price, to obtain it. Thus Louisiana was transcendently Jefferson's policy and Jefferson's achievement, and therefore Jefferson's responsibility to defend against political opponents. He was happy to accept it and confident of his support.

There were two different constitutional issues involved in the Louisiana Purchase. In the first, Jefferson acted unconstitutionally and relied upon the popularity of the measure and his own standing in the country to sustain him; in the second, he favored an *ex post facto* amendment until he was persuaded that it would not be necessary. In both cases he acted so directly contrary to the established "Jeffersonian" position on strict construction that some of his more doctrinaire followers were dismayed. In another year or two, indeed, they were to desert him.

The first and more immediate problem was that of payment to France. The Congress had voted to give the President a discretionary fund of $2 million with which to purchase a permanent right of deposit at New Orleans or, perhaps, to gain sovereignty over the city itself and some surrounding territory. Monroe had gone to Paris in the spring of 1803 armed with instructions to use this money as wisely as he could according to the opportunities he might be offered by the French government. He found that the French were already talking to Minister Livingston about selling all their holdings on the North American continent. Livingston was staggered by the proposal; Monroe, to his credit, bucked up Livingston and went through with the deal. The price he negotiated was some $14 million more than he was authorized to spend. However, relying upon his close friendship with the President and with Secretary of State Madison, he undertook on behalf of the United States to pay the sum agreed upon. Livingston signed only under protest.

Thus when Jefferson learned that his agents had purchased

Louisiana, he found himself in the position of having to defend to Congress the expenditure by the executive of an immense sum that had not been authorized or appropriated. The violation of the Constitution was flagrant. Jefferson's tactic was to meet the issue obliquely and thus blunt its edge. Relying on the delight of the Republican majority in the success of the deal with France, he proceeded to tell the Congress quite simply and with supreme self-assurance that he assumed their intent to pay whatever was required for the purchase. In his Third Annual Message, October 17, 1803, he put the whole matter in terms of the acts of Congress in the previous session, a period when the right of deposit at New Orleans had been for a time suspended. Fearing lest the nation be in constant danger "while so important a key to the commerce of the western country remained under foreign power," Jefferson reminded the Congress that it had "authorized" what he called "propositions" for obtaining "the sovereignty of New Orleans, and of other possessions in that quarter interesting to our quiet." These other possessions of the French, he unobtrusively added, were to be acquired "to such extent as was deemed practicable." Both he and the Congress well knew that no one had at the time thought of acquiring the whole of Louisiana as the "extent practicable." But Jefferson characteristically left the Congress to suppose that it was their wisdom that had allowed so much discretion to the Executive!

As for the matter of payment, the President spoke of "the provisional appropriation of two millions of dollars." This, he reminded the Congress, was "to be applied and accounted for by the President of the United States, intended as part of the purchase price." Nothing in the act stipulated that the sum was to be "part of the purchase price" for Louisiana, but then, nothing said it was not, either. Jefferson simply proceeded with the logical inference. He had, he said, "considered" the appropriation "as conveying the sanction of Congress to the acquisition proposed." Because the "enlightened government of France saw, with just discernment, the importance to both nations of such liberal arrangements as might best and permanently promote the peace, friendship, and interests of both," they had transferred the "property and sovereignty of all Louisiana" to the United States. Under the circumstances a treaty had been signed and

would be submitted to the Senate for its "constitutional sanction" and thereafter "to the representatives also, for the exercise
of their functions, as to those conditions which are within the
powers vested by the Constitution in Congress." In brief, they
would be asked to appropriate the money. An impolite twen-
tieth-century phrase aptly describing Jefferson's language would
be "double talk." But however elegantly or inelegantly the message was characterized by those to whom it was addressed or may
be described in retrospect, it worked. The President, the arch
apostle of strict construction, carried off the loosest construction
yet attempted by unflinching reliance upon his own popular
leadership and the popularity of his unconstitutional act.[2]

The second constitutional aspect of the Louisiana question was
raised by Jefferson himself and, in fact, pressed by nobody else.
His motives for doing so, despite the availability of all his papers,
remain somewhat obscure. The issue, as he said he saw it, was
whether the Constitution gave the Congress the power to acquire
and govern any territory other than those territories within the
bounds of the states in 1788. This problem troubled him so
greatly, he said, that he thought it best to ask for an amendment
to the Constitution to clarify the matter. He tried his hand at
drafting such an amendment and circulated it among his advisers.[3]

Because acquiring territory has always been the prerogative of
a sovereign, and, beyond any dispute, the United States was a
sovereign else it could not have entered into the treaty with
France at all, it is difficult to see why Jefferson thought there was
a problem. The usual explanation is simply that he was such a
stickler for constitutional correctness and strict interpretation
that he leaned over backwards in this instance. This view does
less than justice either to Jefferson's legal knowledge or his
political sense. But if his proposal to amend the Constitution is
looked upon in terms of Jefferson's political tactics, rather than
in terms of his presumed doctrinaire approach to the Constitution, a great deal of sense can be made out of it. The real problem was to get Congress to sanction the purchase both by Senate
ratification and by Congressional appropriation of the funds to
which the President had committed it. Committing large sums of
unauthorized and, of course, unappropriated money was a highly
dangerous precedent. Not only was it not sanctioned by the Con-

stitution, but it constituted a genuine threat to constitutional government. Faced with a choice of losing the opportunity offered by France, if he should wait for Congress to act, or else acting directly contrary to constitutional requirements, Jefferson had thought the public interest would be best served by acting. But once the decision was taken, the wisest course would certainly be to call as little attention as possible to its unconstitutionality. The opposition would have been handed not only a troublesome but a genuine issue. They might be turned some degree away from the main point by a constitutional diversion. Thus it seems reasonable to suppose that by giving so much attention to the constitutionality of acquiring the territory at all, Jefferson could hope to diminish concern about the constitutionality of the means used to acquire it. In a private letter to his old associate John Dickinson he coupled the two points in a revealing way. "Our confederation is certainly confined to the limits established by the Revolution," he wrote, though he assigns no reasons for the dictum. And the "general government has no powers but such as the Constitution has given it." Since it has not been given "a power of holding foreign territory, and still less of incorporating it into the Union," an amendment "seems necessary." But in the meantime, he continues, "we must ratify and pay our money, as we have treated, for a thing beyond the Constitution, and rely on the nation to sanction an act done for its great good, without its previous authority." When the stir he thus deliberately created quieted down for lack of any serious interest in it, the whole matter was passed over, and what might have been a major constitutional crisis never arose. Making full use of his partisan popularity Jefferson did lead the nation "to sanction an act done for its great good" and "without its previous authority," having himself decided what was "a great good" and well knowing that his irreconcilable opponents had quite other notions as to what was good for the nation—or at least for them![4]

3. *Monroe's formula for securing internal improvements he believed unconstitutional. His prestige brought to bear on the Missouri question* ϕ⸱ When he was faced with an important constitutional issue, Jefferson's protegé, James Monroe, showed himself a disciple both of old "Jeffersonian principles" and of

Jefferson's politics of presidential leadership. But Monroe's leadership was nevertheless strikingly different from his master's. In one case he applied Jeffersonian principles in order to avoid action while stating that he favored it; in another he overcame constitutional scruples, as he thought, to save the Union.

The question of the use of federal funds for "internal improvements" was raised in the first instance by Jefferson in the early stages of his administration. He foresaw, as early as 1802, a time when the national debt would be paid off and a surplus would accrue to the Treasury, a surplus derived not from taxes, which were repealed, but only from customs duties and from the sale of public lands. He proposed to use this extra national income to improve the whole nation by building a great system of roads and canals and by establishing a national university. Because Congress had no power to legislate for such purposes, under the express grants in the Constitution, Jefferson proposed the adoption of a constitutional amendment to grant the power. Meanwhile he authorized the building of the Cumberland Road by grants of federal money to the states, under the appropriation power, to construct their separate links in the road. The purpose of the Cumberland Road was to connect the new state of Ohio overland with the Eastern seaboard; its construction was in fact a condition under which Ohio was admitted. It is curious that the power to build "Post Offices and Post Roads" (I, 8, cl. 7) was not at that time invoked. But it was not, and no objections were made to the method used. However, no amendment was adopted to cover federal planning and sponsorship of a program of internal improvements. Madison, some years later, vetoed an internal improvement bill as unconstitutional, while advocating, as Jefferson had done, an amendment to remedy the situation.

When Monroe came to the Presidency in March, 1817, he immediately let it be known that, like Madison, he favored internal improvements, thought Congress lacked the power to proceed, and advocated an amendment to permit the government to go ahead. To Madison he wrote that he thought "it would be improper in me, after your negative, to allow them to discuss the subject and bring a bill for me to sign." Instead he would ask "the procuring an amendment from the states, so as to vest the right in Congress in a manner to comprise in it a power also to institute seminaries of learning." Speaking thus in a private letter to one of his closest political associates, Monroe makes it clear that his view of the problem is neither partisan nor sectional, but controlled by his sense of the public interest, on the one hand, and strict construction of the Constitution, on the other.[5]

Congress, however, was quite unwilling to consider Monroe's appeal for an amendment. The majority, favoring internal improvements, went ahead with various bills, knowing the President would veto. In the spring of 1818, for example, they passed a resolution declaring Congress' power to "appropriate money for the construction of post roads, and of canals, and for the improvement of water courses." At the same time they considered, without passing, bills to continue the Cumberland Road, buy stock in the Chesapeake and Delaware Canal Company, and build roads in Alabama and Tennessee. Monroe wrote to Madison that this session of Congress had been "unusually oppressive on every branch of the Executive department," in large part because of the disagreement on Congressional power over internal improvements.[6]

But between the time of Jefferson's broad-visioned proposals and the succession of Monroe to the Presidency, the matter of internal improvements had moved from the realm of hope and speculation to the realm of practicability and controversy; it had become a sectional issue. An account of the 1818 Congressional debate in *Niles' Register* analyzes the division of opinion. The New England states were generally opposed to the internal improvements program because they were well advanced in programs for their own development and resented the notion of their tax money being spent to the benefit of the West. The South had less need than other sections for extensive roads and canals, since it was well served by natural waterways in exporting its cotton and tobacco crops. Like New England, the South objected vigorously to the expenditure of public money for what seemed the special advantage of one section. The Middle States, however, generally favored internal improvements in the West, because the proposed roads and canals would benefit their commerce directly. It was remarkable how constitutional scruples deterred Southerners and some New Englanders from supporting internal improvement bills, while in the minds of Western and Middle

States Congressmen no constitutional difficulties seemed to exist!

Thus the popular, unpartisan President was faced with a frustrating dilemma. If he approved internal improvement bills, he would do violence to his own sincere beliefs about constitutionality and, at the same time, offend two major sections of the Union, including his own. But if he blocked the program, he would offend his own long-time supporters in the West as well as the populous states like New York and Pennsylvania, where the Republican Party had always been strong, indeed, whose adherence to Republicanism he had himself vigorously encouraged in the old partisan days. And by opposing internal improvements he might in the long run be failing the national interest. Under these circumstances Monroe brooded long and prayerfully on the proper course.

One approach to the problem occurred to him almost by accident during his Northern tour of 1817. At Plattsburgh, New York, he found the old road to the St. Lawrence in such wretched condition that his party could not make use of it. In what amounted to a snap decision, he ordered the War Department to undertake immediately a full-scale repair and development of the road. Since the road involved access to the borders of a foreign nation, there could be no question of its relevance to national defense. Monroe, in other words, acted in his capacity as commander-in-chief of the armed forces. The state of New York, and no doubt the nation, benefited from this decision. But it laid the President open to scathing attack from Henry Clay, the great proponent of an "American System" of internal improvements. In one of his more telling bursts of oratory, the eloquent Speaker of the House demolished the President's arguments about states' rights and strict construction:

The President ordered a road of considerable extent to be constructed or repaired, on his sole authority, in a time of profound peace, when no enemy threatened the country, and when, in relation to the power as to which alone that road could be useful in time of war, there exists the best understanding, and a prospect of lasting friendship, greater than at any other period. On his sole authority the President acted, and we are already called upon by the chairman of the committee of ways and means to sanction the act by an appropriation.

With stinging sarcasm he continued:

This measure has been taken, too, without the consent of the state of New York; and what is wonderful, when we consider the magnitude of the state-rights which are said to be violated, without even a protest of that state against it. On the contrary, I understand, from some of the military officers who are charged with the execution of the work, what is very extraordinary, that the people through whose quarter of the country the road passes, do not view it as a national calamity; and they would be very glad that the President would visit them often, and that he would order a road to be cut and improved, at the national expense, every time he should visit them.

Clay went on to point out that "other roads, in other parts of the Union, have, it seems, been likewise ordered, or their execution, at the public expense, sanctioned by the executive, without the concurrence of Congress." But Monroe was not harmed, politically, by Clay's attack. To the contrary, as Clay's remarks indicate, the President's action was popular, at least in some quarters.[7]

However, a whole system of internal improvements could not be rested upon military need, or even on the power to build post roads. The impasse between the Congress and the President continued without a significant break until 1822, when Congress finally agreed upon a bill to repair and improve the Cumberland Road and sent it to the President. This highly controversial measure precipitated, at least in the President's mind, a constitutional crisis. He could not deny that the road was in desperate need of repair nor that there had been federal support for it from the beginning. The difficulty was that Congress now wanted the federal government to take over the maintenance of the road directly, as a turnpike, by establishing a system of gates and tolls with federal penalties for failure by patrons to pay. Clearly if Monroe signed this bill on the ground that the purpose it served was worthy, Congress would assume his consent in the future to other internal improvement bills. Under the circumstances he decided he would have to veto. On May 4, 1822, he sent the bill back to the House with what became a famous veto message. "A power to establish turnpikes," he said, "with gates and tolls, and to enforce the collection of tolls by penalties, implies a power to adopt and execute a complete system of internal improvements."

He went on to refer to necessary ancillary activities to support a turnpike—taking private property, protecting the road from injuries—and asserted that such activities could as logically be carried on with respect to any road. He then listed all of the powers under which it had been urged that the Congress might pass such legislation—to build post roads, to declare war, to regulate commerce, to pay the debts and provide for the common defense and the general welfare, to make all laws necessary and proper to carry out specified powers, and to make rules respecting property and territory of the United States. "According to my judgment," he said, "it cannot be derived from either of those powers, nor from all of them united, and in consequence it does not exist."[8]

If Monroe had left it at that, he would have placed himself squarely against both the specific purpose of the bill, whose merit he granted and everyone knew to be genuine, and the longer range national interest, which he himself believed called for federal assistance to internal improvements. Since an amendment was no longer a feasible alternative, Monroe put his mind to other possibilities. To the Congress he sent a long and thorough examination of the whole question, in the form of an informal communication. Although he once more pleaded for an amendment that would grant Congress full power to plan and construct, he devoted careful attention to the use of existing powers that no one disputed. In addition to the powers to act for the national defense and to carry the mails, Monroe gave special attention to the appropriation power. If Congress could not *construct* roads or canals, except under strict limitation as to purposes, there was no similar limitation as to *appropriation* of the public money. "My idea is," he said, "that Congress have an unlimited power to raise money, and that in its appropriation they have a discretionary power, restricted only by the duty to appropriate it to purposes of common defense and of general, not local, national, not State, benefit." From this power Monroe concluded that there were several ways in which Congress could use the public money to assist internal improvement. One was to make grants to the states for their use, as in the case of the Cumberland Road, in building or maintaining portions of roads or canals passing through their territory. A second possibility was to enter into compacts with individual states whereby the state legislatures would by law delegate to the federal government the power to build or repair. Still a third way of proceeding was for the federal government to buy shares in private corporations organized for building internal improvements.[9]

By these suggestions, against the background of his strict construction of the Constitution, Monroe succeeded in maintaining substantial support on both sides of the controversy. His position was ridiculed once more by Henry Clay, but it was adopted by the Congress. In response to a request in his Sixth Annual Message, Congress made a direct appropriation of money to be applied by the states for repair of the Cumberland Road. Monroe, of course, signed the bill. The next year he asked for an appropriation for the army engineers to survey possible road and canal routes from the Ohio to Lake Erie. Again Congress granted the request, and Monroe signed the bill into law. Finally, the day before he went out of office, March 3, 1825, Monroe signed a bill authorizing the Treasury to buy stock in the Chesapeake and Delaware Canal Company.

If Monroe's strict Jeffersonian views of the Constitution had the effect of blocking a great national effort at internal improvements, which he himself favored, they nevertheless pleased the strict constructionists and those who, regardless of their constitutional views, opposed general improvements. At the same time, his liberal interpretation of the appropriation power made possible certain substantial improvements that helped the President to maintain the good will of those who favored the larger program under greater use of implied powers. If he did not give vigorous leadership, at least he headed off the worst manifestations of sectional rivalries and maintained his own position as the symbol of national unity.

And it was probably well that he did, for the long-drawn-out controversy over internal improvements was far less of a threat to the Constitution or to national unity than was the Missouri question, which was being debated at the same time. Whereas on this ominous issue Monroe's views were influenced by events and pressures, and actually altered during the crisis, his inconsistency ended with an act of statesmanship that he might not have been able to perform had his approach to his office in general, and to sectional issues in particular, been partisan. It cannot, of course, be said that Monroe's nonpartisan popularity brought about the Missouri Compromise, but his politics of maintaining himself and his office as the national rallying point was certainly a decisive factor in its adoption. That Monroe was re-elected almost unanimously just as the Missouri crisis mounted—and at the bottom of the depression of 1819–1821—evidences not only the groping of public opinion for reassurance when faced with new and frustrating problems, but the remarkable interaction between the people and their trusted chief. If Monroe was the only man the people would entrust with the Presidency, this was because he stood for unity in the midst of threatened disunity, for national as against sectional purposes. That the issues were ultimately irreconcilable was no reason for not making the effort to transcend them. This conviction, shared with their troubled old patriot-President by a great majority of Americans, was what saved the Union for the next forty years.

When Missouri formally applied for statehood in 1820, a smouldering fire of sectional controversy burst for a terrifying moment into a blaze. It had long been the practice to admit slave and nonslave states to balance each other. Since Maine was applying at the same time, it at first appeared that the tested device of balancing the two admissions could be invoked once again. But Missouri presented a new kind of problem, as Northern Congressmen were quick to point out. It was the first state to be carved out of the Louisiana Territory, except for Louisiana itself; this involved the westward expansion not only of the nation as a whole but of slavery, since it was the first territory asking for statehood into which slavery had been introduced. What would be the implications for the future? If Missouri were admitted without restriction, what would prevent slaveholders from migrating beyond Missouri north and west into the empty land and establishing more slave states in the future? Indeed, the admission of Missouri as a slave state seemed to invite the spread of slavery.

And so an effort was made to refuse admission to Missouri unless it excluded slavery. The argument, by men like John W. Taylor of New York in the House and Rufus King, also of New York, in the Senate, was rested on the Constitution. Since Congress had the power to admit new states, it therefore had the power to establish restrictions on admission. Since Congress had power to make all needful rules and laws for territories, it therefore had the power to apply the antislavery clause of the Northwest Ordinance to any and all other territories. The Southern reply, made by men like Nathaniel Macon of North Carolina, was to claim that the North was making specious use of the Constitution for political purposes, namely, to concentrate national power in the interests of industry and finance. As for the Constitution, said the Southerners, it expressly recognized slavery in the "three-fifths" clause and conferred upon Congress no power whatever to determine whether a new state or territory might permit slavery. Since the North already had a majority of the votes in the House, the Southern men feared that any further weakening of the Southern position by the unbalanced admission of free states would upset the fundamental balance of power upon which they believed the Union rested. It is worth observing that no one talked abolition during the Missouri debate, not even King, though he did anticipate William H. Seward by invoking "natural law" in support of his contention that slavery was an evil that should not be allowed to spread. The Southerners, with one or two exceptions, made no moral defense of slavery as such but only of their right to hold and enjoy their property anywhere in the new lands. But if moral lines were not yet irrevocably drawn, by the winter of 1819–1820 there was a bitter and menacing political deadlock in both houses of Congress.

The President, meanwhile, watched developments fearfully. Underlying the more obvious motives of the Northern men, he was sure he could see a covert effort to build a new party, led by King, which might flourish by exploiting Democratic-Republican divisions and perhaps come to power with a sectional majority. King had, after all, made a run for President against Monroe in 1816 and was known to be ambitious still. "Before the arrival of Mr. King," Monroe wrote to Madison, "the discussion was managed with moderation. . . . His own exhibition has lessened his reputation for talents, and patriotism and indeed for morality." What was more significant, if true, "he had declared to some, in whom he confides, that it was an effort for power." The plot,

Monroe had heard, involved "propositions . . . to some of the
members of Penna., to induce that state to unite, on this new
combination." He even had heard that Gideon Granger, who had
been Jefferson's Postmaster General, was involved "in this business" as a member of the New York Assembly. Monroe's state of
mind, as this confidential letter suggests, was unhappily reverting
to his moods during the party quarrels of the 1790's when he had
looked for conspiratorial significance in every word or deed by
every public man. If Rufus King did in fact have any hope of
building a new party to challenge the President, that hope was
not shared by any significant group in New York or anywhere
else. Vice-President Daniel Tompkins was firmly in control of the
situation in New York, despite the noises of De Witt Clinton and
the oratory of King. Elsewhere political preoccupation was with
the *succession* to Monroe in *1824*, not trying to *defeat* him in
*1820*.[10]

But the movement to restrict slavery, of which King was an
extreme spokesman, had nevertheless substantial numbers in the
Congress. The issue was sharply drawn, and Monroe saw that he
might well have to resolve it by doing what he called "a painful
duty." By this he meant that he would veto a bill calling for exclusion of slavery in the admission of Missouri. He was opposed
to restriction as a device for upsetting the sectional balance, and
he was persuaded that it would be unconstitutional. He prepared
for this "painful duty" by drafting a veto message with which to
return any bill admitting Missouri only with restriction.

His arguments were cogent and stated with clarity. First, he
denied Congress had the right to restrict a new State:

That if conditions of a character not applicable to the original States
should be imposed on a new State, an inequality would be imposed or
created, lessening in degree the right of State sovereignty, which
would always be degrading to such State, and which operating as a
condition of its admission, its incorporation would be incomplete,
and would also be annulled, and such new State be severed from the
Union should it afterwards assume equality and exercise a power
acknowledged to belong to all the original states.

Second, he vigorously attacked the notion of restricting territories
that would later become states:

That the proposed restriction to Territories which are to be admitted
into the Union, *if not in direct violation of the Constitution,* IS
REPUGNANT TO ITS PRINCIPLES, since it is intended to produce
an effect on the future policy of the new States, operating unequally
in regard to the original States. . . .

Not long after he drafted this document, Monroe was writing
confidentially to friends like Judge Spence Roane that he was
honestly unsure about the constitutionality of restricting the
territories. He had evidently forgotten that as a young Congressman in 1784, he had endorsed Jefferson's land ordinance that forever outlawed slavery in the western lands. Now, in 1820, he
thought that it was "very unjust to restrain the owner from
carrying his slave into a Territory." But injustice and unconstitutionality, he conceded, were not the same thing. "How far it
may be proper to go on this principle, I shall duly weigh," he
said. "If the right to impose a restraint exists, and Congress
should pass a law for it, to reject it as to the whole of the unsettled Territory might, with existing impressions in other quarters, affect our system." He left no doubt that he meant that a
veto would affect the "system" adversely.[11]

The President was changing his mind. A possible compromise
was being discussed, and, genuinely alarmed at the danger he
felt for the Union, Monroe was listening carefully and weighing
the terms of the proposal against the national interest as well as
the Constitution. The compromise would admit Missouri as a
slave State but thereafter forbid slavery to expand into any of the
territory of the United States north of 36° 30', that is, the southern boundary of Missouri imagined to be extended westward
indefinitely. Since Arkansas would come in as a slave state later
on, and the Texas territory, with slavery established, might ultimately revert to the United States, the admission of new free
states would not for a long time again threaten the precarious
balance of the sections. Monroe did not like these measures. He
would have greatly preferred to admit Missouri without qualification and leave the question otherwise open for the unfolding
of an unknown future. But he saw that the forces on both sides
were too strong and too deeply aroused to allow for national
unity on such terms. By the middle of February, 1820, he ap-

parently came to the conclusion that compromise was necessary.

Having made up his mind, Monroe acted at once to foster the spirit of compromise while maintaining his own status above the conflict. He confided his changing views to his son-in-law, George Hay, in Richmond. Hay, mindful of an impending Republican caucus that was to nominate Monroe for a second term, feared that his father-in-law's leaning toward compromise would have unhappy political consequences. He took the liberty of returning the letter, which had apparently been intended for circulation. "I rejoice," he said, "that you sent your letter to me. In the present state of things, the effect of such a communication, indicating hesitation or doubt, would be fatal." He added that he knew "the temper of the people." They were, he said, "prepared for any struggle." Monroe accepted Hay's judgment and made no further effort to educate the Republican legislators until after their caucus had unanimously renominated him. The caucus, as Hay reported, assumed that Monroe would veto a restrictive Missouri bill. Thus Monroe's tactic, or at least Hay's, was equivocal.[12]

But the stakes were very great. And Monroe did presently make his views known in Virginia through another medium. To the Richmond *Enquirer,* a paper known to express Monroe's views, he sent several "extracts" from letters "from a gentleman in Washington to his friend in Richmond." At one time Monroe was supposed to have written these letters himself, but their style makes such an identification seem doubtful. What is not in dispute, however, is that the letters expressed the views he wished to spread in Virginia and throughout the South. One of these letters concludes with perhaps the most effective plea for the Missouri Compromise made by anyone during the entire controversy. It is worth citing at length, bearing in mind that not only the editors but the readers of the *Enquirer* understood that it contained the views of the President. In the light of the position he took in these paragraphs, it is not difficult to imagine what he must have written to Hay that so jarred that young man's political sensibilities:

> The crisis is indeed a most auspicious one, and nothing but the prudence and wisdom of practical men can avert the dangers which it threatens. If either party completely triumphs, it is much to be

feared that the other will not submit; and I am penetrated with the deepest regret and horror at seeing that too many on both sides view disunion with so little repugnance.

This was the crux of the matter. At this tense moment the President evidently wished to make a special appeal to his fellow Virginians. Their "pride natural to such highminded people," said the letter, made them "too apt to overlook the consequences." These might well be the separation of the Atlantic from the other states. If "individuals" could be forgiven for looking upon such a possibility without too great a concern, "politicians" could not. "It is dangerous for a politician to yield himself up to the indulgence of such a spirit." There is really no sensible alternative except a compromise, and compromise is the special art of the politician. The letter goes on to make a direct appeal:

Your pride revolts at the idea of a compromise of any kind, and thus it is most completely rendered the instrument of promoting the views of Mr. King and his friends, who are drawing the highest advantages from the stand you are taking, whilst it aids them, also, in their endeavors to put down those of our northern friends, who, in opposition to the popular current in their respective States, are firmly identifying themselves with us on the present occasion. Is nothing due to the magnanimity of those gentlemen?

Next the author discusses the meaning of the compromise itself. "It is singly whether you will save any part of the country." More specifically, he declares:

By the compromise you would give up nothing which you can retain; while, by seeming to yield to it voluntarily, you would, by manifesting your own moderation, place your opponents so much the more in the wrong, there being a large majority in the House of Representatives in favor of restricting the States as well as the Territories. You have nothing to hope from that quarter, and I can assure you that there is a very decided majority in the Senate in favor of excluding from all unsettled territory north of 36½ degrees north latitude, and I believe, if a compromise does not take place, the exclusion will be general.

The final point was a flatly realistic statement:

If it should not happen this year, from the disproportionate increase of the non-slaveholding population, it must eventually succeed.[13]

Holding these views in mid-February, 1820, it was predictable that Monroe would accept the compromise bill if it should pass and reach his desk. On March 3, the bill passed. After asking the views of his cabinet colleagues in writing, Monroe signed the bill into law. The new issue, raised later in the year by Missouri's constitutional clause forbidding migration into the State of free Negroes, was anticlimax. The second Missouri Compromise, so-called, amounted simply to a Congressional declaration that Missouri could not mean what it said. Monroe was distressed that the controversy had flared up again. He told Madison that the House fight over a new Speaker, Clay having temporarily left Congress, indicated "a disposition to review the Missouri question in the temper displayed in the last session." But early in 1821 Clay returned and gave his attention to finding a compromise formula. His proposal, which was adopted, amounted to no more than requiring Missouri to declare that it would pass no laws contrary to the Constitution of the United States. Since what was constitutional remained a matter of opinion unless tested by the courts, Missouri accepted the condition. Monroe signed the bill and proclaimed the admission of Missouri on August 10, 1821. Thus ended the Missouri crisis.

There have been many harsh assessments of the Missouri Compromise. The first, by Thomas Jefferson, was perhaps the harshest. "This momentous question," he told Monroe, "like a firebell in the night, awakened and filled me with terror." It was, he said, "the death knell of the Union." And so, perhaps, it proved. But to judge Clay and Monroe in the perspective of the Civil War is unfair to both men. If the Missouri Compromise failed in the end, it nevertheless provided some forty years in which wiser or more courageous men, if such there had been, might have acted to save the nation. Whatever judgment is made of the historic consequences of the compromise, Monroe's statesmanship must be granted. His anxiety to minimize party squabbles and sectional differences, and his politics of nonpartisanship aimed at maintaining national unity with himself as the symbol of that unity, found an appropriate objective in the tense necessities of the first awesome sectional crisis. It may not be too much to say that Monroe's success is still unsurpassed as the high point of achievement among Presidents who elected the role of popular nonpartisan in their exercise of the politics of presidential leadership.

4. *Jackson uses the Constitution to wreck Clay's American system and Biddle's Bank of the United States. Jackson's nullification stand saves the Constitution and the Union* ৽৯

Though he was an unreconstructed Jeffersonian, in principle and temper, James Monroe could and did amend his constitutional views when he was convinced that the national interest required him to do so. At a moment of supreme crisis he converted his somewhat tepid nonpartisan popularity into an act of statesmanship. The last of the great Jeffersonians, Andrew Jackson, was inflexible on the continuing question of internal improvements. That inflexibility, coinciding as it did with the rapid development of the steam railroad, effectively ended the controversy. But under quite different circumstances, Jackson found the Constitution a valuable weapon in winning a highly partisan victory over the forces of finance and business, which for a time seemed to rival the power of the national government itself. In so doing Jackson converted his great partisan popularity into an act of vigorous executive leadership. If that act was, at the same time, perhaps lacking on the score of statesmanship, as his opponents angrily maintained, no such thing could be said of Jackson's stand in the far more serious constitutional struggle over nullification. In that crisis there was no doubt about his statesmanship.

Jackson was involved in constitutional questions, either by events or by his own choice, from the very outset of his administration. By the beginning of his third year in office, indeed, he was so embroiled in controversies and squabbles about constitutional interpretation that he found it hard to conduct the government at all. He wrote to a Tennessee friend that "between Bank men, nullifiers, and internal improvement men it is hard to get a Cabinet who will unite with me heart and hand in the great task of Democratic reform in the administration of our government." Of the three annoying subjects he had only himself to blame for his troubles over the last.[14]

Jackson prided himself on being an "old Jeffersonian." He was even friendly with John Randolph, that highly unstable Virginian who, holding that Jefferson was not sufficiently "Jeffersonian," had formed the "Tertium Quids" against Jefferson in 1804. Jackson himself had leaned toward Burr in the great Republican feud of 1804–1807 and had incurred the dislike of Jefferson. Thus his "Jeffersonian Republicanism" was a kind of vestigial democracy that cherished a vision of something pure and universally believed in by all honorable men and doubtless had never existed in this or any other country. But however it may have been unrelated to past realities, Jackson made of his belief in the vision a very present political force. His fight against John Quincy Adams and Henry Clay, his campaign in 1828, and his First Inaugural Address made plain what Jackson's principles were. He waited only until his First Annual Message in December, 1829, to apply them to the matter of internal improvements.

There were no controversial improvement measures pending at that moment requiring him to act. Rather, like Jefferson and Monroe, forseeing a surplus in the Treasury and anticipating that demands would be made for it to be spent in internal improvements, he took occasion to explain to the Congress and the nation what his views were. He favored broad general improvement, what would be called "development" in the terms of the twentieth century. "Every member of the Union," he said, "in peace and war, will be benefited by the improvement of inland navigation and the construction of highways in the several states." He proposed that "the most safe, just, and federal disposition which could be made of the surplus revenue would be its apportionment among the several States, according to their ratio of representation." He knew well enough that such a system would make national planning impossible and, in effect, give over the struggle to the enemies of internal improvements. Thus he was quite clearly serving notice that he was opposed to anything like an "American System" such as Gallatin and Jefferson had proposed as long ago as 1807 and Clay was continuing to champion. But Jackson was not content simply to oppose; he suggested that even such allocation was unconstitutional. "It would be expedient," he said, to "propose to the States an amendment authorizing it." Such an amendment might, of course, have passed, since it was only a declaration that Congress could divide up the surplus public money according to population with no strings tied to its use by state government. But from the point of view of national improvement it would be useless, while at least on the basis of precedent under Jefferson and Monroe, it was unnecessary.

However, Jackson was not merely engaged in narrow anti-improvement politics; he was, on the contrary, moving directly and skillfully to support the bridge already built between himself and the people, which spanned the river of Congress. "I regard an appeal to the source of power," he said, "in cases of real doubt, and where its exercise is deemed indispensable to the general welfare, as among the most sacred of all our obligations." So much for the opinions of Congress!

Upon this country more than any other [he continued] has, in the providence of God, been cast the special guardianship of the great principle of adherence to written constitutions. If it fail here, all hope in regard to it will be extinguished. That this was intended to be a government of limited and specific, and not general, powers must be admitted by all, and it is our duty to preserve for it the character intended by its framers.

His next sentence he wielded like a bludgeon to club the Clay men:

If experience points out the necessity for an enlargement of these powers, let us apply for it to those for whose benefit it is to be exercised, and not undermine the whole system by a resort to overstrained constructions.

This, at the level of general principle, was "Jacksonian Democracy." If in practice the same term meant something more like seeing to it that government servants were unswervingly devoted to the President, the general principles were not the less appealing to the plain people they were meant to impress. From this point on, Jackson made it his own particular brand of the politics of power to exploit his personal popularity by appealing over the heads of Congress to his "constituents," the people. Nor need the success of his politics raise any question about his sincerity. The man and the principles, as in the case of Jefferson, were identified not only in the public mind but in the private mind of the President.[15]

A year later Congress, under Clay's leadership, did challenge him. In exasperation Jackson wrote to his intimate friend John Overton, that "large appropriations are proposed for private and local roads, such as from Maysville, Kentucky, to Lexington, with the view to compel me to oppose them, and thereby acknowledge Mr. Clay's doctrine." The only alternative, he said, was to "disapprove them upon constitutional grounds." The vigor of his famous veto of the Maysville Bill shows how he welcomed the challenge and how glad he was to rest the whole argument on the Constitution.[16]

The veto began and ended with the characteristic Jacksonian appeal to the people. At the outset he gave lip service to the political amenities. He regretted that any difference of opinion on the subject of improvements, in which everyone believed, should exist between himself and Congress. He had "an unfeigned respect for the high source" from which the bill in question arose. But, more important, he had "an anxious wish to be correctly understood by my constituents in the discharge of all my duties." The bill was not only unconstitutional, in his view, but objectionable because it would increase the national debt. Internal improvements, he reminded Congress, had always been envisoned as flowing from the expenditure of a treasury surplus for the benefit of the whole nation. Here was a proposal to borrow from the public and spend the money for a local purpose. Congress had no power to incur such debts. If the Congress was so sure it had, then let them go to the people with a constitutional amendment to express the power beyond doubt. Jackson, for his part, was confident that no such amendment would be offered by the Clay men. But the suggestion enabled him to prevent a program he believed unsound from coming into being, while, at the same time, he reinforced his own position as the people's champion against any and all special interests. The traditional Republican interpretation of the Constitution, which he himself devoutly believed in, was made to order for this kind of politics.

Jackson referred specifically to two constitutional questions. First, did the people wish that "the construction of roads and canals should be conducted by the Federal Government?" Second, did the people, on the contrary, prefer "that the agency of the Federal Government should be confined to the appropriation of money in aid of such undertakings?" Both of these questions could only be settled by asking the people directly, that is, by placing an amendment before them. The President was contemptuous of the common argument that to secure an amendment was too cumbersome a task. "The time has never yet been," he said, "when the patriotism and intelligence of the American people were not fully equal to the greatest exigency, and it never will when the subject calling for their interposition is plainly presented to them." If Henry Clay thought this kind of appeal demagogic, he must have been infuriated by the conclusion of the message. Referring to the attempt made by Clay and his followers in the "American System" to tie internal improvements to protective tariff support of industry, Jackson laid it down that

such a course would certainly indicate either an unreasonable distrust of the people or a consciousness that the system does not possess sufficient soundness for its support if left to their voluntary choice and its own merit. Those who suppose that any policy thus founded can be long upheld in this country have looked upon its history with eyes very different from mine. This policy, like every other, must abide the will of the people, who will not be likely to allow any device, however specious, to conceal its character and tendency.

At any rate Jackson would reveal how specious it was! What must have galled Clay was the certain knowledge that the people would, if solicited directly, side with the President. The battle, in fact, was over, and the President had won. But it was more than just a political victory. What Jackson had done was to establish beyond doubt his role, not as chief of state merely, not as chief executive merely, not as party leader merely, but as all three combined, for the first time in American history—as President of the United States.[17]

It was as President in this new sense that Jackson undertook to smash the Bank of the United States. In this most sustained and controversial effort of his administration he again used with skill and vigor his twin weapons, his partisan popularity with the "plain people" and his old Republican reading of the Constitution.

There was no intrinsic reason why banks should have been incompatible with Republicanism; in fact, the Republicans had chartered the second Bank of the United States in 1816. But there was nevertheless strong and persistent Republican prejudice against bankers as a class and against banks as their instrument. Jefferson thought all bankers were by nature undemocratic. Because they lived upon income from the investment of other people's money, he thought of them as parasites. His attack on Hamilton's national bank thus expressed deep personal prejudice as well as sincere constitutional scruples. Perhaps his attitude arose in part from his being typically and miserably in debt most of his adult life. Andrew Jackson shared Jefferson's prejudice to the full, though his own financial situation was never allowed to deteriorate as had Jefferson's. Like Jefferson, again, Jackson had a strong aversion to financial paper of any sort, including bank-notes. He was convinced that paper money was a kind of device of hocus-pocus to steal away the earnings of honest men. Nothing other than specie could be relied upon to have its face value when used as a medium of exchange. Banks, therefore, were to Jackson the epitome of all that frustrated the legitimate ambitions of common men and kept the United States from reaching the idyllic state of republican-democracy to which it was otherwise destined. The small farmer in the West and South, the artisan and the small businessman in every section, and the working men of the cities—the people, in short, who were on the wrong side of the credit line—profoundly agreed with their President. If, contrary to Jackson, many of them wished cheap government or private paper, not specie, and if others had little or no understanding of the intricacies of a credit system, all could and did unite with the President against the Bank of the United States as the distant Shylock upon whom to blame their misfortune—or their incompetence.

If Jefferson had resented Jackson's association with Burr and felt somewhat vaguely that Jackson's ambition was too evident and too lacking in *noblesse oblige,* he would certainly have forgiven him much, and applauded enthusiastically from the sidelines, when Old Hickory went after Nicholas Biddle and his Bank of the United States. An ironic sidelight on the bank war of the 1830's is that Biddle, the brilliant and effective adminstrator who had brought the bank out of its postwar doldrums in the 1820's, had been a disciple of Jefferson, a staff member of Monroe's second mission to Europe, and a close friend of the latter for more than twenty years. His credentials were as Republican as Jackson's. But he was, like Jackson, an ambitious man, and the Bank provided him with a means to power that, like Jackson in the Presidency, he could readily identify with the public interest. In Biddle's rise Jackson saw a rival to himself. More important, in the rise of the Bank he saw a rival to the Presidency. This issue—more real than imaginary, given the temper of the times— was what Jackson undertook to resolve by levying war. The heaviest artillery was on the side of the President. This was because Biddle's constituency, so far as he had one, was not popular. Nor was his cause. In the nature of the struggle Biddle could not win, any more than Jackson could lose. If the nation was the real loser in the end, the people did not think so. Instead they cheered on their hero and returned him in triumph for a second term.

Jackson looked upon closing, or at least replacing, the Bank of the United States as a binding campaign pledge and a solemn constitutional and "republican" duty. There was never the slightest equivocation in his attitude. His administration had scarcely commenced when he began to solicit the advice of his friends on what might be the best expedient for discharging the desirable functions of the Bank without allowing it to continue in private hands. Men such as Secretary of the Treasury Samuel Ingham and Attorney General John M. Berrien gave advice hesitantly and cautiously. Ingham knew the uses of the Bank and was not happy at the  notion of a makeshift replacement for it. Berrien was not at all sure that the Bank was unconstitutional, especially after the Supreme Court's decision in *McCulloch* v. *Maryland* (1819), and he was mindful that it had been Madison and Monroe who permitted the revival of a national bank after its first charter had lapsed. Berrien was equally doubtful about the political expediency of tackling the Bank at the beginning of Jackson's term. Other friends, like Felix Grundy and Col. James Hamilton, gave Jackson replies more to his liking. Their views were alike in favoring national banking but agreeing that private ownership and control should be abolished.[18]

Despite Berrien's caution, Jackson resolved to give warning of his bank policy in his first message to Congress. Pointing out that the charter of the Bank would expire in 1836, he said he wished to avoid "precipitancy" in dealing with "a measure involving such important principles and such deep pecuniary interests." The President felt that "in justice to the parties interested" he must place the whole question before the Congress and the people as soon as possible. This, of course, was a direct challenge to the friends of the Bank and was so intended. Jackson went on immediately to say that "both the constitutionality and the expediency of the law creating this bank are well questioned by a large portion of our fellow citizens." He asserted flatly, and inaccurately, in a studied offense to Biddle, that "it must be admitted by all that the Bank has failed in its great end of establishing a uniform and sound currency." He suggested that if, "under these circumstances," a national bank was thought to be "essential to the fiscal operations of the government," the Congress ought to make an attempt to find a formula that would be constitutional—that is, in accord with Jackson's interpretation of the Constitution.[19]

In the months and years thereafter Jackson's attitude was so vehement and often so militantly negative on the whole matter of the Bank that it will be useful to have in mind what, under other political circumstances, he would have liked to do about building a substitute. In a private letter of the summer of 1830 he stated his views with directness and characteristic economy of words:

. . . my own opinion is, that it should be merely a *national Bank of deposit,* with power in time of war to issue its bills bearing a moderate interest, and payable at the close of the war, which being guaranteed by the national faith, pledged, and based upon our revenue, would be sought after by the monied Capitalist, and do away, in time of war, the necessity of *loans.* This is all the kind of bank that a republic should have.

Jackson's distinction between such a bank's "bills bearing a moderate interest" and "loans" is, to say the least, abstruse. But the principle of his plan would have been workable if not adequate. It would, in effect, have set up precisely the subtreasury system that Van Buren first brought into being and Polk, the last Jacksonian, in the end established on a permanent basis.[20]

However, as the battle raged, Jackson devoted all his efforts to destroying the Bank of the United States and none to replacing it. By the spring of 1832 Congress was moving, under the leadership of Clay and Daniel Webster, toward passage of a recharter bill. In the Senate, Thomas Hart Benton led the Jackson anti-Bank forces, while James K. Polk was the House leader against the Bank. At the height of the struggle Benton wrote Jackson that "the charge of my being friendly to the Bank . . . until I found it could not be used for my political purposes, . . . is one of the foulest and basest calumnies ever uttered." Calumnies, of one degree or another, were common during those tense days. And Benton need not be doubted when he goes on to say, "I have always been opposed to it upon constitutional grounds as well as expediency and policy." But in the Congress these views did not prevail. Though not without some financial "assistance" from Biddle (at least in the case of Webster), a majority of both houses voted for recharter and sent a bill to the President on July 4, 1832. His disposition of it was a foregone conclusion. He had, in fact, made it clear long since that he would make the Bank the great issue of the 1832 campaign.[21]

In the last hectic days before the Bank bill was passed, an effort was made to see if a compromise could be reached between the Biddle forces and Jackson. The President was asked whether he would approve any kind of bill at all. His reply reveals not only why he would veto the recharter but how he would place the matter before the people in the election. "I would approve no bank," he said, "that violated the Constitution." On the other hand, "I would approve any bank charter that was presented where none of its provisions violated the principles of the organic law." His standards of judgment were these:

I have always viewed that the powers granted by the Constitution to our Federal Government were for general purposes, for national not local objects—these powers are delegated and precisely marked that those to whom they are entrusted may not exercise any power but in strict conformity with the limits of their trust. Under this rule the Bank must be national, not for a few stockholders and the charter securing to this few exclusive privileges from which all the rest of the community are excluded—to be constitutional its benefits must be, and enure to the whole nation as the taxes do. . . .

The only kind of bank he would approve, therefore, would be "a bank of deposit and exchange, purely national, without stockholders." He defied the Congress to ask for a constitutional amendment. "I say now to Congress, that before it usurps any power not expressly granted and before creating a Bank with stockholders and the United States becomes a member of the corporation, which grants exclusive privileges to a few stockholders, let them submit to the people by way of amendment of the Constitution, and ask them (in the true spirit of the Sages who formed it) whether you will grant this power." Jackson was sure what the answer would be. "If they say nay, then I say to Congress, now and then, 'touch not, handle not, this accursed thing.' "22

To the Bank men, of course, neither of Jackson's proposals represented any sort of compromise. A national depository was no bank, while to ask for an amendment would be to confess that there was reasonable doubt as to the constitutionality of the existing bank. And so, hoping for enough votes in the end to override it, they sent up their bill for the promised veto.

They got it. They got, in fact, one of the most vigorous, politically charged, and frequently quoted vetoes ever to come from a presidential pen. Jackson's message managed to combine strict construction of the Constitution with a blunt attack on special privilege, an attack upon anti-Jacksonians in Congress, an attack upon the Supreme Court, and a moving Jacksonian appeal to the people over the heads of the Congress. It was as partisan a paper as could readily be imagined, yet it was not without elements of statesmanship. If it was bad economic philosophy and at many points lacking in a certain essential understanding of the necessary relations between institution building and the national government, it was immensely effective as a political statement. It could and did serve amply as a platform on which to run for re-election. Above all, it showed Jackson's confidence that the majority would support him against what he considered the forces of privilege and monopoly.

The veto message begins with an extended analysis of the

financial advantages the Bank provides its stockholders. There is a strain of nativism in Jackson's concern that much stock is flowing out of the country into European hands. In the process, control of the Bank is further and further removed from the citizens. Twenty of the twenty-five directors are to be elected by the citizen stockholders, foreign holders being disqualified from the franchise. But this provision of the law actually reduces the power of the citizens:

In proportion . . . as the stock is transferred to foreign holders the extent of suffrage in the choice of directors is curtailed. Already is almost a third of the stock in foreign hands and not represented in elections. It is constantly passing out of the country, and this act will accelerate its departure. The entire control of the institution would necessarily fall into the hands of a few citizen stockholders, and the ease with which the object would be accomplished would be a temptation to designing men to secure that control into their own hands by monopolizing the remaining stock.

Jackson's tone is well suggested by the phrase "designing men." The political tactic of the message is to identify the President and the "citizens" as together the objects of mistreatment and exploitation by schemers, by unscrupulous men of wealth acting behind the screen of the Bank of the United States. If such "designing men" were content to share their malign influence with foreign investors, so much the worse. Jackson carried the point to an extreme—imagining a wartime situation—which was certainly unrealistic but none the less politically effective:

Of the course which would be pursued by a bank almost wholly owned by the subjects of a foreign power, and managed by those whose interests, if not affections, would run in the same direction there can be no doubt. All its operations within would be in aid of the hostile fleets and armies without. Controlling our currency, receiving our public moneys, and holding thousands of our citizens in dependence, it would be more formidable and dangerous than the naval and military power of the enemy.

But this appeal to the fear of foreigners was not the central argument. Nor was the well-founded assertion that the act of recharter would enrich the holders of the bank's stock by an ill-hidden government subsidy. The main point was that the whole enterprise of the bank was unconstitutional and thus a danger to republican democracy.

First there was the question of the Supreme Court's finding that the national bank was constitutionally justified. Jackson, like Jefferson before him, insisted that the coordinate branches of the government must have equal authority to determine what is or is not in accord with the Constitution. "The Congress, the Executive, and the Court," he said, "must each for itself be guided by its own opinion of the Constitution." If this view meant that government might be paralyzed by disagreement among the branches, Jackson was quite willing, at least in this matter, for such paralysis to occur. The President laid it down that "each public officer who takes an oath to support the Constitution swears that he will support it as he understands it, and not as it is understood by others." It seems unlikely that he did not realize how anarchic such a principle would be in practice. It would, for example, have gone hard indeed with anyone in the Executive who chose to interpret and act upon the Constitution in a manner different from the President's! But this message was a weapon, and the ringing assertion at least sounded plausible.

However, the President was willing and able to tackle both the jurisdiction and reasoning of the Supreme Court in other terms, too. "It is as much the duty," he said, "of the House of Representatives, of the Senate, and of the President to decide upon the constitutionality of any bill or resolution which may be presented to them for passage or approval as it is of the supreme judges when it may be brought before them for judicial decision." If this proposition is allowed, the logical conclusion is that

The opinion of the judges has no more authority over Congress than the opinion of Congress has over the judges, and on that point the President is independent of both. The authority of the Supreme Court must not, therefore, be permitted to control the Congress or the Executive when acting in their legislative capacities, but to have only such influence as the force of their reasoning may deserve.

Jackson was certainly aware that on this reading of the constitutional provisions for the three branches, the Congress was entirely within its rights to pass a bill believed by either the President or the Supreme Court to be unconstitutional. But because, in the legislative process, the President would have the last word in all cases in which he could persuade one third plus one of each House to go with him, Jackson was quite willing to give the "loose construction" men their head. As for the Court, perhaps both Congress and President could agree in their own interest to ignore its pretension to authority over legislation.

As for the "reasoning" of the Court, Jackson noted that in the *McCulloch* case the Court had said that Congress had the power to create a national bank if such a bank were *necessary* for the government to carry on its powers. The Court had also said that it would not enter into the province of the Congress by trying to decide whether any institution erected by the Congress was more or less necessary. "To undertake . . . to inquire into the degree of necessity," the Court had written, "would be to pass the line which circumscribes the judicial department and to tread on legislative ground." Thus the Court had in reality left the crucial question undecided. The reasoning of the Court could not properly be relied upon in the matter of the recharter. Since the President was a part of the legislative process, he could and would decide, in the Court's terms, upon the "degree of necessity" of the Bank as chartered under the bill. Therefore, simply enough, it was not constitutional under the "necessary and proper" clause. So much for the Supreme Court and *McCulloch v. Maryland.* Thus, no doubt to the ghostly approval of Thomas Jefferson, Andrew Jackson dismissed John Marshall and his presumption to vindicate the defeated Federalists by judicial process. So much, too, for the Congress.

There was more, much more. The President explored in detail what grounds there might be for asserting that the Bank was either *necessary* or *proper.* He found none. As to propriety, he observed, cogently enough, that since the Bank was presumed to be an instrument for the use of the Executive and was defended as constitutional because needed by the Executive to carry on the fiscal business of the government, the Executive ought to make the decision. Instead, the Executive had not even been consulted. But this and other points were really secondary to the grand assertion of presidential prerogative in deciding what was or was not constitutional, and to the direct appeal to the people with which he began and ended his message.

The final appeal, familiar as it is, is worth repeating, for it underlines the special nature of Jacksonian democracy and thereby expresses what was new in American presidential politics:

It is to be regretted that the rich and powerful too often bend the acts of government to their selfish purposes. Distinctions in society will always exist under every just government. Equality of talents, of education, or of wealth cannot be produced by human institutions. In the full enjoyment of the gifts of Heaven and the fruits of superior industry, economy, and virtue, every man is equally entitled to protection by law; but when the laws undertake to add to these natural and just advantages artificial distinctions, to grant titles, gratuities, and exclusive privileges, to make the rich richer and the potent more powerful, the humble members of society—the farmers, mechanics, and laborers—who have neither the time nor the means of securing like favors to themselves, have a right to complain of the injustice of their government.

Their President could be counted upon to prevent such injustice. "If sustained by my fellow citizens," he said, "I shall be grateful and happy; if not, I shall find in the motives which impel me ample grounds for contentment and peace." When the ballots were counted at the end of the year, Jackson was "sustained" by a great majority of the "humble members of society." The electoral count was 219 for Jackson to 49 for Clay. In the new Congress there was no mood to revive the Bank question; in the old, there were not enough diehard Bank men to override the triumphant President's veto. Thus the partisan President successfully appealed to his partisans, converting his popularity with them into power to smash the Bank and to enforce his interpretation of the Constitution.[23]

When next Jackson appealed to the people on a constitutional question, it was not as a partisan of party but as a partisan of Union, and his appeal was to all the people. If he had expected to alienate some on the Bank question and welcomed the opposition of the bankers and the men of wealth and privilege, he regretted that any man should wish to nullify the law of the land. If his stand on the recalcitrance of South Carolina made enemies for himself and for the Union he was defending, this was not because he wished it so. When the Union was in question, the partisan politician was a nonpartisan statesman. And his popularity, again, was sufficient to the purpose.

The nullification controversy arose over the high tariff law of 1828, though it did not reach dangerous proportions until almost four years later. By that time some planters were badly hurt, and such politicians as Vice-President Calhoun, out of favor with Jackson, were seeking to solve the economic problem and perhaps revive their own political fortunes by raising an issue of states' rights under the Constitution. Jackson, as a good Jeffersonian, was strong for states' rights, and when he saw how seriously the protective tariff hit the cotton- and tobacco-producing states, he was greatly troubled. But by April, 1830, he had evidently made up his mind on the stand he would take. At that time Senators Robert Hayne of South Carolina and Thomas Hart Benton of Missouri, for somewhat different reasons, joined in organizing a Jefferson Day dinner in Washington at which the old Jeffersonian states' rights philosophy would be celebrated and identified with the Democratic Party. The trick was to have each formal toast offered in the course of the evening underline the states' rights position. Jackson, sitting at the dinner with mounting impatience while twenty-four speakers went through this ritual, concluded that he was the victim of political chicanery. When at last his own turn came, he stood and dramatically reversed the tenor of the evening with the famous toast: "Our Union: it must be preserved." From that moment the President was at the head of the Union party.

As a matter of economic policy Jackson was opposed to protective tariffs. He believed in the old Jeffersonian doctrine of free trade, with only such exceptions as seemed to be in the national interest. But in his Annual Message in the fall of the year he took pains to assert his belief that the protective tariff was constitutional even if unwise. Sentiment to interpose state authority or nullify the tariff law nevertheless grew, especially in South Carolina. In short, there was a developing movement, led by John C. Calhoun, still Vice-President of the United States, and Governor James Hamilton of South Carolina, to disobey the law, claiming that it was of no force.

Early in 1831, Senator Hayne, who had been one of Jackson's firm supporters, challenged him and drew from him a strong

statement of the national supremacy position he intended to take
—and did take a year later when actual nullification and even
secession threatened. At the outset Jackson reaffirmed his own
belief in states' rights, for which, he said, "no one has a higher
regard and respect than myself; none would go farther to maintain them." The real question was whether states' rights could
be maintained separately from the Union. States' rights could
"certainly" not be preserved by "conceding to one state authority
to declare an act of Congress void . . . far from it." On the contrary, the proper, constitutional, and sensible course to take if a
state felt itself aggrieved by an Act of Congress was to go to the
people and seek change by democratic means. This was the whole
point of the American system. "The remedy is with the people,"
he said. The people, "by their free suffrage at the polls," Jackson
laid it down, "will always in the end, bring about the repeal of
any obnoxious laws which violate the Constitution." Such abuses
as these, he was confident, "cannot be of long duration in our
enlightened country where the people rule." That "tribunal will
decree correctly." In a direct riposte to Calhoun and Hayne,
Jackson went on to say that he had never believed "that a state
has the power to nullify the legislative enactments of the General
Government . . . nor have I ever understood Mr. Jefferson to
hold such an opinion." What Jefferson would in fact have said
at this historic juncture no one can know for certain. But there
is a clue in the painfully careful opinion written out by the aged
Madison in his "Notes on Nullification," holding that the Union
was a Constitution formed by the "people of the states," not a
compact among state governments. It is certain, in any case, that
when Jefferson proclaimed in the Kentucky Resolution of 1798
that the alien and sedition laws were unconstitutional, he was
leading a fight not against a national policy but against a calculated obstruction to the democratic process of determining national policy.

Jackson's interpretation of the situation in 1831 draws the distinction clearly. "The time," he hoped, was "far distant when
the abuse of power on the part of Congress will be so great as to
justify a state to stand forth in open violation and resistance to
its measures." Such action would be revolutionary, not constitutional. If revolution could be justified as the natural right of an

oppressed people, it could not find any sanction at all when a democratic remedy exists. "In all republics," said Jackson, "the voice of a majority must prevail." Though Hayne and his colleagues were not to accept this proposition in the 1830's, Calhoun was clearheaded enough and honest enough to admit the force of Jackson's statement and to take the only logical alternative—to reject the republican idea itself. Calhoun, in 1850, used the term *democracy* rather than *republic,* but he conceded that the essence of the South's complaint was that the United States had become a "great national consolidated democracy." This was what Jackson was saying to Hayne. It was what Webster, in 1850, said to Calhoun, what Lincoln said to Douglas in 1860, and what hundreds of thousands of Americans died thereafter to settle.[24]

In 1832 no one died in the struggle. The President saw to it that the Union would stand against the threat of South Carolina or any other state. After the South Carolina convention had authorized the Governor to proclaim the tariff unconstitutional and void, Jackson made the necessary military preparations to enforce the law. In a confidential memorandum to Secretary of War Lewis Cass, Jackson predicted that an attempt would be made "to surprise the forts and garrisons [in Charleston harbor] by the militia." He ordered the army to repel any such attempt "with prompt and exemplary punishment." That he believed a political solution would be found, however, is clear from a private letter to Martin Van Buren. Talking about his forthcoming annual message to Congress, Jackson told Van Buren that "as to nullification in the South [he meant] to pass it barely in review, as a mere bubble." "All we want," he said, is "peaceably to nullify the nullifyers." Meanwhile he drafted a proclamation, with the assistance of Secretary of State Edward Livingston, and ordered a bill to be prepared authorizing all necessary military measures to preserve the Union.[25]

Jackson's Nullification Proclamation was issued on December 10, 1832. It was in three main parts: a detailed argument against interposition and secession, an exhortation to the people of South Carolina, and a summons to the whole American people to rally to the Union. There was nothing at all original about the argument. But its language, chiefly the work of Livingston, was felicitous, and the case for union against confederation has

seldom been better stated. Addressing himself to the South Carolina ordinance authorizing nullification, Jackson began by giving
implicit recognition to the right of revolution. But "the ordinance is founded," he said, "not on the indefeasible right of
resisting acts which are plainly unconstitutional and too oppressive to be endured, but on the strange position that any one state
may not only declare an act of Congress void, but prohibit its
execution; that they may do this consistently with the Constitution; that the true construction of that instrument permits a
State to retain its place in the Union and yet be bound by no
other of its laws than those it may choose to consider constitutional." The notion that one state may determine whether a law
is constitutional is incompatible with the right of appeal. If there
is no appeal, then the decision of the State becomes the supreme
law of the land. "But," said the President, "reasoning on this
subject is superfluous when our social compact, in express terms,
declares that the laws of the United States, its Constitution, and
treaties made under it are the supreme law of the land." He went
on to point out that the Constitution also provided that " 'judges
in every State shall be bound thereby, anything in the Constitution or laws of any State to the contrary notwithstanding.' " This
was crucial to the very existence of the nation. "And it may be asserted without refutation," said Jackson, "that no federative government could exist without a similar Provision." He underlined
his summary of the federal position in what was to become one
of the landmark passages in presidential history:

> I consider, then, the power to annul a law of the United States,
> assumed by one State, incompatible with the existence of the Union,
> contradicted expressly by the letter of the Constitution, unauthorized
> by its spirit, inconsistent with every principle on which it was founded,
> and destructive of the great object for which it was formed.

Jackson then proceeded to examine at length the application
of this principle in the specific case of South Carolina. If the
analysis that followed was neither fresh nor original, this kind of
official statement by the President was nonetheless needed. The
construction of the nullifiers was, said Jackson, wholly "sophisti-
cal" and must be rejected. The Constitution, he said, "shall
descend, as we have received it, uncorrupted . . . to our posterity;

and the sacrifices of local interest, of State prejudices, of personal animosities, that were made to bring it into existence, will again be patriotically offered for its support." The Constitution had been made by the whole people, Jackson maintained, not by the states as such. The government of the United States was and must remain a government, not a league.

Turning to the people of the disaffected state, the President made a direct plea:

> Fellow-citizens of my native State, let me not only admonish you, as the First Magistrate of our common country, not to incur the penalty of its laws, but use the influence that a father would over his children whom he saw rushing to certain ruin. In that paternal language, with that paternal feeling, let me tell you, my countrymen, that you are deluded by men who are either deceived themselves or wish to deceive you.

These deceivers, Jackson went on, "are not champions of liberty, emulating the fame of our Revolutionary fathers, nor are you an oppressed people, contending, as they repeat to you, against worse than colonial vassalage. You are free members of a flourishing and happy Union."

It is interesting to compare the peroration that concludes the appeal to South Carolina with the draft Jackson originally wrote and sent to Livingston for advice. Here is the draft:

> Seduced as you have been my fellow Countrymen by the delusive theories and misrepresentation of ambitious, deluded and designing men, I call upon you, in the language of truth and with the feelings of a father to retrace your steps. As you value liberty and the blessings of peace, blot out from the page of your history a record so fatal to their security as this ordinance will become if it be obeyed. Rally again under the banner of the Union whose obligations you, in common with all your countrymen, have with an appeal to heaven, sworn to support and which must be indissoluble, as long as we are capable of enjoying freedom.
>
> Recollect that the first act of resistance to the laws which have been denounced as void by those who abuse your confidence and falsify your hopes is *Treason* and subjects you to all the pains and penalties that are provided for the highest offence against your country. Can the descendants of the Rutledges, the Pinckneys, the Richardsons, the Middletons, the Sumters, the Pickens, the Bentons, the Taylors, the

Haynes, the Gadsdens, the Winns, the Hills and the Crawfords, with the descendants of thousands more of the Patriots of Revolution that might be named, consent to become Traitors? Forbid it Heaven!

This florid, excited passage, breathing the spirit and anger of Andrew Jackson, was raised, still impassioned, to the level of an historic state paper by the skilled pen of Edward Livingston:

There is yet time to show that the descendants of the Pinckneys, the Sumters, the Rutledges, and of the thousand other names which adorn the pages of Revolutionary history will not abandon that Union to support which so many of them fought and bled and died. I adjure you, as you honor their memory, as you love the cause of freedom, to which they dedicated their lives, as you prize the peace of your country, the lives of its best citizens, and your own fair fame, to retrace your steps. Snatch from the archives of your State the disorganizing edict of its convention; bid its members to reassemble and promulgate the decided expressions of your will to remain in the path which alone can conduct you to safety, prosperity, and honor. Tell them that compared to disunion all other evils are light, because that brings with it an accumulation of all. Declare that you will never take the field unless the star-spangled banner of your country shall float over you; that you will not be stigmatized when dead, and dishonored and scorned while you live, as the authors of the first attack on the Constitution of your country. Its destroyers you cannot be. You may disturb its peace, you may interrupt the course of its prosperity, you may cloud its reputation for stability; but its tranquillity will be restored, its prosperity will return, and the stain upon its national character will be transferred and remain an eternal blot on the memory of those who caused the disorder.

Finally, Jackson appealed to the whole people to support his stand on Union. "The momentous case is before you," he said. "On your undivided support of your Government depends the decision of the great question it involves—whether your sacred Union will be preserved and the blessing it secures to us as one people shall be perpetuated."[26]

In January, 1833, Jackson asked Congress to enact a "Force Bill" that would provide troops and authority to put down insurrection if South Carolina should actually disobey the tariff law. But though the debate was acrid and the situation still tense, there was no longer any doubt that South Carolina would yield to the President.

The partisan leader of the majority in a divided country thus successfully put aside disputes of policy when a dispute of procedure threatened the system whereby policy is made. When the democratic process was functioning, Jackson could use it for sharply partisan purposes. And he did not hesitate to insist upon a narrow interpretation of the Constitution, both as a matter of conviction and as a weapon of political maneuver, when the stakes at issue were matters of policy and program. He was happy under such circumstances to be a partisan President relying upon the popular partisan majority behind him to win his and their battles. But if nullification were to prevail, there would be an end to the majority rule that made partisan leadership appropriate. Conditions must be preserved, above all, in which a President, or a party, would be free to rally a majority if he could. Thus the Union, as Webster had said in the Senate, was inseparable from liberty.

Behind the partisan leader the partisan ranks of both parties closed on the issue of Union. If Jackson retained his personal popularity only with his long-time partisans, the popularity of the stand he took on nullification was so great that many long-time enemies acknowledged his leadership. And so it may be said that in his greatest moment the skillful practitioner of the politics of partisan popularity won a nonpartisan victory that ensured, for a time at least, that free politics of any sort might continue. He had fairly demonstrated the sincerity of the ringing words in his Second Inaugural:

For myself, when I approach the sacred volume and take a solemn Oath to support and defend this Constitution, I feel in the depths of my soul, that it is the highest, most sacred and most irreversible part of my obligation, *to preserve the union of these states,* although it may cost me my life.[27]

5. *Eisenhower's popularity and the Little Rock civil rights crisis* ঔ৯ Jackson's powerful attack on the nullifiers succeeded in ending the threat of interposition between the Southern states and Congress so long as the issue did not go to the question of slavery. For twenty-five years after Jackson acted, matters of even the deepest division were kept at the level of debate. But when

the Compromise of 1850 failed to stem the antislavery tide and bloody Kansas spoke the language of defeat to the Southern apostles of an expanding slave economy, the call for nullification was heard once more, this time in the form of a presumed right to secede from the Union. James Buchanan, presented squarely with an act of secession in 1860, had neither the qualities of leadership the times called for nor the personal popularity to make a successful appeal to the people. A timid politician, despite his rich experience in high office, Buchanan knew well the techniques of negotiation but had no taste for aggressive leadership. When the issue was nonnegotiable, as it was when South Carolina announced it would withdraw from the Union rather than accept the authority of Congress, he was helpless. But the Buchanan case is not in point in a consideration of the ways in which a President uses his popularity. His victory over General John C. Fremont in 1856 was narrow, and, in any case, Buchanan's followers were neither united nor enthusiastic.

Lincoln, whose victory in 1860 provided the conclusive factor in South Carolina's decision to secede, certainly had a mandate from his supporters to preserve the Union. And, of course, he proceeded to do so with a leadership no less vigorous and inspired because he was the protagonist of high tragedy. But Lincoln had even less of a popular majority to which he could appeal than had Buchanan. He had been elected only because the Democratic Party was hopelessly split on the slavery-secession question. In a four-cornered race, Lincoln had received not quite 40 per cent of the popular vote. That when the crisis actually came, a majority of the whole people would rally to the Union was certain, but there was no broad dedication otherwise either to Lincoln or to his principles. Thus his building of an Administration capable not only of governing the quarreling elements that stood by the Union but of prosecuting and winning the war was one of the supreme achievements in the history of democratic government. But it was accomplished despite a lack of personal popularity and followership. Lincoln's victory was won as commander-in-chief in a military situation, not as a popular leader in a political situation.

The defeat of the South in the Civil War brought an end to interposition efforts for almost a hundred years. But in the 1940's and 1950's the accumulating decisions of the Supreme Court, holding various forms of discrimination against colored Americans unconstitutional, brought such bitter resentment among Southern segregationists that when the Court, in its climactic decision of May 1954, proscribed discrimination in the public schools, the doctrine of interposition was revived. This time there was no threat of secession. But there was already grave danger of local violence, arising out of resistance to school integration, when Southern members of the House and the Senate enacted a resolution declaring the Court's decision itself unconstitutional, and when, by February, 1956, four Southern state legislatures had passed resolutions of interposition declaring the Court's decision not binding in those states. And so, a century and a quarter after Jackson, another President had to decide what course he should take in the face of nullification.

The President, of course, was Dwight Eisenhower. Like Jackson, he was an old soldier who had become an immensely popular President. But there the similarity ended. Jackson had gone into the nullification crisis of his time the partisan leader of an intensely partisan majority. He had had to transcend partisanship in order to win a contest for the supremacy of the Union. He had, in a sense, to become nonpartisan. Eisenhower had an even larger majority behind him, but his appeal had been to all interest groups and all sections. He was as nearly a nonpartisan President as the two-party system will permit. In his campaign of 1952 he had capitalized on the split in the Democratic Party on civil rights. His opponent, Adlai E. Stevenson, had gone into the South to state his position in favor of the extension of civil rights and the ending of all forms of discrimination. At Richmond, Virginia, Stevenson had made a dramatic statement of his views. Perhaps as a consequence, in the election he lost that state as well as several other traditionally Democratic Southern and Border states.

Eisenhower, though he several times stated that he stood for equality of all Americans, said nothing specifically about either civil rights or discrimination. In the South he spoke chiefly of the dangers of Communism and corruption in government, the need to end the Korean War—and promised to give the states the tidelands oil. He made no reference to racial problems. Carrying four states of the old Confederacy, as well as Oklahoma, he ran better in all of them than had any Republican since Herbert Hoover, who had benefited from Southern concern over Alfred E. Smith's Catholicism. In his first Annual Message Eisenhower called for extension of equality before the law. He ordered progress to be made in desegregating both the armed services and the District of Columbia. But though he makes much of this in his memoirs, the measures had been initiated by his predecessor. And Eisenhower ran little risk of alienating Southern feeling by such action, since he was not proposing to interfere with state "prerogatives."[28]

In the first year of his administration the Gallup poll showed that Eisenhower's popularity continued strong among all Americans except Negroes. When the Supreme Court's landmark decision on school segregation was handed down in the spring of 1954, he had already weathered such storms as the McCarthy attacks on his foreign policy and the Dixon-Yates scandal. There had been a considerable economic recession for which the people seemed to consider the President in no way responsible. While liberal periodicals like the *New Republic* and Democratic critics like Stevenson had some success in showing that the Republican Congress was failing and the Republican program inadequate, they were quite unable to persuade the citizens that Eisenhower as President was inadequate.

Thus the Court's historic finding against segregated public schools posed for the President a dilemma he could not effectively resolve. If he announced his vigorous support of the Court and his personal agreement with its decision, he would immediately alienate much of the following he had built up in the South and among those Northerners who shared Southern prejudices against people of color or, to some degree, feared the breakdown of racial barriers forecast by the Court. If, on the other hand, he refused his support to the desegregation movement as ordered by the Court, he would alienate a presumably larger number of Americans who agreed with the Court and wished to see drastic improvement in the field of civil rights. The movement against discrimination had gained momentum with the economic gains of the Negro in New Deal days and in the wartime and postwar boom. It was already axiomatic that political success in the large cities of the North, the West, and the Pacific Coast required a liberal attitude toward civil rights. Before the Court spoke, Eisenhower had held a majority support on both sides of the issue by avoiding it. In the North and West the general assumption was that the President's statement of his belief in "equality" meant his endorsement of the civil rights claims of Negroes; the South assumed that his failure to stress civil rights meant that he was not eager to break down segregation customs and institutions.

Under these painful circumstances, Eisenhower elected to try to maintain his unpartisan image by refusing to involve himself directly, while at the same time he acknowledged in general terms his constitutional responsibilities. At his first press conference after the school decision, he was asked if he had any advice to give the South as to how "to react to this recent . . . decision banning segregation." "Not in the slightest," he said. He went on to quote Governor James Byrnes of South Carolina, "Let's be calm and let's be reasonable and let's look this thing in the face." Byrnes, of course, was an arch-segregationist who had led the Democratic rebellion against civil rights and had refused to support Stevenson in 1952. Eisenhower called Byrnes's words "a very fine statement." If this was calculated to give encouragement to the Southerners who were reacting with bitter resentment to the Court's decision, the President's next words no doubt reassured others. "The Supreme Court has spoken," he said, "and I am sworn to uphold the constitutional processes in this country; and I will obey." To say that he would "obey" a decision of the Supreme Court certainly suggested, perhaps was intended to suggest, that he had no enthusiasm for his task. At any rate he gave no hint that he favored the Court's position. What he "favored" was Governor Byrnes's statement.[29]

His initial reaction had the effect, apparently as he wished, of eliminating Eisenhower from the first stages of the great public controversy over school desegregation. As late as August he was maintaining a posture of strict aloofness. When asked whether he would recommend to Congress legislation "backing up the Supreme Court decrees," he answered, "The subject has not even been mentioned to me." No one was inclined to pursue the subject by asking whether the President had by chance thought of the "subject" for himself. Somehow Eisenhower's position outside the controversy carried conviction. Hardboiled Washington reporters who would not have feared to press either Franklin Roosevelt or Harry Truman were content to drop the subject. Or perhaps they were convinced that the effort to involve the President in so crucial an issue simply could not succeed if he did not already feel himself involved.[30]

For almost two years Eisenhower succeeded in his purpose of staying out of embroilment on civil rights. He mentioned the subject only when it was absolutely necessary and then only to reiterate his belief in "equality" and his intention to do his duty. Duty, as he saw it, did not call for any sort of leadership by the President. It was in this frame of mind, against a background of rapidly increasing tension on the whole racial matter, that Eisenhower was called upon to react to the revival of "interposition." On February 29, 1956, at his press conference, the President, who had not previously reacted to the news that Southern legislatures were passing interposition resolutions, was asked directly what he thought about them and whether he intended to initiate any federal action. Here are the questions and the answer Eisenhower gave to them:

Q. As you may know, four of the Southern state legislatures have passed interposition resolutions stating that the Supreme Court decision outlawing segregation has no force and effect in their states; and I was wondering what you thought about this concept of interposition, and what you thought was the role of the Federal Government in enforcing the Supreme Court decision?

A. Well, of course, you have asked a very vast question that is filled with argument on both sides. You have raised the question of States' rights versus the Federal power; you have particularly brought up the question whether the Supreme Court is the last word we have in the interpretation of our Constitution.

Now, this is what I say: there are adequate legal means of determining all these factors. The Supreme Court has issued its own operational directives and delegated power to the district court. I expect that we are going to make progress, and the Supreme Court itself does not expect revolutionary action suddenly executed. We will make progress, and I am not going to tell them how it is going to be done.

Regardless of constitutional doctrine it was easy enough to draw the conclusion from this statement that whatever "progress" was made in desegregating the schools would be made without the assistance of the President so long as Eisenhower could avoid it. Whether he meant to convey this impression or not, Southern prosegregation leaders did in fact draw that conclusion, and events proved that they were not mistaken.[31]

But doctrine, too, was important in the President's statement, both to the citizens of the United States and to the peoples of other nations who were closely watching to see how the Americans would deal with their critical internal problem. It was a remarkable doctrine. The President seemed to be saying that there were "adequate legal means" to determine whether the Supreme Court is "the last word we have in the interpretation of our Constitution." If this is what he meant to say, then either the Supreme Court was the legal means or some other body, such as a state legislature, was superior to it. But since this issue had been settled, first by executive leadership under Jackson and then by the Civil War, it is unlikely that Eisenhower really meant to side with the interpositionists. What then did he mean to say? The conclusion is hard to escape that his words were an intentional obfuscation of the issue. T. V. Smith at one time celebrated the political device of "strategic obfuscation," and perhaps he could have cited Eisenhower's handling of "interposition." Any thoughtful student of politics would no doubt agree that to obfuscate an issue is often to treat it wisely and to confuse deliberately may have the effect of quieting tempers and inducing an atmosphere in which some sort of rational compromise can be reached. It is reasonable to suppose that Eisenhower, like Monroe in 1820, had some such intention. Certainly he believed his best contribution would be to keep calm, refuse to take sides, and set an example of reasonableness. But the issue posed by the interposition resolutions was no more compromisable in 1956 than it had been in 1832 or 1860. The President might seek to extricate himself from the controversy by confusing it, but he could not make the controversy disappear.

A month later Eisenhower was confronted with a question about accepting the support in 1956 of Southern Democrats who had supported him in 1952. His handling of this matter was nearly identical with his treatment of interposition and thus throws considerable light on the fundamental position he was attempting to hold. Reminded that "a number of prominent Southern conservative Democrats" who had been for him in 1952 had "indicated their defiance of the Supreme Court's decision on segregation," he was asked directly if he would accept the support of such men under the new circumstances. The President's answer should be cited in full:

A. I don't believe they expressed their defiance. I believe they expressed their belief that it was in error, and they have talked about using legal means to circumvent or get along, whatever the expression they have used.

I do not believe that anyone, the ones that I know, have used the words "defy the Supreme Court," because when we carry this to the ultimate, remember that the Constitution, as interpreted by the Supreme Court, is our basic law.

The one thing is, though, the basic law appears to change, as I pointed out last week. It was one thing in 1896, and it is a very greatly different thing now.

So, there are emotions, very deep emotions, connected with this problem. These people have, of course, their free choice as to what they want to do.

As far as I am concerned, I am for moderation, but I am for progress; that is exactly what I am for in this.

Again, it is difficult to understand "exactly" what the President was "for." His assertion that the Southern leaders in question had not defied the Court was either an intentional quibble or stated under unbelievable misinformation, for all of the Southern pro-Eisenhower members of Congress had signed the so-called "Southern Manifesto," declaring the decision of the Supreme Court not only in error but beyond the jurisdiction of the Court to make. All had expressed their approval of the interposition resolutions of the Southern legislatures. On this issue, at least, all of them were asserting that the Constitution, as interpreted by the Court, was *not* the basic law. When Eisenhower said that these Southern leaders were "free" to decide what they would do, he appeared to be saying that their choice of interposing the state legislatures between the Supreme Court and the local school districts was a defensible choice. But if the Court was the "ultimate" source of authority, as he also said, then interposition was not an available choice. Thus Eisenhower's assertion that he was for "progress" was made in the context of an implication that he condoned the views of those who were not for "progress." If anything is clear in the whole statement, it is that the President was bound that he would not, if he could help it, take a position that would alienate any supporter.[32]

But when the issue went to so crucial a matter as the constitutional rights of citizens as construed by the Supreme Court, and implemented by orders of the courts, Eisenhower could not avoid alienation of some followers except by refusing to give leadership to the country. And this was precisely what he did. On February 27, 1956, Adlai Stevenson, campaigning for the Democratic presidential nomination, made a statement on the civil rights problem that included a specific suggestion. "The office of President of the United States has great moral influence and great prestige," he said, "and I think the time has come when that influence should be used by calling together white and Negro leaders from the areas concerned in the South to explore ways and means of allaying these rising tensions." At about the same time such people as Senator Richard Neuberger of Oregon, Representative Adam Clayton Powell of New York, Governor LeRoy Collins of Florida, and many clergymen of all faiths urged Eisenhower either to hold such a conference as Stevenson suggested or a conference of Southern governors and attorneys-general. The President at first seemed to see some merit in these ideas, but he postponed a decision, meanwhile asking Congress to set up a bipartisan commission charged with exploring how much progress was being made in carrying out Supreme Court orders. Such a commission, eventually established as the Civil Rights Commission (1957), would, of course, not involve the President. Indeed, it could serve to keep the President out of it. Pressure from various sources was, however, continually applied to Eisenhower to take leadership in one way or another. On April 24, Governor Collins was informed by the White House that the President was still weighing his suggestion. But on May 23, 1956, it was finally announced that Eisenhower would call no conference of any sort and would not undertake any positive action for fear of "inflaming racial feelings."[33]

And Eisenhower maintained this posture throughout the remainder of the year. When he was asked in August if he favored including in the Republican platform "a specific endorsement of the Supreme Court decision" on public school desegregation, he said he had not "given any thought" of his own to the matter. He was content to reiterate his allegiance to the Constitution. When he was asked at the same time whether, in view of the fact that Southern schools were not preparing to comply with court orders in the fall, he had plans for administration action, he took pains to point out that the matter was up to the courts. He reminded his questioners that "the pattern of the South was built up from 1896 to 1954 in what they thought was absolute accordance with the law." He went on to observe that "we have got to make certain reforms by education, . . . no matter how much law we have." If this kind of language left the President still committed to his constitutional duty, it was certainly calculated to show sympathy with those who disagreed mightily with him as to what the Constitution was. Finally, on September 5, he was asked point blank whether he would "endorse the finding of the Supreme Court on segregation or merely accept it as the Republican platform does." He answered, "I think it makes no difference whether or not I endorse it. The Constitution is as the Supreme Court interprets it; and I must conform to that and do my very best to see that it is carried out in this country."[34]

In November the election results showed conclusively that President Eisenhower had succeeded in maintaining his almost unprecedented popularity with people of all sections and most interest groups. To his 1952 list of Southern state victories he added Louisiana and the border state of Kentucky. But the disastrous events at Little Rock one year later raised sharply the question whether the President's nonpartisanship had not been costly. It would, of course, be impossible to say with any certainty what effect upon the developing crisis the direct intervention of the President might have had. What can safely be said is that the President's repeated statements disassociating himself and his office from the issue did not discourage those in Little Rock and elsewhere who were determined to defy the courts.

Less than three weeks before the Little Rock crisis erupted,

Eisenhower was asked whether he had "any plans to take a personal part in the problem this fall, for example, by speaking on it or getting in touch with Governor Faubus of Arkansas." He replied that his speaking would, as always, urge "Americans to recognize what America is, the concepts on which it is based, and to do their part as far as they possibly can to bring about the kind of America that was visualized by our forbears." He did say, somewhat hesitantly, that he thought the reasoning of the Supreme Court was "probably . . . correct" when it asserted that Negro children would have "emotional difficulties" in "equal but separate" schools. "At least I have no quarrel with it," he added. But he stressed the fact that there "are very strong emotions on the other side." In the long run, he said, "we are going to whip this thing . . . by Americans being true to themselves and not merely by law." He said nothing about talking with Governor Faubus, though the Arkansas Governor had repeatedly announced his intention to defy the court order desegregating Central High School in Little Rock and had said he would use the National Guard if necessary to his purpose.[35]

Within three weeks the President had called out the army to suppress violence in Little Rock, children were being escorted to school by federal troops, and the National Guard had been put on federal service. The President was most assuredly doing his constitutional duty. When necessity required it, he moved with efficiency and swiftness. But even under these extreme conditions he was not prepared to say to the nation that he favored the integration that was proceeding under the guard of the troops he had ordered to the scene. Instead, he told the nation in his solemn address on the Little Rock events that "our personal opinions about the decisions have no bearing on the matter of enforcement." He did, however, show his concern for world opinion. He cited the Charter of the United Nations in its affirmations of faith in fundamental human rights and the dignity of human beings "without distinctions as to race, sex, language or religion." And he urged the people of Arkansas to obey the law so that the troops could be withdrawn. "Thus will be restored," he said, "the image of America and of all its parts as one nation, indivisible, with liberty and justice for all."[36]

After Little Rock no extreme action by segregationists again forced Eisenhower's hand during the remainder of his term. It was his successor, John F. Kennedy, who had to use troops to carry out court orders in Mississippi and Alabama. And, again, it is not possible to determine whether the spirit of resistance so desperately expressed by such men as Governors Ross Barnett of Mississippi and George Wallace of Alabama was encouraged by the hands-off attitude of the Eisenhower presidency. All that can be said is that Eisenhower himself never changed his position on the civil rights question. He sought always to avoid taking sides and consistently, even stubbornly, refused to say whether he favored the decisions of the Supreme Court. In 1958, for example, he told his press conference that he would "weaken public opinion" by discussing such cases as those on desegregating the schools. In 1959 he said he did not "believe it is the function or indeed is it desirable for a President to express his approval or disapproval of any Supreme Court decision." And in the 1960 presidential campaign, as he went about the nation on behalf of Richard Nixon's candidacy, he again spoke only in the most general terms about equality for all Americans. Not until he published his memoirs in 1963 did Eisenhower state categorically a belief that the Court was right on desegregation of the schools.[37]

Although the polls in 1960 showed that his personal standing with the people remained high, even that he could defeat any Democrat if he were running for another term, he was unable to transfer his popularity to a favored successor. To the victor, Kennedy, Eisenhower bequeathed a continuing problem of tension and agitation over constitutional rights. Whether he could have moderated that problem or, perhaps, put it on the road to resolution by asserting vigorous leadership, by asking for and working to obtain legislation, by placing himself unequivocally at the head of the anti-interposition forces as Jackson had done, or simply by announcing his agreement with the Court on desegregating the schools and actively endeavoring to persuade Southerners to comply—these questions must remain unanswered.

What emerges from an examination of Eisenhower's handling of a major constitutional problem, however, is clear enough. Nonpartisanship, or unpartisanship, may help a President to retain his popularity even among groups and factions who are violently opposed to each other. But if the problem at issue involves a matter so fundamental as the meaning of the Constitution, unpartisanship may constitute a kind of abdication of responsibility that is not compensated for by repeated assertion that the President will do his duty. No President has ever refused to do his duty in accordance with his oath of office. It cannot, therefore, be said that doing his duty is an adequate position for a President to take. The problem will not go away because a President ignores it or avoids implicating himself in it. Indeed, it may become more exacerbated precisely because he does not act. Unpartisan popularity may thus become a hindrance to leadership, not an advantage to the leader. A politics of withdrawal may turn out to be a politics of defeat for the essential democratic politics of persuasion. In a moment of constitutional crisis national leadership, as Jackson had showed long before, requires the President, whatever his party, whatever his politics, to be not only a supporter but a partisan of the Constitution.

### 6. *Franklin Roosevelt finds that the Constitution is more popular than the President*    Franklin D. Roosevelt's dramatic clash with the Supreme Court in 1937 fortunately did not have about it the quality of national crisis that made Dwight Eisenhower's attitude toward the Court so fateful. But it is none the less instructive as an example of presidential leadership in matters involving the Constitution. Whereas President Eisenhower had no part in precipitating the civil rights crisis of the 1950's but, on the contrary, was forced to deal with it by a decision of the Supreme Court ultimately requiring executive enforcement, Franklin Roosevelt was not only responsible for the controversy of 1937 but deliberately brought it about. It was a highly partisan issue, and Roosevelt was a vigorous partisan.

Over several years his annoyance with decisions of the Supreme Court invalidating laws he considered at once vital to his program for recovery and mandated by his great popular support, had increased to a point where Roosevelt was persuaded that the Court was using the Constitution as a political weapon to defeat the will of the majority. After the Court had invalidated such measures as the NRA, Roosevelt anticipated that it would strike down the "gold clause" in the law that had enabled the executive to devaluate the dollar. Such action by the Court, he thought, would be intolerable. The address he prepared to deliver for the expected occasion shows how his attitude toward the Court was developing. "To stand idly by," he said, "and permit the decision of the Supreme Court to be carried through to its logical, inescapable conclusion would so imperil the economic and political security of this nation that the legislative and executive officers of the Government must look beyond the narrow letter of contractual obligations, so that they may sustain the substance of the promise originally made in accord with the actual intention of the parties." In these words Roosevelt seemed, in effect, to commit himself to an act of Presidential nullification. Although the Court did presently find a portion of the law unconstitutional because it permitted the abrogation of contracts in the case of United States bonds, the Court also held that holders of the bonds had not sustained enough injury to warrant their suing in the Court of Claims. At the same time the Court upheld the right of Congress to legislate regarding private contracts. Thus the emergency Roosevelt envisaged never came about.[38]

But his temper had hardly cooled when the Supreme Court invalidated the New Deal agricultural program by striking down the AAA. In other cases the Court also struck down the Guffey Coal Act, sometimes called the "little NRA," and declared the Railroad Retirement Act unconstitutional because it exceeded the powers of Congress under the commerce clause. In the campaign of 1936 Roosevelt repeatedly called for new legislation to replace what had been impaired or invalidated by the Court, and the Democratic Party platform called for amendment to the Constitution to "assure power to enact those laws, adequately to regulate commerce, protect public health and safety, and safeguard economic security." Afterwards, when he had decided to attack the Court directly, the President maintained that the platform had called for amendment only as a last recourse. But this was something of a quibble, as the point of the platform was to commit the party to new action in the face of Supreme Court intransigence. Nothing in the platform or in Democratic oratory, including the President's, even hinted at a plan to pack the Court.[39]

Thus the public generally was startled and many Americans were quite frankly shocked when Roosevelt sent to Congress on February 5, 1937, a plan to reorganize the judiciary that would allow him to appoint an additional justice of the Supreme Court, to a total of 15, for every justice who did not retire on reaching age 70. The President had frequently criticized the Court; he had ridiculed it as "the nine old men"; he had accused it of forcing upon the country "the private, social philosophy of a majority of nine" against the wishes of the elected Congress and the elected President. But he had never proposed to tamper with it.

Roosevelt's strategy was to claim that since he had a mandate from his landslide victory of 1936 to continue a program of social and economic legislation that the Court was blocking, it followed that his mandate included measures to put an end to the blocking. Since no one questioned the right of the Court, under existing law, to act on constitutional cases, Roosevelt saw only two alternatives available to carry out this mandate. One was to take the leadership in obtaining an amendment to the Constitution that would validate in advance the kind of measures the New Deal was trying to effect; the other was to put onto the Court judges who would be responsive to the "temper of the times." The former alternative was both cumbersome and uncertain. As Roosevelt wrote to an old friend, "If you were not as scrupulous and ethical as you happen to be, you could make five million dollars as easy as rolling off a log by undertaking a campaign to prevent the ratification by one house of the Legislature, or even the summoning of a constitutional convention in thirteen states for the next four years. Easy money." To get a two-thirds vote in Congress on an amendment, he said, "is next to impossible." And he was probably right. This was because Roosevelt's New Deal majority, a coalition of Northern Democrats with a handful of Republican liberals, was only just large enough to put legislation through the committee system and get it to a favorable vote. A strong conservative minority on the Democratic side held most of the seniority in the committees and, with the help of the Republican conservatives, could in all probability muster better than the necessary one third to obstruct passage of an amendment. But even if an amendment could be got through the Congress, a difficult and time-consuming process would be necessary to get it through three fourths of the state legislatures or state constitutional conventions.[40]

And so the President chose to try to "pack the Court." The political ammunition he sought to use on his opponents was his popularity and the popularity of his program, as demonstrated in one of the most overwhelming victories in presidential history. Roosevelt, it should be remembered, had carried every state except Maine and Vermont and had a popular majority of more than 11 million. In the campaign he had been frankly and joyously partisan. He had made no effort to unite the country behind his program. On the contrary, he had lambasted the "economic royalists" from one end of the nation to the other. He had appealed directly to independent farmers, to small businessmen, and, above all, to wage workers. He had boasted of the social measures that had been enacted between 1934 and 1936, often known later as the "Second New Deal"—the Wagner Labor Relations Act, the Social Security Act, and the creation of the Rural Electrification Administration, the National Resources Committee, and the National Youth Administration. He had called for more and greater progress and in a hundred ways attacked the conservatives who were standing in the way. Thus when the returns were in, Roosevelt had greater assurance than perhaps any President since Jackson that his leadership and his program had been vindicated by the partisan majority behind him.

Roosevelt has often been criticized for failing to consult at length with Congressional leaders before taking so drastic a step as asking for power to pack the Supreme Court. It is alleged that he offended some important leaders in both Houses who might otherwise have supported his proposal. But Roosevelt's judgment in political matters seldom betrayed him. Fresh from his massive triumph, he gambled that a surprise attack would catch his opponents off guard, disarmed by the voters, while his friends, even if they did not like the measure, would feel obliged to go along with him. He was right about his enemies but wrong about his friends. At first the conservatives in the Senate, where the plan was introduced, were confused and divided. But though

Majority Leader Joe Robinson dutifully went to work for the President, the veteran New Deal Senator Burton K. Wheeler immediately announced his opposition and started a counterattack. Within a matter of days the proposal to tamper with the Supreme Court had split the Democratic Party down the middle, united the Republican minority, and greatly confused the people at large.

Roosevelt personally took the leadership in the effort to rally a majority behind the plan, which provided for optional retirement of the judges at age 70, power for the President to appoint additional judges up to a maximum of 15 when judges reaching 70 stayed on, sending of appeals on constitutional questions directly to the Supreme Court, and strengthening the lower courts by the addition of up to 50 judges. The President, of course, met privately with members of Congress and instructed his staff to use every influence and pressure they could muster upon Senators who might be in doubt or might be subject to persuasion.

On March 9 he went into the homes of his constituents, the people, via a fireside radio chat. The purpose of his rhetoric, as it had always been, was to persuade the people to identify *his* idea as *their* idea. He spoke of the American government as a three-horse team. "The three horses are, of course, the three branches of government—the Congress, the Executive, and the Courts." It had been "intimated," he said, that he himself wished to be the driver of the team, but those who say so "overlook the simple fact that the President, as Chief Executive, is himself one of the three horses." Then came a typically Rooseveltian crescendo:

It is the American people themselves who are in the driver's seat.
It is the American people themselves who want the furrow plowed.
It is the American people themselves who expect the third horse to pull in unison with the other two.

He was sensitive to the charge that he was interfering with the independence of the judiciary. "I want," he said, "as all Americans want—an independent judiciary as proposed by the framers of the Constitution." But somehow he was able immediately to identify "independence" with a "Supreme Court that will enforce the Constitution as written—that will refuse to amend the

Constitution by the arbitrary exercise of judicial power—amendment by judicial say-so." If what the President in fact wanted
was, perhaps, something very like a Court that *would* amend
the Constitution by "judicial say-so" in order to make the commerce clause, for example, a good deal more inclusive than the
"framers" could possibly have intended, it was no doubt much
better politics for him to suggest that the Court was already
amending the Constitution by disagreeing with the President and
Congress. "It does not mean," he said, "a judiciary so independent that it can deny the existence of facts universally recognized."

Taking full personal responsibility for the Court reorganiza-
tion plan, Roosevelt told the people that he had reviewed the
situation and "by a process of elimination" had reached the
conclusion that the only method of securing the kind of legislation the people wanted was "to infuse new blood into all our
courts." What he meant by new blood was "judges who will
bring to the Courts a present-day sense of the Constitution." In
short, no doubt aware of the play with ideas in which he was
engaged, he wanted new judges who would "amend" the Constitution. But they would "reject the legislative powers which the
courts have today assumed."

Next he went directly to the charge that he was proposing to
"pack" the Court. "It is charged," he said, "that I wish to place
on the bench spineless puppets who would disregard the law and
would decide specific cases as I wished them to be decided." The
best way to meet that charge, Roosevelt evidently felt, was with
indignation. "I make this answer," he declared, "that no President fit for his office would appoint, and no Senate of honorable
men fit for their office would confirm, that kind of appointees
to the Supreme Court." Although some Roosevelt haters would
no doubt agree enthusiastically with the notion that he was not
"fit" for his office, and some others might assert that his appointees to the Court, shortly to be made, were "spineless,"
Roosevelt was nevertheless certainly vindicated by such eminent
justices as Hugo Black, William O. Douglas, and Felix Frank-
furter, all of whom had "a present-day sense of the Constitution" and none of whom feared to oppose any President's wishes.

If Roosevelt's position on the character of justices who ought
to be serving on the Supreme Court involved an element of

paradox, it was perhaps no more than the paradox that always inheres in the conflict between order and liberty. He assuredly wished to see on the Court justices who would agree with his views as to program and policy—as must any President. But he no less assuredly wished to see on the Court justices "worthy and equipped to carry out impartial justice." The point, as he put it, was that "we cannot yield our constitutional destiny to the personal judgment of a few men, who, being fearful of the future, would deny us the necessary means of dealing with the present."[41]

Though he asserted, finally, that his plan was "no attack on the Court," but rather sought "to restore the Court to its rightful and historic place in our system," his speech left his followers still confused. In their confusion they could not and did not unite to back his plan. They could agree with his intentions but not with his means. All his oratorical skill, all his deeply sincere and obvious devotion to the welfare of the common man, could not quite persuade his majority that he was not attacking the Supreme Court in itself. When a dynamic, aggressive, beloved partisan leader attempted to translate his partisan popularity into an act that seemed to be aimed at the Court, he found that his partisans were on this issue mainly nonpartisan. Devotion to the idea of a Supreme Court independent of the Congress and the Executive transcended concern about the votes of individual members of that court. Devotion to this idea of the Court was nonpartisan devotion and could not be shaken by an appeal to partisanship, even when the appeal was to the immediate self-interest of the majority of the people.

Even as he appealed to the people to back him and apply the necessary pressure to Congress, Roosevelt was losing the battle. He had signed on March 1 a bill permitting justices to retire at 70 with full salary, and Justice Willis VanDeventer presently announced his intention to do so. Since the Court had been typically divided 6 to 3, Roosevelt could now appoint a "liberal" justice who might be expected to narrow the gap. And Chief Justice Charles Evans Hughes, seeing, perhaps, that a time had indeed come for a swing toward more liberal construction of the Constitution, and perhaps also seeing a way to protect the "independence" of the Court, engineered a series of unexpected decisions upholding important New Deal measures—the Social Security Act, the Wagner Labor Relations act, state minimum wage laws, and others. Between the first of April and the first of June so many cases were decided in favor of the administration, often by 5 to 4, with Hughes himself altering the balance, that many friends of Roosevelt's court plan concluded that it was no longer a vital matter.

Franklin Roosevelt had told the country that "the Court itself can best undo what the Court has done." In this he was right. He said also, after the Court battle was lost in the Senate, that in losing the battle he had won the war. In this, too, he was right. There can be no serious doubt that Roosevelt's direct attack upon the Court by threatening to "pack" it had reversed the trend of judicial policy-making. Such a reversal would certainly have taken place in time, but the President's leadership gave history a sharp push, forcing the judges to sit up and take notice that they were too stubbornly frustrating the popular will. And so, in an important sense, Roosevelt succeeded in what he had set out to do. His mandate was translated into action.

But the mandate that was thus carried out was the will of the people, expressed in the election of 1936, that Franklin Roosevelt should continue the war against poverty, should continue to advocate and bring about measures to improve the public welfare, and should further strive to regulate business in the public interest; it was not, as Roosevelt had tried to make it appear, a mandate to "pack" the Supreme Court or to tamper with it in any way. Roosevelt's will to bring the Court into line with his views was no part of the views of the people who supported him. His immense popularity was not convertible into a political blank check upon which he could write any program he chose. It was identified with a liberal attitude toward the function of the Executive, with a program of social welfare, and it was legal tender only for transactions directed to those ends. It had no other currency.

Roosevelt, unwilling to forgive his opponents, tested the matter even beyond his defeat on the Court plan. A year later he made an aggressive effort to bring about the defeat of several of his Democratic Congressional opponents in their local primaries. In every case the opponent of his Court plan was re-elected. Indeed the Congressional election of 1938 returned the ancient coalition of conservative Democrats and Republicans to the power they had enjoyed almost continuously since 1877. After the Fair Labor Standards Act was passed in 1938, the New Deal was over. No one can say to what extent Roosevelt's attack on the Court affected the 1938 elections. It may well be that the progressive trend was about to diminish in any case. But it is equally likely that the Court fight so stained Roosevelt's popularity among his great partisan majority that the thrust and dynamism of his leadership, on domestic matters at least, could never again have quite the same effectiveness.

Thus, in a sense, Franklin Roosevelt's experience with constitutional questions was the reverse of Dwight Eisenhower's, and both instances have much to say about the nature of presidential leadership and the politics of popularity. On the one hand, nonpartisanship, because it seeks to appeal to diverse and sometimes sharply conflicting interest groups and sections, may bring about a kind of paralysis of the will to lead. Eisenhower, plainly, could not have taken the leadership on civil rights without altering the character both of his popularity and of his conception of the Presidency. He either could not do so or did not wish to, and so he was content simply to say over and over again that he would do his duty. When the crisis erupted into violence, he did so. Neither his honor nor his patriotism can be questioned. But the shrewdness of his politics in maintaining himself on a plane above the battle did not, in the end, give evidence of a wisdom, or courage, that might have saved his country much misery. Nor, on the other hand, did the aggressive partisanship of Franklin Roosevelt, sustained by immense partisan popularity, bring greater satisfaction either to himself or to the country when he sought to take action beyond the bounds of his partisan popularity. If Eisenhower could not translate nonpartisan popularity into partisan leadership, neither could Franklin Roosevelt translate partisan popularity into action on a matter on which the country was nonpartisan.

On constitutional questions, at least, there is abundant reason to believe that presidential leadership requires a deep understanding, crossing party lines, between the President and the great majority of the citizens who wish to stand by the Constitution and by the institutions that support it. Jefferson could go beyond the Constitution to purchase Louisiana only because the majority was certain that he intended no arrogation of power detrimental to the liberties of the people. Jackson could put down the nullifiers because the great majority of the citizens saw in nullification an imminent danger to the liberties of everyone and to the very existence of the republic. Monroe made possible the Missouri Compromise by appearing not to take sides when the nation was almost evenly divided, while at the same time he gave crucial if anonymous support to the Compromise and then signed it into law. Franklin Roosevelt could not establish the necessary understanding across party lines that would have been necessary to alter the size or character of the Supreme Court and therefore failed in his immediate objective despite his great and recent victory at the polls. Eisenhower, making no effort to achieve such an understanding, could not act at all until it was too late to achieve peaceable solutions to the constitutional problems of his time. Leadership on constitutional questions requires no less vigorous action by the President than upon lesser matters. But the evidence thus far, at least, is that the Constitution is more popular than the President, no matter what his politics may be.

# IV

## Presidential Popularity and Domestic Policy

1. *The inability of Monroe to turn his nearly unanimous popular acclaim into Congressional support of domestic manufactures* ❧  When John C. Calhoun told the Senate in 1850 that the United States had become "a great national consolidated democracy," he spoke more wisely than he could have realized. He was, of course, bewailing the power of the people in their majority to project through Congress a policy unfriendly to the spread of slavery. But his words covered much more than that. The American revolution of the nineteenth century that he deplored—and wished to undo—was the revolutionary diminishing of the state governments and the consequent expansion of the powers and responsibilities of the national. With this transformation went a change in the Presidency, in its institutional functions, in the popular notion of it, and in the conceptions of the office held by Presidents themselves. In the early days of national growth a popular President like Monroe could safely assume that he was not responsible for economic depression and would not be held responsible by the people, but by the beginning of the twentieth century another popular President, Theodore Roosevelt, could assert that the President is the people's "steward." By the 1960's President Lyndon B. Johnson was announcing his intention to "make war on poverty," thereby acknowledging that if the President was not responsible for the fact of poverty, he was at least obligated to try to end it.

Thus the experience of early Presidents in the field of domestic policy is not, for the most part, instructive from the

vantage point of the Presidency today. The terms of comparison
are not commensurate. But the politics of popularity that pre-
occupies contemporary Presidents activated their early predecessors, too, even if the issues and the expectations of the people
were wholly different. And the ways in which men like Monroe
and Jackson treated their popular standing with the people are
easily and usefully disengaged from the long-dead issues.

Monroe, as Secretary of War during the War of 1812, had seen
at first hand the importance of domestic manufactures. Even
Jefferson, who had for years been opposed to the development of
a manufacturing economy in the United States, had changed his
mind to a considerable extent when he saw its uses at the time
of his embargo policy. When Monroe assumed the Presidency, he
thought fit to state immediately his view that domestic manufactures should be encouraged. In so doing he was bound to
offend some of the "Old Republicans," especially those who had
for years looked to him, for no very good reasons, as their best
hope of a return to the Jeffersonian principles of the 1790's. He
would offend, too, those planters who feared that the growth of
manufacturing at home would cut down their markets abroad.
Doctrinaire free-traders properly assumed that national support
of domestic manufacturing would mean raising tariffs. To offset
such expected unfavorable reactions, Monroe could count on ap-
plause from the manufacturers themselves and from the working-
men of the towns and cities for whom jobs would be more
plentiful and wages might rise with the growth of industry.

Monroe left no record of his views on the divisive character of
supporting domestic manufactures. Thus it is not possible to say
that he calculated the effect his announcement would have on
groups or sections. But it is possible to see in the record of his
actual statements of policy both the caution that was characteristic of his Presidency and a change in emphasis after his all-but-
unanimous re-election. In his First Inaugural he rested the case
for building up domestic industry on the dangers of war:

> Our manufactures will . . . require the systematic and fostering care
> of government. Possessing as we do all the raw materials, the fruit of
> our own soil and industry, we ought not to depend in the degree we
> have done on supplies from other countries. While we are thus de-

pendent the sudden event of war, unsought and unexpected, can not fail to plunge us into the most serious difficulties.

If preparedness for an emergency could thus justify adopting a policy diametrically opposed to old Republicanism, Monroe could at least try to show how such a policy would benefit those who opposed it. He sought the investment of domestic, rather than foreign capital, "as its influence . . . instead of exhausting . . . would be felt advantageously on agriculture and every other branch of industry." Finally, it was "equally important . . . to provide at home a market for our raw materials, as by extending the competition it will enhance the price and protect the culti-vator against the casualties incident to foreign markets." Thus the new policy was promising for everyone. Monroe, of course, knew well enough that the policy of encouraging native industry was deeply divisive. But having determined from observation and reflection that it would prove generally beneficial, he took care that his words would assuage any wounds they might open. It was a masterful exercise in the statement of a divisive policy in terms of a national interest.[1]

But when it was a question of taking action, or even of rec-ommending action, Monroe preferred to shift the responsibility entirely onto the Congress. He could not himself make any specific recommendations without stirring up an opposition he wished to avoid and had avoided by the language of his In-augural. Thus in his first message to Congress he was content to say simply that "our manufactories will require the continued attention of Congress." Since there was already considerable capi-tal invested in domestic industry and much useful knowledge about machinery and fabric had been acquired, he told the Congress that "their preservation" was "connected with the high interests of the nation." That preservation "depends on due en-couragement," he added, but said nothing about what such en-couragement should be. In fact he said nothing more about the subject.[2]

Two years later, when the panic and depression of 1819–1820 were under way, Monroe reported at length to the Congress on the misfortunes that had overtaken the factories. He spoke of the shortage of money, the constriction of markets, and the ruinous competition of foreign goods. But he was reporting only, not

recommending. He said nothing of the widespread unemployment that was the chief cause of the slumping market, nor did
he suggest any remedy whatever. On the contrary, he again left
the whole problem up to Congress:

> It is deemed of great importance to give encouragement to our do-
> mestic manufacturers. In what manner the evils which have been
> adverted to may be remedied, and how far it may be practicable in
> other respects to afford them further encouragement, paying due re-
> gard to the other great interests of the nation, is submitted to the wis-
> dom of Congress.[3]

The President's "wisdom" may have been less adequate to the
purpose than that which he attributed to the Congress, but he
left no doubt that he was well aware that any remedies attempted would be considered anything but remedial in some
quarters. In fairness it must be remembered that Presidents were
not expected in those days to act as stewards of the nation's
prosperity. Jefferson had written drafts of bills on many domestic
subjects and had made other specific recommendations to Congress when he thought the public interest required them. But in
doing so he had acted as party leader, not as President. Madison
had never had such unquestioned influence over his party, and
the party system had collapsed entirely in Monroe's time. Even
had he wished to do so, Monroe could not have guided a legislative majority in the House and Senate merely by assertion of
party leadership. That he could have done so by appeal to the
people is arguable. He had not stood upon any specific platform
when he was elected in 1816; no concrete proposals were identified with his name. There was no reason to suppose that the
popular majority that sent him to the White House in emphatic
preference to Rufus King expected more from him than calmness
and dignity and a desire to let the nation develop in peace. At
any rate Monroe evidently assumed that his mandate called only
for such qualities of representation, not for active leadership, at
least in domestic affairs. He made no appeal to the people to
support home manufacturing. Indeed, as we noticed in Chapter I,
the only appeals he made to the people were in precisely those
terms of national unity, patriotism, and peaceful progress that
would avoid discussion of specific programs. Nor did he ever
spell out a program for Congress—or Congress ever act!

His fourth annual message, on November 14, 1820, the last of his first term, is a fair example of Monroe's constant intention to minimize divisive issues and to hold together the massive, if restive, coalition of disparate groups and sections that composed the nation and had just re-elected him. As he spoke, there was no end in sight to the economic depression, and thousands of people were either unemployed or in severely reduced financial circumstances. Yet Monroe began by saying that he addressed the Congress "with great satisfaction, because, taking all circumstances into consideration . . . I see much cause to rejoice in the felicity of our situation." He did not claim that there was "an unvaried prosperity" or that "every interest of this great community" was happy. He acknowledged that there was still a depression, even a severe depression. But he consoled himself and the Congress with this remarkable sentiment:

A free, virtuous, and enlightened people know well the great causes on which their happiness depends, and even those who suffer most occasionally in their transitory concerns find great relief under their sufferings from the blessings which they enjoy and in the consoling and animating hope which they administer.

A century later even so Monrovian a President as Herbert Hoover could not have indulged in this kind of rhetoric. But Monroe got away with it.[4]

Four months later, secure in his re-election, and secure in the fact that he would not again be running for office, Monroe took a better-defined position. In his Second Inaugural he took direct cognizance of the national economic misery and of the depleted funds of the Treasury. He recommended the re-enactment of internal excise taxes and called upon the people to support him:

I have never dreaded, nor have I shunned, in any situation in which I have been placed making appeals to the virtue and patriotism of my fellow-citizens, well knowing that they could never be made in vain, especially in times of great emergency or for purposes of high national importance. Independently of the exigency of the case, many considerations of great weight urge a policy having in view a provision of revenue to meet to a certain extent the demands of the nation, without relying altogether on the precarious resource of foreign commerce. I am satisfied that internal duties and excises, with corresponding imposts on foreign articles of the same kind, would, without imposing any serious burdens on the people, enhance the price of produce, promote our manufactures, and augment the revenue, at the same time that they made it more secure and permanent.

Since this was the first appeal Monroe had ever made to the people of the United States, his manner of stating his confidence in their reaction can be put down to the then customary demands of formal rhetoric. What is interesting is that Monroe did in fact make the appeal, and on a decidedly unpopular matter. What is still more interesting is that he did not make it during his first term, even though the national economic situation would have been greatly improved if he had done so and Congress had responded to his plea. To have made such an appeal, however, would have placed him in the position of dividing his following, perhaps even encouraging an opposition candidate in 1820. The politics of his nonpartisan popularity, whether he consciously meant to consult it or not, would have dictated the very avoidance of the issue he practiced. But after his unanimous re-election, with only retirement ahead, he could afford to take risks with his popularity that had not seemed available before. At any rate, whatever his motives, he took the risks.[5]

In the fall, in his annual message, Monroe re-emphasized his policy of restoring internal taxes and raising duties. He looked forward to the United States becoming "at no distant period . . . a manufacturing country on a large scale." In the abundance of raw materials and in the skill of the people he saw "every improvement calculated to lessen the demand for and the price of labor." Thus the Americans could meet any demand of "fair competition." With this prospect, imports would diminish, and so, under existing tax laws, would the federal revenue. And so his new policy was appropriate. "If domestic manufactures are raised by duties on foreign," he said, "the deficiency in the fund necessary for public purposes should be supplied by duties on the former."[6]

Congress, however, ignored the President and nothing was done. As interests shifted in the sections, the political currents were swirling and eddying to such an extent that no drive for higher tariffs or for internal taxes could be generated in Congress. When the Tariff of 1816 was enacted, there had been strong opposition from New England merchants. Daniel Webster had argued against protection and for free trade. For the South, John C. Calhoun had stood for a protective tariff to support a domestic cotton industry that at that time seemed likely to flourish in Southern towns. But by the 1820's manufacturing had become an important part of the economy of New England, which now joined the middle states in favor of protection. In the South, planters had been unhappy with the modest tariffs of 1816 and were anxious to return to free trade. The West remained unchanged in its attitude. But no region favored internal taxes. Under these circumstances, the President had gone as far, in his message of 1821, as he was prepared to go. It was evident that his popularity was not sufficient to stimulate a great pressure of citizens upon Congress. However, Monroe continued to express his views in his formal addresses to Congress. In 1822 he said that he was "persuaded that a further augmentation may now be made of the duties on certain foreign articles in favor of our own and without affecting seriously any other interest." The following year in his annual message he reminded the still passive Congress that he had previously several times recommended that "encouragement . . . be given to our manufactures." But he was not emphatic. He had "only to add," he said, "that those views remain unchanged."[7]

Not until 1824, when a new presidential election was to be held, was Congress at last willing to act. And it was not Monroe's leadership, nor popular demand stimulated by the President, that caused the legislators to change their minds. It was, rather, the jockeying for position by the candidates to succeed Monroe that altered the legislative balance. Indeed, it is perhaps not too much to say that after 1823 Monroe's administration was something of a political and administrative shambles. The near reverence with which the President had been held in the earlier years of his term gave way to indifference and, finally, to neglect and even contempt on the part of many officials closely associated with him. Crawford, in a notorious episode, even went so far as to threaten Monroe with a poker! The public at large seemed to forget the President entirely except for the poignant moment in February, 1825, just before his retirement, when he received Lafayette at the White House. There were Jackson people, Clay people, Adams people, Crawford people, and Calhoun people, but there were no Monroe people. And so Monroe was not responsible for the Tariff of 1824. The views of the popular, unpartisan President were irrelevant to the most significant act of domestic policy during the whole of his second term.

Much has been written about the one-party experiment of Monroe's administration and about the collapse of the Democratic-Republican Party. Whether Monroe could have held the party together had he tried is an unanswerable question. What is certain is that he did not try. Instead he took Jefferson's smooth words of 1801 seriously—"we are all Republicans, we are all Federalists." Convinced that the war had brought permanent disgrace upon the Federalist cause and buoyed up by the enthusiasm of his popular reception as he toured the country in 1817 and 1819, he chose to cast himself in the role of chief of state and to conduct the Presidency on a plane above partisanship. The need for partisanship, he thought, had dwindled away with the unifying events of the years. Thus he failed to establish effective communication between himself and the people who stood behind him, except in terms of vague moral and patriotic sentiment.

The politics of nonpartisan popularity, as we saw in Chapter 2, helped Monroe to maintain a posture suited to a President forced to preside over a nation desperately divided by concern for the future of slavery and while that issue was still compromisable. But the same politics could only disconnect him from other vital currents running in the country. On lesser domestic issues he at first held himself aloof. And so he could weather the depression of 1819. But when in the later years, he arrived at a conviction about fundamental economic policy, he found that he had no following. The unanimous support that returned him to office in 1820 simply disappeared when he attempted to exercise substantive, not ceremonial, leadership.

2. *Jackson relies on his partisan majority against even his own Cabinet as he forces removal of the deposits from the Bank of the United States* ৡ৯ It was probably not accidental that when the American party system was rebuilt, its chief architect was Andrew Jackson, the most aggressively partisan of the

candidates of 1824. Not that Jackson was anxious to *stir up* opposition, but he saw that a President, or a presidential candidate, who wished to lead the country toward more or less well-defined goals would have to work to build a majority in agreement with him and would have to *expect* opposition. The more specific the program, the more vigorous the opposition. The vigor, both of Jackson's leadership and of the opposition it engendered, is well illustrated not only by his relentless attack on the Bank of the United States before he vetoed its recharter, as we have already seen, but in the tenacity with which he afterwards pursued his policy of removing the federal deposits from the Bank.

Within two weeks of his inauguration to a second term, Jackson made a formal address to his cabinet asking their opinions in writing on the question of the deposits. In particular, he asked them to state whether they thought a new bank should be chartered, whether the deposits of the federal money were secure in the old Bank, which was to be in existence for another three years, and, if not, whether they would favor transferring federal funds to state banks. He precluded any truly free interchange of ideas, however, by offering the "results" of his "own reflection." These results were five in number:

1. That the charter of the present Bank ought under no circumstances and upon no conditions whatever to be renewed.
2. That the ground gained by the veto ought to be firmly maintained, and that my assent ought to be withheld from any bill authorising the establishment of a Bank out of the District of Columbia. [*Jackson believed that a bank operating only within the District of Columbia would be within the powers of Congress to make all laws for the federal district (Art. I, Sec. 8, cl. 17)*].
3. That if my assent is given to the establishment of a new Bank it ought to be one located in the District of Columbia, having the right to establish Branches in the different states and in such places thereof only with the permission of the different states . . . that the Government shall have the right to appoint the President and as many Directors of the Principal Bank and the Branches thereof as will secure fidelity . . . that Congress should retain the right to repeal or modify the charter . . . as a security against the corruptions and evils which are now experienced from the uncontrollable authority of the present Bank.

4. That such an institution ought not to be recommended until full and fair experiment has been made to carry on the fiscal affairs of the Government without a national Bank of any description.

5. If this last view of the subject be adopted it will be necessary now to devise and settle a new system for the deposit and distribution of the public funds thro' the agency of the State Banks, to go into operation at such a time as shall upon a careful consideration of the subject be thought most advisable.

In effect the President was not asking for advice but only seeking to know whether the principal officers of the government would support the decisions he had already made.[8]

This was exactly the opposite of that "staff process" upon which, a century and a quarter later, another general relied. Dwight Eisenhower, endeavoring to apply his experience with military procedures to presidential decision-making, asked not for support of his own views, nor for opinions he could weigh against one another, but for an opinion on which his principal advisers had agreed and he could then adopt or reject as he thought best. Between the Jackson and the Eisenhower extremes lies the procedure adopted by such presidents as Jefferson in early times and by Franklin Roosevelt and John Kennedy in recent years—the somewhat disorderly churning over of ideas and opinions among people in whom the President has confidence, with the President himself taking part, often extensively, until he is satisfied that the best wisdom, practical and political, has been generated.

Jackson, in placing the question of the federal deposits before his cabinet, was laying down the ground rules for a tough campaign to carry out a policy to which he was already fully committed and that he believed he had a mandate to carry out. Jackson's mandate was no doubt debatable, but it was a good deal fairer inference from election returns than was the mandate Franklin Roosevelt claimed to have in 1937 to pack the Supreme Court. In the latter case an overwhelming victory at the polls had certainly given Roosevelt endorsement for his program, but that program contained no provision for meddling with the Court. In the 1832 campaign, on the other hand, Jackson had certainly asked in the most clear-cut manner for an endorsement of his attack on the Bank of the United States. He got it, resoundingly. If the voters were not directly asked their opinion about handling the federal money in the future, it was certainly fair to infer that they were willing to leave this matter to the wisdom of the triumphant President.

At any rate Jackson so interpreted the election and proceeded to act accordingly. Indeed, without waiting for the opinions of his cabinet, he sent Amos Kendall, one of his closest political associates, to talk in confidence with officials of state banks in the larger cities, preparatory to transferring the deposits. Kendall at that time was only Fourth Auditor in the Treasury, a position that would hardly have warranted his negotiating with the state banks on so momentous a matter as their replacement of the Bank of the United States as public repositories. But Kendall was an inner-circle Jacksonian, and well known so to be. He could, in fact, speak with greater authority than the Secretary of the Treasury himself. That the proposed removal of the deposits was primarily a political move was amply revealed by Kendall's role.[9]

From the cabinet Jackson got a variety of responses that showed how confused the question really was. All of the members wished to give the President political support. But only Taney, then Attorney-General, was prepared to accept the President's views unequivocally. Treasury Secretary McLane was at the other extreme. While he continued to agree with Jackson that the Bank of the United States should not under any circumstances be rechartered, he nevertheless favored a national bank, preferably a nationalized bank in which the government owned all the stock. Pending the establishment of such a bank, he favored leaving the federal deposits in the old bank. Inviting Jackson's wrath, he said that he considered the "intimations" with which the President accompanied his request to the cabinet as "for the purpose of free examination and discussion, and not to preclude or embarrass the investigation." McLane proceeded to argue for a national bank and against removal of the deposits. He felt, however, he said "too much respect . . . for the sincere conviction and patriotic motives" with which the President's opposition was expressed in his veto message to press the matter. He would "do no more than respectfully advise a revision of the subject at the proper time." As to the removal of the deposits, McLane underlined the fact that a great majority in the House had sustained a report by the Ways and Means Committee that found the Bank solvent and well managed. He pointed out also that a special investigator of the Treasury had reached the same conclusion. He therefore advised keeping the deposits in the Bank until a permanent solution to the problem should be reached.

Since Jackson had already asked him to replace Edward Livingston as Secretary of State in June, McLane knew when he wrote his long opinion that he would not be called upon to undertake the removal of the deposits himself. He might therefore have attempted to duck the issue. But his forthright and thoughtful paper evoked neither anger nor retaliation from the President. Jackson, in fact, endorsed the paper with this comment: "There are some strong points of view—all ably discussed." He was so impressed that he presently circulated McLane's paper among his political intimates. Francis P. Blair, for example, then editor of the pro-Jackson *Globe*, provided Jackson with a detailed analysis and refutation of McLane's views. Though he made some effective comments on the arrogance of the Bank's leadership. Blair's chief point was political. In effect he swept away McLane's careful theoretical and practical considerations by asserting that "the President with 'manifest propriety' referred the whole subject to the people and their representatives." McLane had pointed out that a majority of the House disagreed with Jackson, but Blair hit the Jacksonian bulls-eye by telling the President that "in re-electing General Jackson to represent them in the Executive Department after the Veto, they [the people] elected him to carry out the principles of that Veto, as their Representative."[10]

As the spring of 1833 wore on, Jackson seems to have wavered somewhat as to the time for removal of the deposits. Despite the advice of McLane and of old and trusted friends like Hugh White, he would not reverse himself on the Bank of the United States. But he was willing to consider that the sensible course, as many people advised, might be to wait until Congress returned to session in December and try to persuade that body to share with him the responsibility for what would amount to a crippling of the Bank. The objections to such a course, as he saw them, were that the pro-Bank politicians would thus be given one more chance to plead with Congressmen in the hope of mustering votes to override the veto and that the Bank itself would be given time to seek more friends by financial favors. To remove the deposits forthwith might be rash in the light of the nation's financial structure; to wait might be disastrous politically. In the decision to act at once, Kendall played a critical part.

When William J. Duane succeeded McLane in June, 1833, it soon became apparent that though the new secretary had favored Jackson's veto of the recharter of the Bank, he shared McLane's views and those of financial men generally regarding the deposits. Thus Jackson was again faced with resistance at the very point of action. Kendall, moving from state bank to state bank to prepare for the impending transfer, seems to have felt the need to exert extra pressure on Jackson to make sure that the President would not lose his political advantage by waiting until winter to act. On June 9, Kendall wrote to Vice-President Van Buren, who was to receive Jackson in New York a few days later, urging him to advise the President to act at once and outlining a method of procedure. Van Buren, previously somewhat hesitant in his own communications with the President, was apparently persuaded by Kendall's effective letter. Since that letter, a confidential communication between two political allies, was to become national banking policy, it is worth special attention.

Kendall begins by saying that there are some "points in this subject on which his [the President's] mind is not settled and on which particularly he will desire your opinion." As Kendall apparently thought Van Buren's advice might be decisive, he proceeded to set forth his own views in full, in the confident expectation that they would presently reach Jackson with the added sanction of the trusted Vice-President. "I shall take it for granted," wrote Kendall, "that the deposits will be removed. The question then arises in what manner and to what banks?" In answer to these questions, "premising that the government must not be placed in a worse condition under a new arrangement than it is now," he outlined a plan to "combine safety of the deposits and convenience to the Treasury." His idea was that one bank in Boston, two in New York, and one each in several other major commercial cities should be designated as official government depositories. These state banks, in turn, might contract with other banks to share the work but not the responsibility. The designated banks would "be responsible to the government

for the whole public deposit of the United States." These banks
would, for their part, provide all the services then being performed by the Bank of the United States and be subject to filling
orders of the Secretary of the Treasury without expense to the
government. They would be required to submit monthly reports
of their financial condition, to report weekly to the Treasurer of
the United States on the state of the deposits, and to pay, on demand of the Secretary of the Treasury, any sum in specie or its
"equivalent."

Next Kendall dealt with the "manner of changing the deposits." He proposed to leave the existing deposits with the Bank
of the United States until they should be exhausted by warrants
for current expenses of the government. Meanwhile all newly
collected funds would be deposited with the designated state
banks. "This had the double recommendation," he said, "of
shielding the government from every charge of harshness toward
the U. S. Bank and enabling the selected state banks to make
terms with their rivals and neighbors before they may be called
on for payments by the Treasury."

Turning to the matter of timing, Kendall told Van Buren that
he was "firmly of the opinion" that the change ought to be soon
enough "to take the last dollar out of the U.S. Bank and present
the new machine in complete operation before the next session
of Congress." This would mean starting the process by the first
of August or, at the latest, the first of September. There would,
of course, be consternation on the part of the adherents of the
Bank, but the government "will have the advantage . . . of . . .
the increased power of the state banks and the weight of the
President's popularity." If Van Buren agreed with these views,
Kendall hoped his "great influence" might be "exerted in every
proper mode, to effect the desired object."[11]

Van Buren's conversation with Jackson at New York during
the following week did indeed have the "desired effect." On June
26, from Boston, the President dispatched his instructions to
Secretary Duane to proceed with the change-over. It is apparent
from the text of Jackson's message that Van Buren had fully
agreed with Kendall. Together, without much difficulty, they
had persuaded Jackson to adopt Kendall's plan. Jackson's plan,
in fact, follows Kendall's almost verbatim. It called for (1) com-

mencing to deposit federal funds in state banks by the first or fifteenth of September; (2) starting with two banks in New York and one each in Boston, Baltimore, and Philadelphia; (3) giving these banks the right to subcontract the handling of the money; (4) giving the Secretary of the Treasury power to change or discontinue the system as he thought best in the national interest; (5) the banks to make weekly reports on the deposits and monthly reports on their own condition; (6) the banks to agree to make payments to the government either in specie or its equivalent at any place in the country convenient to the Treasury; (7) the banks to render every service "which can now be lawfully required of the Bank of the United States" without charge to the government; finally, (8) the government to deal as equitably with the state banks as possible. To negotiate the agreements between the Treasury and the state banks, Jackson suggested that Duane appoint Kendall! As Duane certainly knew that Kendall had been making a bank-to-bank preliminary survey, he could not have been surprised at the nomination. But since Kendall was a subordinate at the Treasury, Duane was also face to face with the fact that Jackson's letter was a political directive as well as an administrative one. Kendall was involved not in his role as a Treasury official but in his role as political confidant of the President.[12]

That the political motivation was uppermost in Jackson's assertion of leadership Duane was told even more bluntly in another communication Jackson sent to him the same day, enclosed in the letter of instruction. In this memorandum Jackson recited for Duane's benefit "the full development of the policy which the President thinks it his duty to pursue in relation to the Bank of the United States." The force of the whole document lay in its reliance upon the outcome of the 1832 election as providing the President with a mandate. He put the matter before the Secretary of the Treasury in these categorical terms:

. . . the Bank petitioned for a renewal of its charter and the Representatives of the people and of the states in Congress by a majority of both Houses, passed a Bill granting their request. Upon this bill the President deemed it his duty to put his constitutional veto. His veto of the Bank bill brought the subject directly before he people who were about to express their opinion of his official acts. By both parties in the contest the principal issue was joined upon the Bank veto, and by a decisive majority the people condemned the bill passed by Congress and approved the act of the President, declaring the Bank to be both inexpedient and unconstitutional. To this decision given by the highest power known on earth it was hoped the Bank and its advocates would cheerfully submit. To the public functionaries who are now called upon to act on the subject, it seems to the President that it ought to be a rule and guide next in authority to the constitution itself, because it was given by a majority of the states and a majority of the people who make the law makers, and have a right to direct them. He therefore considers it a settled question so far as public sentiment is concerned that the present Bank of the United States is not to be rechartered.

Before proceeding to argue—rather, to lay it down—that the Kendall plan was best for the country, Jackson again called Duane's attention to the relation between the President and his constituents. "The President has no doubt," he said, "that the proposed experiment will serve to satisfy the people that a national Bank can be dispensed with without serious injury or embarrassment to the public service or to the substantial interests of the country." He was quite prepared, in this as in all other matters, to abide by the clear expression of public opinion. "If the result be otherwise," he went on, "it will then become the right and duty of the Government and people to decide between enlarging the authority of the Federal Government and the exercise of that which it possesses within the District of Columbia." At the conclusion of the long paper Jackson saw fit to say that because of the subject, he expected it to be handled by the Treasury Department, but the President would "take upon himself the responsibility of a course which involves much private interest and public considerations of the greatest magnitude."[13]

Duane replied to Jackson in a letter dated July 10. He refused, in effect, to carry out the President's wishes. Though he agreed that the Bank of the United States was not to be rechartered, he argued that the matter of a new system of federal banking should be put up to Congress. In the interim he preferred to leave the deposits with the old Bank. Jackson's reaction was, in the first instance, patient—at least for Jackson. He pointed out that Duane had not indicated his own views as to a proper substitute for the banking functions of the U.S. Bank and asked the Secretary to furnish him with a statement on this matter. He also asked the Secretary to "call upon [the President] on Monday morning to converse further upon the matter." That conversation, if it ever took place, was not decisive. In fact the impasse between the President and his Secretary of the Treasury was allowed to continue until the 23rd of September.[14]

It would be tedious to recapitulate all of the letters and memoranda that passed between Jackson and Duane, between Jackson and Van Buren, and between Jackson and Kendall during the two months in which Jackson chafed at the delaying tactics of Duane and of other members of his Cabinet who thought it would be unwise to remove the deposits before Congress could act. But there were recurring themes, and there is abundant evidence of Jackson's rising temper. In the Cabinet, only Taney was foursquare for removing the deposits, and removing them quickly. As he told Jackson on August 5, he thought "the step should be taken before the meeting of Congress because it is desirable that the members should be amongst their constituents when the measure is announced and should bring with them when they come here the feelings and sentiments of the people. . . ." He added that he relied "at all times with confidence on the intelligence and virtue of the people of the United States . . . I think they will sustain the decision." This, of course, was what Jackson wanted to hear. He continued to get similar support from Kendall and Van Buren, as well as other close political associates, but again for clear-cut political reasons, he did not wish to take action with his Cabinet in open opposition. He had seen how Monroe's administration crumbled because of dissension in the Cabinet, and he was bound that his own leadership should not founder in the same way. [15]

Under the circumstances he had two practicable alternatives: he could fire his recalcitrant colleagues, or he could search for new means to persuade them. With the help of Kendall and the government directors of the Bank he followed the latter course as far, at least, as he could. It was far enough, as it turned out, to persuade everyone except Duane!

Through the government-appointed directors of the Bank Jackson sought to learn in detail how much money the Bank had been spending for various kinds of printing intended to present its side of the fight with the President. On the surface such information ought, perhaps, to have been easy to obtain. But Nicholas Biddle, whether for good or ill, did indeed run the Bank with the autocratic power and disdain of supervision of which Jackson had always accused him, and a good many expenditures were simply noted in the books as made by the president of the Bank on his own order, with no indication as to how the money had been spent. It was necessary, therefore, to have clerks examine all the cashier's receipts and make up a special report on printing expenses. On August 19, the job was completed and the government directors reported to the President. Their findings fully supported Jackson's contention that bank money, of which one fifth, he insisted, was public money, had been used in substantial amounts to try to frustrate the policy of the President of the United States. Jackson's notion that one fifth of the Bank's assets and income belonged to the United States was perhaps defensible in moral terms, since the government owned one fifth of the stock and had the right to appoint five of the twenty-five directors. However, the legal basis for Jackson's claim that the president of the Bank had no power to spend that rather hypothetical one fifth was certainly shaky.

But shaky or not, Jackson pressed the claim and was able to show the Cabinet, from the report of the government directors, that Biddle's expenses for "printing" had risen sharply, directly parallel to the growing intensity of Jackson's attack on the Bank. In the last half of 1829 printing costs had been $3,765.94. After Jackson's first annual message the figure had risen to $7,131.27 in the first half of 1830 and to $6,950.20 in the second half. This money had been used for printing and distributing throughout the country pamphlets by Albert Gallatin and others on the virtues of the Bank. In March, 1831, the Board of the Bank had authorized Biddle to "cause to be prepared and circulated such documents and papers as may communicate to the people information in regard to the nature and operations of the Bank." Following this action, which set no limits to Biddle's budget, the Bank had spent $29,979.92 in the first half of the year and $13,-224.87 in the second half for printing and distributing literature favorable to the Bank's side in the raging battle. In 1832 Biddle had similarly spent a total of $38,677.88, and in the first half of the current year (1833) he had spent $9,093.59. The government directors were not able to show that all of this money, amounting to well over $100,000, had been spent to fight the President. But the cashier's receipts showed that a great portion of it had been so spent. Thus when Jackson, in a letter to Van Buren, asserted that the figures showed Biddle had spent $60,000 "for corruption," he was probably not far off. A few days later, in a confidential letter to Polk, he raised his estimate to $80,000, which may have been too high.[16]

Armed with such figures, Jackson proceeded with his campaign to persuade the Secretary of the Treasury and the Cabinet to support his decision to remove the federal deposits from the Bank. His temper had been rising for weeks and months. In August he told Van Buren that every investigation "develops some more corruption of this mammoth of power." He was determined, he said, "to meet it boldly, and fearlessly, regardless of its threats of the senate to reject my nominations, or that Congress will order the deposits restored to it." Again writing to Van Buren he denounced Duane for his failure to accept the President's views. He would give him one more chance and then, "should Mr. Duane refuse to yield to the wishes of the Executive, and retire, I pledge myself that no one superintends that Department hereafter but one whose whole opinions I *know* correspond with my own." He added that he would "give the agency to Mr. Taney who is right, and with me *in all points.*" When he asked Van Buren to return to Washington and help in the struggle, the Vice-President gave a good demonstration of his own political shrewdness. "I shall be governed in that matter," he wrote the President, "altogether by your wishes. You know that the game of the opposition is, to relieve the question, as far as they can, from the influence of your well deserved popularity with the people, by attributing the removal of the deposits to the solicitations of myself and a monied junto in New York." Since his appearing in Washington would "play into enemies' hands," Van Buren assumed that the President would not insist. There could never, of course, be a serious doubt of Van Buren's loyalty to Jackson. It does not escape notice, nevertheless, that the Vice-President managed to extricate himself from the painful meeting of the Cabinet Jackson held a few days later.[17]

Kendall, meanwhile, had been both lining up an impressive list of banks that would be willing, indeed happy, to receive the deposits, and also taking careful political soundings. He reported faithfully to his chief every scrap of gossip. It is probably not remarkable that what he heard about Duane was not likely to please Jackson. At any rate he lost no chance to let the President know what was being said. He reported, for example, a conversation he had in Philadelphia with a banker who said that "Mr. McLane had procured the appointment of Mr. Duane, and by so doing, placed himself at the head of two departments." His over-all impression, however, was that the majority of the Jackson people were with the President. "With the exception of a few friends of the Bank," he told Jackson, "a few timid politicians and now and then a merchant, the whole mass of our political friends appear, so far as I can learn, to be in favor of a removal of the deposits." The press, too, was on the President's side. "I believe every Republican paper east of Pennsylvania, many of them in that state and most of them in the West have come out in strong terms."[18]

It was on this kind of grass-roots opinion-sampling that Jackson relied in his appeal to the people over the heads of both Congress and his own Cabinet. If Kendall's techniques were somewhat less scientific than the political polling of a later time, they produced results not only pleasing to Jackson but remarkably accurate. Jackson's own political antennae were also at work. He told Duane that he was entirely satisfied that public opinion was with him both on eliminating the Bank of the U. S. and on removing the deposits from it but that he would not press his independent treasury plan because he found too little popular support for it. Duane, perhaps overly sensitive to the wishes of financial men with whom he had necessarily to work, feared that the same public opinion would rebel against Jackson precisely if he did remove the deposits. Kendall and Jackson were, of course, right, and Duane, McLane, and the others wrong.

On September 18 Jackson read to the Cabinet a long paper reviewing the whole bank question, underlining the Bank's independence from government control, and reporting in detail how the Bank had spent "public" money for propaganda against the government. He demanded, and got, the Cabinet's support for summary action to deposit federal funds in the state banks with which Kendall had negotiated. Duane said he would need to think over the matter still further. "I made my determination known to my cabinet yesterday in writing," wrote Jackson to Van Buren, *"as the measure of the Executive and on my own responsibility,* etc., etc., it is a strong paper; and Mr. Duane has said so . . . and has asked until tomorrow to decide whether he will execute it." Jackson added, "I expect *now* he will act with energy, or retire friendly, which to me is desirable."[19]

But Jackson was to be disappointed yet once more. Duane not only refused to carry out the President's wishes but also refused to resign. Jackson gave him still another chance to reconsider, but Duane was wholly intractable. On September 23 Jackson summarily dismissed him. The same day he appointed Taney to the Treasury. To Van Buren he communicated his private feelings:

> I have this morning, from imperious necessity been compelled to dismiss Mr. Duane from the Treasury Department. His conduct has been such of late that would induce a belief that he came into the Dept. as the secret agent of the Bank, to disclose the cabinet secrets for its benefit, rather than to aid the Executive in the administration of the Government.

And so the decision was made. On the 26th Taney carried it out.[20]

But Jackson still had to fight the Congress. On the day after Christmas Henry Clay introduced two resolutions in the Senate, one censuring the Treasury for its action and the other accusing the President of undertaking an unconstitutional responsibility. Debate continued, off and on, until March 28, 1834, when both resolutions were adopted. Jackson sent a special message to the Senate asserting that he had been in effect tried for an impeachable offense without a hearing. Meanwhile in the House, Polk rallied Jackson forces to enact four counter-resolutions supporting the President's action.

In the fall election the President himself took no part, but the removal of the deposits was nevertheless a prime issue. If he had been vindicated in 1832 for his veto of the Bank recharter bill, he was almost as resoundingly sanctioned in 1834 for his policy on the deposits. In 1832 the Democrats had won the House by the great margin of 147 to 93. In 1834 they held it by nearly as great a majority, 144 to 98. In the new Congress Polk, one of the most devoted—and astute—Jacksonians, was elected Speaker.

The Senate continued its vendetta with the President by refusing to confirm Taney as Secretary of the Treasury. But during his interim appointment he had launched the new policy from which there was to be no turning back despite Biddle's retaliatory calling in of loans. In fact the spreading of the huge federal deposits among the state banks ("pet banks," as they were soon known) precipitated an inflationary boom that Biddle was powerless to stop. Before long he was forced to follow the lead of the state banks and again extend competitive credit. Taney, too, was vindicated when the new Senate confirmed him as Chief Justice of the United States.

As for the Clay resolutions censuring Jackson, Thomas Hart Benton, tough Missouri Jacksonian, kept them under fire on the Senate floor and in the cloakrooms until on January 16, 1837, just seven weeks before Jackson retired, the Senate reversed itself and expunged them from the record. In the end Jackson's victory was total. If he left a legacy of financial uncertainty that produced the Panic of 1937 for Van Buren to contend with and that was not relieved until Polk's administration, the responsibility had to be shared by Biddle for his equally vindictive policy. And Jackson scored some important triumphs for democratic government and a strong Presidency.

At the least, Jackson's handling of the question of the deposits showed how effective popular leadership could be under the American constitutional system. At best, it showed that a President who defines the issues clearly, for good or ill, and wins the support of a popular majority can, with determination, carry out his policy even against concentrated private economic power. He demonstrated, too, that a President's political power need not be limited by the disapproval of his official advisors. If it is not conducive to either efficient or stable government, for the President to fire a succession of Cabinet secretaries, it is at least better than diffusing his power, as weaker Presidents have often done, among men who owe their authority to him and to him alone.

*3. Polk's "Constitutional Treasury": how a President can convert the popularity of an issue into political weapons to persuade the Congress* ॐ    The causes of the Panic of 1837 are still debated, but whether or not the "pet bank" system had a fair trial, it is certain that it failed and that a substitute had to be found. Van Buren, as President, turned to the independent treasury idea that Jackson had favored but abandoned because he feared it was not popularly supported. Again following Jackson, Van Buren insisted on hard money in government financial transactions. In May, 1837, with a bad financial situation getting worse, he decided to call a special session of Congress for September. At that time he laid before it his plan for a subtreasury to receive all federal funds, with only gold and silver coins to be accepted. The Senate passed the measure by a small margin. But despite the efforts of Speaker Polk the bill was pigeonholed in the House. The President had only a doubtful two-vote margin in the House and wholly lacked a personal popularity he might bring to bear on wavering Representatives.

Because of his rigid opposition to paper money Van Buren's measure was unpopular even in Democratic areas of the West. A friend of Polk's, for example, wrote the Speaker that it made no difference how sound the Van Buren policy was; "the people are governed by habit and want paper money." Correctly predicting that the "party will go down" with the plan because, he said, the people could not understand it, he urged Polk to use his influence to get treasury notes into circulation. Polk, however, was loyal to the President. At the end of the session, he retired from Congress to run successfully for Governor of Tennessee, but his party "went down" in the Congressional election, when the Whigs captured the House by 132 to 103. The 26th Congress, unable to muster the votes to recharter the Bank of the United States, did at last authorize Van Buren to create a subtreasury. Evidently hoping that Harrison, and afterwards Tyler, would approve a national bank, the same Congress repealed the subtreasury in the early months of the Whig administration that followed Van Buren's defeat. When Tyler, a one-time Democrat, refused to support a national bank, the federal finances were once more in a precarious state.[21]

Thus the election of 1844 was a kind of referendum on the problem of banking and of handling federal money. James K. Polk, unexpectedly becoming the Democratic candidate, immediately made it known that he favored the opposite of Clay's "American System"—he was for a low tariff, against internal improvements, and for a subtreasury. Polk called it the "constitutional treasury."

Although Polk was not personally popular as Jackson had been, his record had made him an impressive candidate, and his forthrightness, especially on foreign policy, as we shall see in Chapter V, gave him a clean edge over Clay in the election of 1844. His well-known stand for a low tariff and an independent treasury were certainly endorsed in the great Democratic sweep of the House of Representatives. In the 29th Congress a previous Whig margin of two votes was converted into a Democratic margin of sixty-three, and Polk had no hesitation in applying the leverage that majority gave him, nor in standing, like Jackson, on his mandate. At the very beginning of his administration, as Secretary of the Navy George Bancroft noted, Polk placed the constitutional treasury second in the list of his "four great measures." In his first annual message he recommended that a "constitutional treasury be created for the safe-keeping of the public money." Heavily emphasizing national power as against private, he continued:

> To say that the people or their government are incompetent or not to be trusted with the custody of their own money in their own Treasury, provided by themselves, but must rely on the presidents, cashiers, and stockholders of banking corporations, not appointed by them nor responsible to them, would be to concede that they are incapable of self-government.

The constitutional treasury went through the House on April 2, 1846, by 122 to 66.[22]

The Senate, nearly equally divided, presented a difficult problem. The Democratic majority was dominated not by Polk–Jackson men but by "deep South" Calhoun men, who had seniority in the committees. Calhoun, after his ouster by Jackson from his high place in the national party, had joined Clay and Webster in support of the Bank of the United States. He later opposed the removal of the deposits and the subtreasury idea, and his influence with men like Dixon Lewis, chairman of the Senate Finance Committee, was a serious obstacle to Polk's program. Lewis, in fact, told Webster that he intended to keep the treasury bill off the Senate floor for a good long while, listing a number of less important measures he would deal with first.

Under these circumstances Polk showed his mettle as a politically sophisticated and toughminded President. Calling Lewis to the White House he spoke very frankly—and persuasively:

> I told him that I had great anxiety for the passage of the Constitutional Treasury Bill and the reduction of the Tariff, which I had recommended in my annual message. I told him that I considered them as administration measures and that I intended to urge them upon Congress as such, and that I considered the public good, as well as my own power and the glory of my administration, depended in a great degree upon my success in carrying them through Congress.

Polk proceeded to the matter of appointments. He told Lewis that he was most unhappy that Southern Democrats were opposing confirmation of certain men from the North, whereas Southerners were not opposed by Northern senators. The plain implication was that the President would have less interest in the future in Southern candidates for federal office unless there was a change of heart among Southern senators. Lewis complained that Calhoun's followers were being ill-treated. But Polk served notice that as far as he was concerned, they were all party men and he was not going to give special advantages to any Democratic candidate for President in 1848. He was concerned with his own administration, not the next one. Finally, he reminded Lewis that he had done more for the South on the tariff than any other President. Men from that section, he said, ought "to cease their opposition upon these small matters in which no principle was involved, for the sake of enabling me to carry out the great measure which involved principle."[23]

If Lewis had intended to kill the bill by delaying tactics, he soon changed his mind. Though he held it back for another month, he nevertheless reported it, without crippling amendments, on June 8. When the vote was finally taken, on August 1, the Administration had the votes to carry it.

Again, the point is not that the subtreasury law was good or that it was bad, but that a strong, highly partisan President, relying on his power as leader of an established national majority, was able to insist upon the passage of a measure desired by his partisan majority. If Polk was not personally popular, he was politically astute enough and aggressive enough to make full use of the area of agreement between himself and his party. Under the circumstances a powerful minority in that party, because it was clearly a minority, was forced to accede to the will of the President and his majority faction. Polk had no hesitation in dividing the country. Indeed, he considered it his duty to divide the country, since what he believed best for the country was bitterly opposed by the minority and no compromise was available. The alternative was to do nothing. But Polk, holding Jackson's conception of the President as the leader of the popular majority, obligated to define the issues, not obfuscate them, was wholly unwilling to let matters drift. More than a century later another President, Harry S. Truman, studying Polk's remarkable diary, saw how it might be possible to be a "strong" President even without the kind of popularity his world-renowned predecessor had enjoyed. But it was to be three generations after Polk before a President would appear who was at once popular and partisan, and who would assert the kind of energetic partisan leadership Polk exerted. Theodore Roosevelt would not, perhaps, have wholly approved a comparison of himself with James K. Polk, but in some essentials of their conception and conduct of the Presidency the two men were instructively alike.

4. *Theodore Roosevelt and the anthracite coal strike: the power and prestige of the presidential office enlarged* 〰 Between Polk and Roosevelt the only President who could be said to have great personal popularity was Grant. The Civil War hero's standing in the nation before his election was above that of any other American. Despite many failures of leadership and

the shocking revelations of corruption among men close to him, Grant maintained his popularity almost unimpaired throughout his two terms. One reason may have been precisely his unwillingness to give leadership in domestic affairs. In his first annual message, for example, he made these characteristic statements:

The appropriations estimated for river and harbor improvements and for fortifications are submitted. . . . Whatever amount Congress may deem proper to appropriate for these purposes will be expended.

In his last annual message, a kind of farewell address, he reiterated the primacy of Congress and apologized for his mistakes.[24]

Between Grant and Roosevelt perhaps none of the Presidents was quite so deferential to Congress, but except for such sporadic incidents of energy as Cleveland's interference in the Pullman strike of 1894, the characteristic pattern of presidential conduct was to "execute the laws" without inviting additional responsibilities.

Whether or not Mark Hanna, Tom Platt, and other Republican leaders consciously intended to shelve Theodore Roosevelt by making him Vice-President in 1900, the death of McKinley and Roosevelt's own character and conception of public service guaranteed that he would not be shelved. With the sole exception of Lincoln during the Civil War, no President after Polk had even seriously considered taking charge of the government as did Roosevelt within hours of his taking the oath of office. In his first term he tackled the trusts and won the Northern Securities case. He went after the railroads for their rebate practices. He pushed forward his project for a Panama Canal. But nothing he did so enlarged the scope of the presidential jurisdiction as his interference in and forced settlement of the anthracite coal strike of 1902.

In 1900 the newly-organized United Mine Workers had made the first industry-wide demands on the coal operators for higher wages and better working conditions. The operators at first refused even to discuss the question. However, Hanna, directing the campaign for McKinley's re-election, persuaded them, under threat of a Bryan victory, to make some temporizing adjustments, so that a strike at that time was averted. But by the spring of 1902 the workers again came to the point of threatening to strike unless more substantial improvements were made in wages and working conditions.

This time the operators of the mines, then chiefly owned by the railroads, flatly refused to bargain with President John Mitchell or his United Mine Workers. Appeals from Hanna, as well as from men like Senator Matt Quay of Pennsylvania, complaining that a miners' strike would hurt the Republicans in the Congressional elections, were rejected summarily. This time the operators were set to "teach their laborers a lesson." George F. Baer, President of the Reading Coal and Iron Company, won himself an unenviable place in history as spokesman for the employers. "The rights and interests of the laboring man," he wrote to a clergyman who had appealed for conciliation, "will be protected and cared for—not by the labor agitators, but by the Christian men to whom God in his infinite wisdom has given the control of the property interests of this country." How complete was the control thus "given" is suggested by a remark of Samuel Gompers. The miners, he said, as children "were brought into the world by the company doctor, lived in a company house or hut, were nurtured by the company store, laid away in the company graveyard."[25]

The impasse resulted in a strike on May 12, 1902. The first efforts to resolve the issues were made by Pennsylvania Republican leaders fearful of defeat in November. But by midsummer there was no sign of a break, there were numerous reports of violence in the coal fields, and the supply of hard coal was shrinking rapidly. There was a growing prospect of a winter without coal for the furnaces of the nation's homes.

As early as June 27, President Roosevelt, responding to appeals from many citizens, ordered Attorney-General Philander Knox to determine whether the President could intervene under the antitrust laws. Knox replied in the negative and advised Roosevelt not to involve himself in any case. So matters stood when Roosevelt visited Senator Henry Cabot Lodge and Governor Murray Crane in Massachusetts at the end of August. Lodge reinforced Roosevelt's own view that the strike would be a serious handicap in the election, while Crane painted a bleak picture of conditions in Massachusetts, where the price of what little coal remained was rising alarmingly. The President resolved to try every means within his power to bring the two sides of the controversy together and end the strike. Despite a serious injury when a trolley car smashed into his carriage, he wrote many letters to influential people and made a tour of the middle west, hoping to stir up public pressures upon both operators and strikers. He returned to Washington on September 24, having abandoned his trip because of an abscess on his leg, a complication of his accident. For the next three weeks, confined like a later Roosevelt to a wheelchair, he busied himself with his favorite hobby—the making of history. "Political" interference, he felt, was not only justified but necessary:

A word as to the interference of politicians. Quay and Hanna are Senators; Odell is Governor [of New York]; I am President. If any one of us interferes in a spirit of mere political trickery, or to gain political ends of an unworthy kind in an unworthy manner, if he threatens or hectors, why he should be condemned without stint. But the heaviest weight of condemnation should be reserved for any one of us who represents the people and who yet fails to do all in his power in the interest of the people to bring to an end a situation fraught with such infinite danger to the whole commonwealth. If during the ensuing week there comes some heavy riot on the East Side in New York, in my judgment the operators, more than the miners, are responsible for it.[26]

In the last days of September Roosevelt sent Hanna and Secretary of War Elihu Root to New York to see J. P. Morgan, asked Senator Quay to redouble his efforts to get the operators and miners together, and privately sought ways in which he could himself take action. As late as September 27 he wrote Lodge in discouragement:

There is literally nothing, so far as I have yet been able to find out, which the national government has any power to do in the matter. Nor can I even imagine any remedial measure of immediate benefit that could be taken in Congress.

He told Lodge that it would be "a good thing to have national control, or at least supervision, over these big coal corporations," but he thought such control would come only as part of the general movement toward greater government control over business.[27]

As he waited for word from New York, hoping that Morgan would use his influence over the operators, Roosevelt meditated his own position in the country. The people, he wrote Lodge, would "hold the government responsible if they do not get enough coal." He himself had no influence with the operators because of their resentment of political interference in 1900 and, more especially, because Roosevelt already had a reputation for being unfriendly to business. He explained his view of the situation to Lodge with characteristic realism:

Unfortunately, the strength of my public position before the country is also its weakness. I am genuinely independent of the big monied men in all matters where I think the interests of the public are concerned, and probably I am the first President of recent times of whom this could truthfully be said.

He drew the inference without hesitation. "Where I do not grant any favors to these big monied men which I do not think the country requires that they should have," he wrote, "it is out of the question for me to expect them to grant favors to me in return." He was, he said, "at his wits' end how to proceed."[28]

Word from Morgan was that the operators were intractable. If Baer and the others would not budge, Mitchell could hardly be expected to send his miners back to work. On October 1 Roosevelt decided to follow a suggestion made by Governor Crane that he bring the two sides together at the White House. He had as yet no plan to intervene himself but hoped, rather, that a summons from the President, with a firm statement that the public interest required a settlement, might provide an occasion for the breakdown of rigid positions on both sides.

Mitchell and his aides and the major coal company presidents responded promptly, and all were present at the conference on October 3. The President made his plea. Mitchell, for the miners, offered to accept the findings of an arbitration panel appointed by the President and to return to work pending the panel's report. To Roosevelt's disgust, which turned to hardly concealed fury, the operators not only refused the proposal but advanced none of their own. Late in the day Roosevelt wrote to Hanna somewhat disconsolately, "Well, I have tried and failed. I feel downhearted over the result both because of the great misery made necessary for the mass of our people, and because the attitude of the operators will beyond a doubt double the burden on us who stand between them and socialistic action." Mitchell, he told Hanna, had shown to much better advantage than had the employers. In fact the latter had denounced Mitchell "with such violence and rancor that I felt he did very well to keep his temper." He added that because he had refused to send troops into Pennsylvania, the operators had "insulted" the President himself. "What my next move will be I cannot yet say," he wrote, but it was clear that there would be a next move.[29]

Two days later he wrote to Grover Cleveland, with whom he frequently consulted throughout the crisis, that he had decided to appeal to Mitchell to send the miners back to work in exchange for the appointment of a presidential fact-finding board whose findings the President would "do whatever in my power lies" to have acted upon. He presently asked Cleveland to serve on the board. But Mitchell thought the risks too great for the strikers and refused to accept the President's proposal. T.R. had not been very hopeful of this solution, as Mitchell had already gone so far in the confrontation with the operators on October 3. But with all hope of conciliation now gone, T.R. had either to withdraw or press forward with an unprecedented arrogation of power. To withdraw would have been unthinkable to Roosevelt, for reasons both of personal character and of politics. The quiet politics of peaceful conciliation had failed. Now was the time, Roosevelt decided, for a demonstration of the nation's power to preserve itself from disaster through the direct intervention of the nation's leader, the President.[30]

Roosevelt called in Knox and Elihu Root and told them he was about to adopt drastic measures. He would remind the operators of the "old common law" principle that "a peasant could take wood that was not his if necessary for the preservation of life and health in winter weather." He was undeterred when Knox disclaimed any knowledge of such a common law principle —as well he might, since T.R. apparently invented it for the occasion.

But the President's threat was not to be confined to warning the operators of what the people might do under the provocation of a cold winter. He proposed also to direct the army to take over and operate the coal mines. "I did not intend," he said afterwards, "to sit supinely when such a state of things was impending." The crisis "was not one in which I could act on the Buchanan principle of striving to find some constitutional reason for inaction." He would give the operators one final chance to accept arbitration by a presidential commission. If they should refuse this time, he would have Senator Quay go to the governor of Pennsylvania and ask him to appeal to the President for federal assistance. Then the President would send in troops, not only to maintain order but to protect the public health by opening and operating the coal mines. Roosevelt underlined his recognition that his action would be "an evil precedent." He gave Knox and Root full opportunity to protest formally. The action, he said, he would take only reluctantly, but

it was the only one which I could see to take which would be effective in such an emergency. . . . I should feel obliged to take it rather than expose our people to the suffering and chaos which would otherwise come. I told them [Knox and Root] that they should both write letters of protest against it if they wished, so as to free themselves from responsibility—for that I should act just as if we were in a state of war.

Root's response was to state that he was prepared to send in 10,000 regular troops upon the President's order, and Knox agreed to support the action.

The President forthwith called in Major General J. M. Schofield and gave him the command assignment. It was a good choice, in view of Roosevelt's shaky legal position, for the general told the President he "would open the mines and would run them despite interference by the strikers, the owners, the courts or anyone else."[31]

As it turned out, there was no need for Schofield to act. The President's plan—in effect an ultimatum—was presented by Root to Morgan in New York for transmittal through his friendly offices to the operators. Meanwhile Roosevelt proceeded to organize his panel of arbitration commissioners. Among others he included Grover Cleveland, Labor Commissioner Carroll Wright, and E. E. Clark, head of the Brotherhood of Railway Conductors. But when Morgan obtained the operators' reply from

Baer, it agreed to the President's terms only with the proviso that the commission be named according to a process of selection laid down by themselves. The President was infuriated at the lack of "reasonableness" of the operators. Mitchell, with whom he discussed his plan and the employers' reply, was, of course, happy to cooperate. But he was adamant that the operators should not be allowed "to pack the commission."

Eventually, on Mitchell's advice, Roosevelt decided to offer a compromise in which he would accept the operators' proposal for five of the commissioners but would add two to be selected by himself without restriction. "That night," Roosevelt recorded, "Bob Bacon and Perkins came on from Morgan, both of them nearly wild." The operators, in an unparalleled act of arrogance, so it seemed, had rejected the compromise. The commission must be appointed on their terms, or they would not recognize it. At the White House, Roosevelt fumed while the business leaders implored him to accept the operators' offer. As the President recalled afterward, Bacon and Perkins almost by accident gave Roosevelt the impression that what the operators wanted was not really a matter of substance but of form, in effect, to save face. It occurred to T.R. at this point that they might accept the quixotic notion that Clark, of the Railway Conductors, was an "eminent sociologist," thereby enabling the President to put on the commission one of his own appointees while appearing to conciliate the employers, who had specified an "eminent sociologist"! The Morgan men jumped at the idea, sure that it would be accepted. To Roosevelt's amazement it was, so thin was the coating of toughness to which the operators had been reduced by the President's strong position. Once this point had been settled, no objection was made to the two additional appointments by the President, who added a Roman Catholic bishop and the Commissioner of Labor. In the end, the only real concession Roosevelt made was to withdraw ex-President Cleveland's name in favor of an Army Engineer favored by the operators. On the 16th of October agreement was reached, and presently the strike came to an end.[32]

In the election the Republicans gained eight seats and, despite a gain of 25 new seats by the Democrats, held the House by a safe margin of 29. Roosevelt's victory was complete.

But more important than winning the election was the expansion of presidential discretion he achieved. By acting energetically and decisively when the great mass of the people wanted action, he underlined the special relationship between President and people and demonstrated how immense is the power of a President, with or without Congressional sanction, when the people, in substantial majority, are behind him. That Roosevelt had power to respond to a call from the governor of Pennsylvania was beyond dispute. Cleveland had sent in troops during the Pullman strike, even without the call of the state governor. But the heart of Roosevelt's plan was that the troops he was prepared to send into Pennsylvania would not simply serve to maintain public order but would take over and operate the coal mines as "government receiver." For the latter action there was neither precedent nor statutory authority. If the experience of President Harry S. Truman fifty years later is a safe indicator, it is probably well for Roosevelt that the mine operators yielded to his threat instead of challenging him to carry it out, for the Supreme Court would in all probability have declared T.R.'s action unconstitutional and ordered the mines to be returned to the operators. But the operators did yield, forced finally to recognize the superior interest of the whole people as represented by the President of the United States.

In rejecting the "Buchanan principle," as he put it, T.R. acted boldly and confidently once he had decided what to do. His indecision in the first instance was owing not to a desire to avoid action but to uncertainty as to what he could do, and he was not helped but hindered by an attorney-general who advised him not only that he had no power to intervene in the strike but that he should not do so in any case. When he finally elected a decisive course, he seems not to have been deterred by lack of constitutional or statutory authority; indeed, he reports enthusiastically General Schofield's defiant resolve to carry out the President's orders in the face of any opposition. He was, as it turned out, developing a theory of the presidency that held that a President could do, in the public interest, anything he was not expressly forbidden to do by statute or by the constitution. This was a more modest view of presidential power than Lincoln had adopted when he issued the Emancipation Proclamation and suspended the writ of habeas corpus. But that had been during the most dangerous of possible national crises, a civil war. Roosevelt, acting in peacetime, took a bolder stand than did any of his predecessors. Indeed, he spoke of acting as though the nation were at war.

The political risk taken by Theodore Roosevelt in his intervention in the coal strike of 1902 was owing to his membership in the Republican Party. There was, in any case, a strong leaning of labor toward the Bryan Democrats, so that T.R. had little to lose on the union side in his insistence on a settlement. There were, in fact, good prospects of gain. On the other hand, the operators were nearly all Republicans—McKinley Republicans, that is—whose financial resources had traditionally been at the disposal of Republican campaign managers. The Morgan–New York finance group would not, they indicated, be disturbed by presidential action. But it was nearly certain that T.R., simply by insisting on a settlement, would alienate at least those businessmen who took their cue from George Baer. And operating businessmen, accustomed to exerting a decisive influence in Republican counsels and encouraged to do so by businessmen-politicians like Mark Hanna, would certainly feel that the President was betraying their trust.

Roosevelt knew this well enough. But three considerations evidently outweighed in his mind the possible losses as he contemplated the situation. First, the loss of direct support would be offset by the lack of any alternative for the operators to express their dissatisfaction politically. They would certainly not support the Democrats, and the loss of their dollars to the Republican treasury could perhaps be made up by heavier drafts on the financial element of the Republican Party. Second, the public interest clearly demanded some sort of settlement so that coal would be produced and distributed by winter. Since it was the operators who were irreconcilable, not the union, it would be necessary to force them into concessions to match those of the union. The cause was of sufficient moment to warrant the use of extraordinary methods. Finally, there was offered to the President an opportunity to spread the influence of the Presidency itself over a larger area of public affairs. T.R. believed, like Lincoln, that the President should act when the people could not act for themselves. He told his daughter that he found himself "thinking what Lincoln would have done." Congress, of course, could act to require compulsory arbitration, but this would have been contrary to Roosevelt's—and the nation's—firm belief in the efficacy, indeed the virtue, of private enterprise and private bargaining. Congress could, perhaps, but would not nationalize the mines, because that would be "socialism." And so Roosevelt took the course of massive presidential intervention, resting on the belief that his purpose was popular and that the people would back him against both the operators and the local politicians they kept in their pockets.

The result was not only the settlement of the strike, not only the Republican victory in the Congressional election of 1902, but, more than these, a decisive step by Roosevelt toward his own election in 1904, with its clear endorsement of his bold new conception of the Presidency. As that election approached, Roosevelt, writing to the English historian, George Trevelyan, put the settlement of the coal strike into the perspective of his popularity, his conception of the Presidency, and his notion of national leadership.

. . . The whole country breathed freer, and felt as if a nightmare had been lifted, when I settled the anthracite coal strike; but the number of votes I shall gain thereby will be small indeed, while the interests to which I gave mortal offense will make their weight felt as of real moment. Thus I could go on indefinitely. However, I certainly would not be willing to hold the Presidency at the cost of failing to do the things which make the real reason why I care to hold it at all. I had much rather be a real President for three years and a half than a figurehead for seven years and a half.[33]

After 1902 a President could always point to precedent when he saw a need for personal intervention in times of national crisis, and strong Presidents have done so in many ways. Wilson used his war powers to maintain labor peace; Franklin Roosevelt cast his weight on the side of the unions during the bitter labor struggles of the 1930's, though he did not directly intervene except in wartime; and Harry Truman tried to settle the steel strike of 1952 by taking over the mills, only to be told by the Supreme Court that he had exceeded his authority. But, strangely, the only

President since Theodore Roosevelt who has actually settled a nationwide labor dispute by presidential intervention, and without the use of force, is Lyndon B. Johnson.

5. *Lyndon Johnson's extension of the T.R. principle in settling the railroad dispute. Both men use their popularity and then test its durability at the polls* ᠑⟩ The settlement of the railroad dispute in April, 1964, established a new landmark in the history of presidential leadership. It may be many years before the evidence of all the witnesses to the event is made available, but the main elements of the picture were clear at the time of decision. The railway brotherhoods had been bargaining with the rail operators without appreciable progress for some five years. The central point of contention was the union's desire to protect the job security of men whose work was rendered obsolete by technological change in railroading. The operators, under a sort of duress that the unions could bring because of their total organization of railway labor, had reluctantly permitted the practice of featherbedding for many years—that is, they had signed contracts agreeing to employ more labor than was needed. But the financial squeeze on the railroads, in part owing to federal regulation of rates in the interest of avoiding inflation and in part owing to the fast-growing competition of trucking and air freight haulage, finally persuaded the operators that they must, in the interest of survival, reverse the hiring policy. And so an impasse was reached. The unions called a nationwide strike for April 10th.

Over the years there had been many attempts at mediation by the national government. Both Presidents Eisenhower and Kennedy had urged the two sides to come to an agreement in the national interest. Two cases reached the Supreme Court only to leave matters in the *status quo ante*. Presidential commissions, arbitration boards, the efforts of three Secretaries of Labor—all had failed.

Under these circumstances, like Theodore Roosevelt before him, President Johnson called the two sides to the White House. There were some important analogies. In both cases the national interest certainly required a settlement, and in both cases the

impasse reflected far-reaching national economic and political
issues. In particular, the railway dispute involved the whole, still-
unanswered question of technological unemployment wherever
automation or partial automation is introduced or jobs otherwise become superfluous. Involved also was the tense political
question of union power to "countervail" the power of management. The unions, secure by law and practice in their bargaining
position as they had not been in 1902, were nevertheless faced
with a prospect of losing power as they lost members or, at
least, the power to secure members' jobs. The operators, for their
part, as in 1902, could not see their way to continuing efficient
operation of their properties unless there were substantial union
concessions. Unlike 1902, however, they were not challenging the
legal or social position of the unions. In short, no solution was
possible, but a resolution was imperative. And the President, like
his predecessor of sixty years before, was in office by virtue of
inheritance and deeply involved in an effort to secure a term of
office in his own right by winning an election.

Unlike Roosevelt, Johnson's first effort met with partial success. The unions agreed not to strike before April 25, and both
sides agreed to continuous negotiations. The President, given
this interval in which to work, evidently used every sort of persuasion he could muster. He did not threaten a government take-
over as Roosevelt had done, but he did, it appears, make clear to
both sides that if they could not agree, he would consider it his
duty to ask the Congress for a compulsory arbitration law.

That Johnson could have obtained passage of such a law seems
likely, in view of his prior record of persuading Congress to enact
a major tax reduction bill and the subsequent success of his civil
rights program, despite delays in the Senate. The Democratic
majorities in both houses were very large, and the prestige of
the President, as measured by opinion polls as well as by performance, was no doubt sufficient to put through a measure so
clearly in the public interest. But such a law would certainly
have had serious political repercussions. Unions in all fields of
labor, without exception, would oppose its passage. They would
be bitterly resentful after passage. If, like the coal operators of
1902, they would have had no alternative to Johnson in the
election, they might nevertheless have supported him with little

enthusiasm and less money. Defections in union labor in the great cities of the North would have been critical for Johnson's hopes. As a Texan, the first Southern President since the Civil War, he had serious handicaps in the North, in any case. As a fervent advocate of civil rights, he had troubles in his native South. His popularity, ranging from the liberal left to the "middle of the road," would certainly have been jeopardized by passage, at his instigation, of a compulsory arbitration law. On the conservative side, his popularity had already been heavily damaged by his advocacy of civil rights. That he stood, in April, 1964, at a high point of acceptance by the people was partly evidence of sentimental attachment to the memory of John Kennedy, whose program Johnson had pledged to carry out, and partly owing to his masterful handling of legislative problems in the early months of his administration. But above all, Johnson had won popular support among the mass of the Democrats and among independents by the sure touch of his leadership and the articulate, progressive direction of that leadership.

Thus there were great risks in his personal intervention in the railway controversy. A veteran newspaper man summed up the story afterwards this way:

The President kept them [the negotiators] at it day and night, worked Secretary of Labor W. Willard Wirtz overtime, and called in experienced outside mediators to help out. Johnson was on top of it all the time. He coaxed but didn't threaten.

He had a big personal and political stake in the outcome himself. He put his Presidential prestige on the line in this one—particularly by making optimistic statements—and a strike would have been an impressive setback.

A settlement would mean the opposite. No wonder he was so delighted when he rushed to a studio to go on the air—although it meant interrupting programs—and announce the result as fast as he could.

The settlement itself involved genuine concessions on both sides, so that Johnson could fairly call it a monument to the free collective bargaining process. The unions received substantial increases in wages and in fringe benefits; the operators achieved the right to reduce employment gradually and systematically. But, of course, it was less the process of collective bargaining than the pressure of presidential power that made a resolution possible. President Johnson gave leadership, "political" leadership of a high order. As the same hard-bitten newsman put it:

> But he is, above everything, a politician and it is as such that he is running the Presidency. . . . There are various kinds of politicians: the sonorous, the pompous, the placid, the active, and the very aggressive who tries, often behind the scenes, to anticipate and shape events. Johnson is the aggressive kind.[34]

6. *Partisanship and innovation: Franklin Roosevelt and Social Security* ᛒᕀ Franklin D. Roosevelt was also an "aggressive" politician who liked to plan ahead, "to anticipate and shape events." His own lack of settled convictions on economic questions and the often divided counsels in the executive branch gave to the first New Deal (1933–1934) a kind of patchwork quality in which there was little anticipation and much improvisation. But by 1934, when emergency measures had been taken and the worst edges of poverty and misery of the depression had been rounded off, the second Roosevelt was ready to listen to advice on long-range matters and to build and win support for a program of national reconstruction. In the Second New Deal, so-called, of 1935 to 1938, the Social Security Act was a major achievement. Its promotion and passage Roosevelt considered "nonpartisan," but by the summer of 1936 he was forced to use the "nonpartisanship" of the social security program as a weapon in a bitterly partisan campaign. Congress, after some delays, had supported social security by an overwhelming majority; but the slowly developing opposition reached such a pitch of activity that in the end Roosevelt had to treat the election of 1936 as a kind of referendum. He welcomed the fight, as he always claimed to welcome any political fight.

The origins of the Social Security Act are to be found in a message to Congress of June 8, 1934, in which Roosevelt spoke of a "task of reconstruction." In it he included security in homes and jobs and against misfortunes "which cannot be wholly eliminated in this man-made world of ours." The "values" in such a program of reconstruction, he said, were not "new and strange," but rather ideals "to some degree forgotten." Six months later he sent to the Congress a second message asking for enactment of a program of comprehensive social security. If the values were not new in themselves, they were certainly new as responsibilities of the national government.[35]

The Democratic platform of 1932 had called upon the states to provide unemployment insurance and old age pensions in a manner similar to the long-established program of workmen's compensation. In the election campaign Roosevelt made no significant amendment of this idea, which was as old as the Progressive programs of Theodore Roosevelt's time. In one or two speeches Franklin Roosevelt did speak of a national responsibility for individual welfare, but in 1932 there was no hint of a full-scale program to achieve it. By 1934 he was persuaded that the states could never command the resources to provide adequate unemployment insurance, assistance to dependent and handicapped children, or pensions for old people. He was ready to see the burden shifted from the states, which had, in fact, never taken it up, to the shoulders of the nation. After his 1934 message he appointed a national Committee on Economic Security, with instructions to consider how the federal government could do the job. It was their report, converted into specific suggestions for law, that lay behind his special message to Congress on January 17, 1935.

In that message Roosevelt asked for a four-part social security system: (1) unemployment compensation, (2) old age benefits, (3) federal aid to dependent children and to the handicapped, and (4) additional federal aid to state and local public health agencies. Unemployment compensation was to be financed by a tax on all employers who were engaged in interstate commerce, and old age pensions would be supported by a payroll tax on employees as well as matching funds from employers, again applying to those involved in interstate commerce. The President estimated that about 30 million people would be covered. The benefits to children and to public health would come through federal grants to the states. The whole system would be planned and administered by a Social Security Board, but the states would retain control over unemployment compensation funds. The national government would make grants to the states for administration of the elements of the system under state control.

On the same day as the message, Roosevelt released the full report of the Committee on Economic Security and gave the press a forthright statement of his belief in the need for immediate enactment of the program. He told Congress that no time should be lost, since state cooperation would be required and some forty-four state legislatures would be in session during the spring of 1935. Both House and Senate leadership were well briefed in advance, and everyone knew that Roosevelt considered the social security program "must" legislation.

Rexford Tugwell, one of Roosevelt's "brain-trusters," afterwards recalled how the social security idea had fitted into Roosevelt's developing philosophy of reconstruction. By late 1934, according to Tugwell, Roosevelt had decided to reject the conception of tightly controlled over-all national planning. He had talked with John Maynard Keynes, the English economist whose views were just then beginning to come into ascendancy in economic thought, and though he was never to go so far as Keynes proposed in the direction of deficit spending, he was persuaded that free enterprise could produce national prosperity if government kept the brakes on inflation and deflation through careful control of credit, supplied capital investment when business slackened, and built in certain guarantees against depression. As Tugwell put it, he "thought of social security as the necessary floor for the laissez-faire to which he was reverting." Thus Roosevelt's stake in the passage of a social security law was very great. He was prepared to use every means available to see it through.[36]

Yet by February there were signs that the committees of Congress would not be responsive. Conservative Southern Democrats were unhappy at the prospect of a great further step toward federal superiority to the state governments. Businessmen disliked the additional taxes they would be called upon to pay. Some people seemed honestly to feel that such a program would weaken the character of Americans who, according to time-honored shibboleth, were expected to provide their own security, not rely upon government. It was easier to make such views felt in the relative privacy of Congressional committee rooms—and cloak rooms—than on the floor of either House or in public places, where the evident desire of the immense majority of the people to be protected against a recurrence of the terrors of depression made the idea of social security one of the most popular in history.

Roosevelt spoke of the social security program in nearly all of his public appearances in the spring of 1935. His majorities in both houses of Congress were such that he needed only to show them that the public demand was great; there was no need for the rougher tactics of patronage manipulation or election retaliation. Throughout Roosevelt relied upon the Democratic Congressional leadership and made his appeal to the people. In his fireside chat of April 28, he explained social security carefully and reminded his audience that the measure was "pending before the Congress." He promised to keep up necessary federal expenditures for work-relief, but the point was that "we must begin now to make provision for the future." Social security, he said, was "an important part of the complete picture."

It proposes, by means of old-age pensions, to help those who have reached the age of retirement to give up their jobs and thus give to the younger generation greater opportunities for work and to give to all a feeling of security as they look toward old age.

The unemployment insurance part of the legislation will not only help to guard the individual in future periods of lay-off against dependence upon relief, but it will, by sustaining purchasing power, cushion the shock of economic distress.

Finally, he needled business by pointing out that "another helpful feature of unemployment insurance is the incentive it will give to employers to plan more carefully in order that unemployment may be prevented by the stabilizing of employment itself."[37]

The response to this kind of direct appeal was a continuing flood of mail upon the desks of Congressmen. In the deluge the plaintive opposition of employers and conservatives was drowned. And at the very moment when the legislators were making up their minds on the President's moderate proposals, they were forced to recognize that millions of Americans were ready to ask for something much more radical. Huey Long of Louisiana, Father Coughlin of Michigan, and pension-promoter Dr. Townsend had all demonstrated their ability to stir multitudes with plausible schemes of national redemption. Roosevelt asked only for national reconstruction.

And so, in August, the Congress passed the Social Security bill by an immense margin and sent it to the President. "Today," said Roosevelt, as he signed the bill into law, "a hope of many years' standing is in large part fulfilled. We can never insure one hundred per cent of the hazards and vicissitudes of life, but we have tried to frame a law which will give some measure of protection to the average citizen and to his family against the loss of a job and against poverty-ridden old age. . . . If the Senate and the House of Representatives in this long and arduous session had done nothing more than pass this Bill, the session would be regarded as historic for all time."[38]

The bill and the session, as Franklin Roosevelt foretold, were indeed historic. In addition to social security, Congress passed the National Labor Relations Act and the Soil Conservation Act, established the National Youth Administration, and authorized the President to set up the Rural Electrification Administration. These were the leading measures of the Second New Deal. Social security was, as Tugwell wrote, the foundation. If NRA, AAA, and other dramatic activities of the First New Deal were to disappear by court edict or by attrition, Social Security was a permanent accomplishment.

But the opposition was neither stilled nor discouraged by the action of Congress. The President himself would have to stand electoral trial in 1936, and if he could be brought down, his program could be brought down with him. The campaign against Social Security gained momentum in the spring and early summer of 1936. The radicals of the right—Townsend, Coughlin, and Gerald L. K. Smith, Long's "successor"—joined forces to run Congressman William Lemke as Union party candidate for President. Their campaign provided abundant opportunity to denounce the social security program as wholly inadequate, while promising the old, the poor, and the unemployed quick prosperity if their schemes were adopted. Roosevelt himself never believed that this array of crackpots could be a serious threat. But other Democrats were not so sure. And publicists prophesied as many as 10 million votes for the Union ticket, most of which would come from the Democratic side.

Also on the right, though no one called them radical, were the men of the National Association of Manufacturers, the Chamber of Commerce, and the Liberty League who saw in Social Security only a major thrust of interference by government in the private affairs of the people.

On the left, Norman Thomas was preparing for his third campaign as Socialist candidate for President with a program demanding that radical measures replace temporizing reforms. For the Socialists the social security system was a palliative intended to cover up the inability of the free enterprise system to provide security for American workers. The Communists, though they had only bitter hatred for the Socialists, said much the same thing through the various "front" organizations they were then sponsoring.

But, of course, the principal opposition had to come from the Republicans. Since most Republican members of Congress had voted for the Social Security Act, it was not an easy matter to mobilize a Republican attack upon it. The Republican presidential candidate, Governor Alf M. Landon of Kansas, himself an old-time Progressive, seemed to have no strong views against the program. But presidential campaigns often, indeed usually, tend to turn men's views into lines and channels much more rigid than they would otherwise be. As Landon listened to the advice of men like former President Hoover, Republican National Chairman John D. M. Hamilton, and others, he began to see in such programs as Social Security dangers to individual liberty that had not previously impressed him.

After the campaign Governor Landon on many occasions observed that "the candidate must trim his sails—not to suit his own personal ideas, but to what seems to fit the political situation." On the matter of Social Security in 1936, he trimmed his sails considerably. From mild concern about technical aspects of the old-age pension fund, he moved to extreme statements denouncing the whole social security program. On September 26, at Milwaukee, he made Social Security a principal target of his campaign against the New Deal. The law, he said, was "unjust, unworkable, stupidly drafted and wastefully financed." He even called the worker's contribution aspect of the pension system "a cruel hoax."[39]

Three days later another eminent Republican, former New Hampshire Governor John G. Winant, who was administering the early stages of the social security program, resigned as chairman of the Social Security Board to enter the campaign on the side of Roosevelt. The President's letter to Winant accepting the latter's resignation reveals something of the way Roosevelt decided to handle the Landon challenge. Because Congress had created a nonpartisan board to administer Social Security, Winant could have stayed on while speaking publicly to "correct" errors and misinterpretations. At first Roosevelt seems to have preferred this course. But then he talked over the matter with Winant and decided to accept the resignation so that Winant could "be free as a citizen, not simply to clear up misconceptions and misinterpretations of the Act, but actively to defend the 'constructive provisions' of the Act and to oppose spurious substitutes." Thus Roosevelt sent an eminent progressive Republican onto the firing line as chief campaign spokesman for the social security program.[40]

Although Governor Landon never went so far as to attack the idea of social security—indeed, he proposed an old-age pension plan of his own—his supporters in the business world pulled no punches. The payroll tax provision of the Social Security Act would be the most direct "interference" by the national government in the affairs of workers yet undertaken by the New Deal. Because every worker covered by the plan would have 1 per cent of his pay withheld—and the amount would be increased over the years—the paycheck itself seemed the best means of reaching the worker with anti-Roosevelt campaign material. By October workers were finding slips of paper in their pay envelopes containing the following enlightening information:

Effective January, 1937, we are compelled by a Roosevelt "New Deal" law to make a 1 per cent deduction from your wages and turn it over to the government. Finally, this may go as high as 4 per cent. You might get this money back . . . but only if Congress decides to make the appropriation for this purpose. There is *no* guarantee. Decide before November 3—election day—whether or not you wish to take these chances.

If so small a deduction seems hardly a threat in this day of multiple withholdings, it must be remembered that in 1936 almost no wage workers were paying any income tax at all, and voluntary deductions for fringe benefits were virtually unknown. Pay envelopes, in any case, contained very little money, so that even 1 per cent in those days was a serious bite out of minimal earnings.[41]

This was not the first time pay envelopes had been used to send frightening messages to workers. In 1900 Mark Hanna had persuaded employers to "suggest" in pay envelope messages that if Bryan were elected, businesses would have to close down. But the 1936 campaign was met by a far more politically effective counterattack than anything Bryan had been able to muster against McKinley. Franklin Roosevelt, identifying himself with the interests of the "forgotten man," brought up the pay envelope trick at every opportunity. He denounced it as unpatriotic and dishonest and the act of frightened men. On the principle that the best defense was a strong offense, he made relentless political war on the businessmen who were using the pay envelope dodge. "Are you willing," he asked his audience at Worcester, Massachusetts, "to turn the control of the Nation's taxes back to special privilege? I know the American answer to that question. Your pay envelope may be loaded with suggestions of fear, and your dividend letter may be filled with propaganda. But the American people will neither be bluffed nor bludgeoned!" That was on October 21. Two days later, in a radio address to a nationwide series of campaign dinners for Democratic businessmen, he said, "We are resolved to keep politics out of business. But at the same time we ask that business refrain from coercion in politics." Seeking to divide good businessmen from bad, as his cousin had divided good and bad trusts, FDR continued, "Not only wage earners but nearly all business men resent the present attempts by a few employers to frighten their employees by misrepresentation."[42]

At Wilkes-Barre, Pennsylvania, on John Mitchell Day, however, he did not hesitate to set coal miner against operator by recalling the strike of 1902. The pay envelope device, he said, was a "repetition of the arrogance and the ruthlessness which the operators utilized to try to break the solid ranks of labor when the miners fought at Armageddon in 1902." Making the advantages of Social Security the main theme of his speech, he outlined the plan in some detail, underlining the fact that the employers were telling "only half the truth." Such tactics, he said, belong "in a class with the coercion of the strong arm squad and the whispering of the planted labor spy." The facts were that the employer pays dollar for dollar on the old-age pension plan and pays the whole tax for unemployment compensation. "Three for one! There's the rub," said the President. "That is what these propaganda spreading employers object to. . . . They are now trying to frighten the workers about the workers' one dollar premium, so that they won't have to pay their three-dollar premium." Angrily he denounced the idea that Congress might not appropriate the money for pensions. "These propagandists—with allies whom I do not have to describe to you who know them—are driven in their desperation to the contemptible, unpatriotic suggestion that some future Congress will steal these insurance funds for other purposes." Then, reversing the common vulgarism that the New Dealers ought to "go back to Moscow," Roosevelt advised the businessmen who had "no confidence in our form of government or its permanence" to "move to some other Nation in which they have greater faith." This sally drew an almost frenzied response from the crowd. In the closing days of the campaign Roosevelt used it as a punch line in many brief speeches.[43]

Another favorite tack was to underline the immense coalition that had supported the social security program. At Brooklyn, on October 30, for example, Roosevelt called the Social Security Act "a new Magna Carta for those who work." Both in its preparation and in its enactment, he said, "it was supported not only by organized labor but by those other liberal groups—workers, employers, churches, private charities, educators who for many years have believed that modern Government can make provision against the hardship of unemployment and the terrors of old age."

The coalition at the time the act was passed included even most of the Republican Senators and Representatives, and Roosevelt never allowed them or his audiences to forget it. He never mentioned Landon by name throughout the campaign, speaking instead only of the "Old Guard" or the "Old Guard candidate." At Brooklyn he told the crowd that "a distraught Republican leadership, driven to desperation and urged on by the same sinister forces which generation after generation have opposed all social legislation, now repudiates its own Representatives and Senators in the halls of Congress and leaves them looking positively silly!"[44]

In what was perhaps the most dramatically partisan speech of an intensely partisan campaign, Roosevelt, in his windup at Madison Square Garden on October 31, told the cheering crowd that the forces of "organized money" had never before "in all our history . . . been so united against one candidate as they stand today. They are unanimous in their hate for me—and I welcome their hatred!" If the crowd was stirred by this hyperbole, it was on its feet in ecstatic enthusiasm with the next words:

I should like to have it said of my first Administration that in it the forces of selfishness and of lust for power met their match. I should like to have it said of my second Administration that in it these forces met their master!

If this was demagogy rather than statesmanship, as even some of Roosevelt's warmest supporters sadly told one another, it was well calculated to unite his followers in their determination to send him back to Washington, like Jackson, as the people's champion. This kind of talk, wholly absent in his first campaign and to be discarded again after 1939, was enough to guarantee division in the nation regardless of the President's pious phrases about being "President of all the people." FDR well understood what he was doing. His program, deeply as he believed it to be good for the whole nation, was a partisan program. He expected to make enemies; he expected his enemies to fight; he enjoyed fighting back.[45]

But he was not only fighting *against* "organized money"; he was fighting *for* his program. Again, in the final speech, he placed Social Security squarely in the center of that program. Once more he outlined its various aspects and emphasized the fact that the cost was to be borne chiefly by the employers. Once more he ridiculed the Republicans for opposing a bill their Congressional representatives had supported only one year before. Once more he lashed out at the employers who used pay envelopes for their attacks on Social Security. And, finally, he asked directly for a vote of confidence in the new system:

I have expressed indignation at this form of campaigning and I am confident that the overwhelming majority of employers, workers and the general public share that indignation and will show it at the polls on Tuesday next.[46]

"Tuesday next," of course, proved to be the most decisive election since 1820. Roosevelt himself carried 46 states and polled more than 27 million votes to 16 million for Landon, while an equally immense victory in the Congressional elections brought the President and his New Deal an overwhelming endorsement. The social security program was secure. There was to be periodic sniping at it in later years, but no serious attempt to repeal it was ever again made. Sixteen years later, at Boise, Idaho, Republican candidate Dwight D. Eisenhower made Roosevelt's 1936 victory "official." The social security program, Eisenhower said, was among those fundamental aspects of the American governmental system that are no longer debatable. Thus partisan policy became in the end nonpartisan, as it had been in the beginning. That a social security program would eventually have become as essential a part of modern life in the United States as it had in Europe was no doubt nearly inevitable. But that it should be so soon and so unshakably established was owing to the partisan leadership of Franklin Roosevelt and to his ability at the historic moment to convert his partisan popularity into public policy.

*7. Unpartisan popularity unavailable for partisan purposes: Eisenhower changes his mind on the Taft-Hartley Act and avoids a fight on federal aid to education* ᣟᣛ It was characteristic of Dwight Eisenhower that his immense popularity was built, at least in part, on his careful avoidance of precisely the kind of partisan issues that F.D.R. had welcomed. Perhaps, by 1952, any Republican candidate would have endorsed Social Security. But such Republican leaders as Thomas E. Dewey or Robert A. Taft would certainly not have avoided debate, as did Eisenhower, on other articles in the heritage of the New Deal. As outspoken leaders of the national minority, these men could not be elected. Eisenhower, in contrast, won by building a new majority, a majority behind himself based on uniting, not dividing, the country. But it was a majority good for popular votes for himself, not for enacting policy.

In his attitude toward Congress, where he had to find the votes to get his program enacted, Eisenhower very nearly reverted to the Whig concept of weak President and strong Congress. He was so insistent on the separation of powers that from the beginning of his administration Congress saw that he would seldom, if ever, make a public issue with it over controversial measures. In his memoirs Eisenhower frankly discussed his views on leadership. "In my view," he wrote, "a fair, decent, and reasonable dealing with men, a reasonable recognition that views may diverge, a constant seeking for a high and strong ground on which to work together, is the best way to lead our country. . . ." In the early months of his first term, in a prophetic political address, he told the National Convention of Young Republicans that it was a "major purpose" of his administration "to do all that it can reasonably do to encourage cooperation and harmony between the legislative and executive branches." This was a characteristic note, a hallmark of the Eisenhower "style." "Government," he said, "must not allow its policies to be caught in the fatal crossfire of a Congress and an Executive warring upon one another. Such a condition is not going to prevail if it is within the power of this administration to prevent it." Finally, he insisted, "our very form of government is in peril unless each branch willingly accepts and discharges its clear responsibilities— and respects the rights and responsibilities of the others."[47]

Probably no President would take exception, in public, to such unexceptionable sentiments. What matters is that Eisenhower emphasized these views and made them a kind of shibboleth. Habitually he talked about harmony and cooperation—not about program; about agreement on high ground—not about resolving controversial issues. As he reviewed his own administration, he looked further back, at the leadership of Franklin Roosevelt, with disapproval. "In the situation where his own party was delighted to hear a daily excoriation of the opposite political party, his methods were adequate. . . ." But in his own time, Eisenhower wrote, "I think it is fair to say that . . . only a leadership that is based on honesty of purpose, calmness and inexhaustible patience in conference and persuasion, and refusal to be diverted from basic principles can, in the long run, win out."[48]

If Eisenhower was disturbed that the Democratic Party should continue to be the national majority when he was winning immense personal victories, he ignored the matter in his speeches and writings, both during and after his administration. Yet there is good reason to believe that his own unwillingness to press for adoption of his program by really vigorous methods was a contributing factor in the Republican failure to develop a wider appeal. His handling of such issues as amending the Taft-Hartley law and federal aid to education affords fair examples of the President's firm intentions dissolving into a kind of wistful piety as the divisive character of the issues was revealed to him by events.

In the campaign of 1952 the Democrats had called urgently for repeal of the notorious labor law that had been passed by the Republican Congress of 1947 over President Truman's veto. Eisenhower, for his part, had defended the law in its main elements but had told the convention of the American Federation of Labor that he favored certain revisions. The act, he said, "could be repressive to labor." Specifically he referred to a "provision that employees who struck for economic reasons, rather than because of unfair practices, lost their right to vote for collective-bargaining agents." He pledged also to ask Congress to require employers to take the same non-Communist oath as labor representatives were required to take under the law. In the course of the campaign Eisenhower appealed to workers in other ways, especially by his attack on inflation. The election results showed that he had made very sharp cuts into traditional Democratic strength in the labor unions.

It was surprising, even shocking, to many Republicans that Eisenhower should appoint a Democratic trade union leader as Secretary of Labor, but the appointment certainly pleased labor. Martin Durkin frankly told the press that he had never known President Eisenhower, that he had supported Governor Stevenson, and that he was at a loss to know why he should have been asked to serve in Eisenhower's Cabinet. But the most instructive aspect of the appointment was the almost total failure of communication between the new Secretary and his chief.

Durkin, president of the Plumbers' Union, was a seasoned labor executive who looked upon his appointment as an opportunity to advance the interests of labor, chiefly by helping to bring about major revisions of the Taft-Hartley law. He knew well enough that in the Cabinet he would be sitting with men whose opinions varied from contentment with the law to the feeling that it had not gone far enough in modifying the Wagner Act to the advantage of employers. Durkin frankly looked upon his position as that of a participant in a kind of continuous collective bargaining process in which he spoke for labor and the rest of the Cabinet for management. He told Eisenhower that he could accept the post only with a clear understanding that the President himself favored modification of the law according to the wishes of labor. He came away from his conference with the President-elect confident that Eisenhower had agreed. The President-elect, for his part, appears to have thought, like Washington, that the presence in the government of leaders of opposing factions would allow him to secure their cooperation. There is no doubt that he intended to ask for amendments to the Taft-Hartley law, and there is no doubt that in his own preliminary thinking there was a good deal in common with the formal views of labor expressed by Durkin. What Durkin did not understand was that Eisenhower was more interested in cooperation than in seeing even his own views prevail.

Shortly after his inauguration Eisenhower set about to make good his pledge to amend the Taft-Hartley law. He appointed a committee consisting of Secretary Durkin, the Secretary of Commerce, a White House staff official, and two Republican members of Congress and asked it to explore the possibilities of amendment to the law. The President, to Durkin's disappointment, gave the committee no advice as to how it should proceed and spoke not at all of his own views. Instead, Eisenhower expected the committee to "submit recommended amendments to me for transmission to the Congress." Durkin immediately found himself indeed in a collective bargaining situation, without the backing of the President and with no allies in the committee. Without top leadership the committee was wholly unable to resolve the issues before it. By May 25, Eisenhower was told that

Durkin and Secretary of Commerce Sinclair Weeks were "poles apart." He was disappointed and apparently surprised.

Presently Durkin concluded that there was no prospect of action favorable to labor and decided to resign. Eisenhower afterward recalled his rupture with Durkin as the "only case" in his eight years in the White House "in which a resignation was tendered because of failure to achieve a meeting of minds" between himself and "any principal subordinate." At first the President attempted to persuade Durkin to stay. In response to Durkin's statement that he would lose his job in his union unless the Taft-Hartley law was amended along the lines he recommended, the President said, "Martin, if you will work along with the rest of us in a common effort to develop fair amendments to the law, your success will assure you a good position in the future—without question." He then told the Labor Secretary, without "accepting or rejecting" Durkin's recommendations, "that if all my advisers on that body could, despite their diverse views, come to a unanimous agreement, I should of course give great weight to their conclusions."

Within two weeks after this conversation Durkin had resigned. The President noted in his memoirs that Durkin "gave no other reason" except a desire to return to his union post. Eisenhower appears simply not to have understood that by telling Durkin he wished "unanimous agreement" of his labor committee, he was forcing the secretary to resign. The issues before the committee were, perhaps, negotiable, but they were not susceptible to a "compromise" in which one union official would yield to the majority views of the business community represented by the other members of the committee. Durkin's "collective bargaining position" was hopeless. His resignation was predictable, as perhaps it had been from the day of his appointment.

In a final interview Eisenhower told Durkin "very earnestly that he was not a 'bargainer' in my Cabinet. He was," said the President, "my principal adviser on labor." In this matter, at least, Durkin was on firmer ground than the President. The Secretary of Labor is, by statute, required to represent the interest of labor, not merely to advise the President. In such matters as labor legislation Durkin's use of the term "collective bargaining" is close both to the spirit and the letter of the law creating the office of Secretary of Labor. The President, of course, retains ultimate responsibility and authority—he chooses the Secretary of Labor. Eisenhower, having chosen a professional union official who was a frank opponent of the Taft-Hartley law, should not have been surprised when he acted like a union official who was opposed to the Taft-Hartley law. At any rate, there was nothing to do but accept Durkin's resignation.

Thereafter, under the new Labor Secretary, James P. Mitchell, the labor committee worked without public displays of disagreement. When the American Federation of Labor Convention was held in September, there still was no committee report, however, and Eisenhower sent the convention a message of regret, together with a new promise that "amendments which would be fair to all" would be submitted to Congress at the next session. In December Secretary Mitchell reported the committee's recommendations to the President at his weekly conference with Republican legislative leaders. Recalling this episode, Eisenhower says in his memoirs, "They were approved and thus we were prepared to make our recommendations at the opening of Congress in 1954."[49]

Eisenhower's conception of presidential leadership is better revealed by the little word *thus* in that sentence than by any of his formal statements on the subject. The fact was that his own initial sense that the Taft-Hartley law contained injustices to labor had been wholly blunted by the nearly unanimous sentiments to the contrary among those with whom he lived his presidential life. He seems never to have considered that not only would businessmen wish to retain in the law any provisions that militated against strikes, but that Republican Congressmen could hardly be expected to accede to a demand for union-sponsored amendments to an act that was the pride of the last Congress they had controlled and bore the name of the Majority Leader of the Senate. But once the overwhelming objections of business and the Republican Congress made itself felt, Eisenhower lost interest; he told Durkin, in fact, that he had never had any firm views on the Taft-Hartley law. What is certain is that he found the issue too divisive to be handled according to his notions of presidential leadership.

As for the Administration's long-delayed recommended amendments to the labor law, they were offered to Congress in January, 1954, as part of the President's program. But they were soon lost in the maelstrom of controversy over the Dixon-Yates contract, the Army-McCarthy hearings, and other matters of the moment. The President himself quietly abandoned the labor proposals to their Congressional fate—which was oblivion. The manner in which he did so is, again, instructive. On January 13 he was asked at his press conference whether any of his recommended measures had special priority:

> I naturally cannot tell you in advance which I am going to consider the most important and the least important. I don't know how they will come up in Congress and how they will be handled. So I am not going to identify particular details as "must" and "not must." . . .

The plain inference seemed to be that the President would attach special importance to measures given special importance by Congress. The President would not, in short, lead; he would follow. He could not, perhaps, have done otherwise without paying a higher price in loss of popular following than he was willing to pay, or thought he ought to pay, as measured against his deep sense of need for national unity.[50]

More than five years later, when Congress, without presidential participation, was at last about to amend the Taft-Hartley law—in ways almost directly contrary to what Eisenhower had seemed to favor in 1952—he underlined his own distance from what was happening by giving his press conference a little homily. "You know," he said, "I am disturbed by what seems to be becoming a habit in this country, to adopt certain theories that Marx advanced. One is that there is inevitably a bitter and implacable warfare between the man that works and the man that hires him." "To my mind," said the President, "this is absolutely and completely un-American. It is not the way a free country must work. Every last workman, down to the lowliest, the most menial task you can think of, is just as important as any manager or any capitalist that invests in a company." "We have got to talk about cooperation," he concluded. "How do labor and management and capital cooperate to produce the wealth that this country needs? That is what we mean by an expanding economy." If the bit about the economy was somewhat obscure, the rest of the President's statement was clear and understandable and acceptable to most Americans. His evident sincerity in such views was a large part of what endeared him to the people. The irrelevance of his views to the business at hand was none the less real because, perhaps, it ought not to have been.[51]

Eisenhower's handling of the problem of federal aid to public schools was a similar case, except that he never changed his view as to what *should* be done; rather, in the face of opposition he changed his mind as to whether it *could* be done.

When he was president of Columbia University in the 1940's, his faculty at Columbia Teachers College had familiarized Eisenhower with the forthcoming problem of acute classroom shortage, as well as the growing shortage of teachers, that would accompany the postwar growth in population. He was quick to see the need for action and vigorously assisted Columbia to raise foundation funds for research into future educational problems. In the early stages of his Presidency (1953–1954) the United States Office of Education, as well as various influential citizen groups, persuaded Eisenhower that the classroom shortage, at least, could not be remedied without substantial federal assistance. Accordingly he asked Congress, in his 1955 legislative program, for more than a billion dollars to be spent over a three-year period in loans and grants to needy school districts. This was intended to help local government to overcome a classroom deficit variously estimated at from 300,000 to 700,000. Eisenhower accepted the smaller figure.

The plan carefully avoided asking for funds to pay additional teachers. "I opposed involving the federal government," he wrote afterwards, "in the operation of the schools, such as in paying teachers' salaries." He feared that financial aid of this sort would sooner or later be accompanied by a movement toward federal control of the schools, which would have been wholly counter to his political philosophy, shared by a great many Americans. But assistance in building classrooms would involve no more than federal oversight over standards of building and posed no threat to local control of the schools. The President sent an effective message to Congress and spoke in favor of the plan both in several public addresses and in his press conferences.

It was a Democratic Congress, elected in 1954, with which Eisenhower had to deal. In the heat of that campaign he had warned that a Democratic victory would produce a "cold war" between Congress and the Executive, but afterwards he had confessed that campaign statements were often exaggerated and had indicated his willingness to cooperate fully with the new Congress. The Speaker of the House, Sam Rayburn of Texas, was a long-time personal friend, and Eisenhower's relations with Lyndon B. Johnson, Senate Majority Leader, were cordial. The Democratic leadership expressed a desire to cooperate on the matter of federal aid to education. Thus the matter was not, in the usual sense, partisan; but it was divisive. In his memoirs Eisenhower wrote only that "despite the need for classrooms, the Congress did nothing."

The fact was that for many years there had been efforts by such legislators as Senator Lister Hill of Alabama to put through a program of federal aid for education. Proposed bills always died in committee, because agreement could not be obtained on such controversial matters as whether to include parochial schools and because powerful lobbies against any form of federal entrance into the school situation had been more effective than the National Education Association or the National Committee for the Public Schools. Without vigorous presidential leadership, Congress, it had long been clear, was unlikely to act.

The President, in the winter of 1955, made no serious effort to persuade Congress to enact his program, but he did undertake to rally the country behind some sort of federal aid plan. The device he employed was a "White House Conference," such as Theodore Roosevelt had called many years before to mobilize national opinion behind his conservation policy. The Eisenhower White House Conference on Education, called to meet in the fall of 1955, was the apex of a conference program that involved every sizable community in the states and territories. Perhaps half a million citizens participated at various levels, local and state. At Washington in November, some two thousand parents, teachers, and school officials took part in discussion and ratification of a policy statement calling for federal assistance in building classrooms for the public schools but opposing the use of federal funds for parochial schools. As an exercise in popular democracy, crossing party lines and involving a great variety of opinion, the White House Conference on Education was impressive. Its statement of policy certainly provided the President with the kind of articulate popular support he would need to go again to the Congress.

In the winter of 1956 the President did so. Again he proposed to spend more than a billion dollars for classroom construction, but spread over five rather than three years. Another provision, however, called for a fund of $750 million for federal purchase of local school construction bonds, so that in all something like an expenditure of $2 billion was contemplated. The money was to go to the "neediest" school districts. In Congress the Democratic committee chairmen took charge. Presently a bill, favored by the majority leadership and known as the Kelley Bill, was drawn up. It would have involved roughly the same amounts of money as the Administration had recommended, but the money would be apportioned according to the school-age population of the various states. Eisenhower was disappointed at this change. He seems not to have understood that an equitable population formula for division of federal funds was far more likely to win approval of the House of Representatives than any formula, however efficient, that asked Congressmen to vote their constituents' tax money for somebody else's constituents' children! The President was nevertheless willing to go along. However, when Representative Adam Clayton Powell of New York, in whose House committee the bill was being debated, amended it to exclude from assistance any state where a school district was not in compliance with the Supreme Court decision against segregation, a new issue was introduced, and the bill became the focal point of deeply divisive controversy.

With opinion divided on at least three issues—the best formula for distributing federal funds to school districts, the question of including or excluding parochial schools from the program, and the use of the funds to force compliance with desegregation orders—it was evident that no bill could pass without firm leadership by the President. Questions not only of education but of civil rights and of church-state relations were involved. It was, indeed, an historic juncture.

But on these issues the popular President commanded at best

only a minority of his own party in the Congress, and only a
minority of the minority would respond to his plea simply because he made it. On the Democratic side were a larger number
of legislators in both houses who were willing to join forces with
the President to support the Kelley Bill. But Southern Democrats
were wholly alienated by the Powell amendment, so that the
Democratic majority leadership itself commanded less than a
majority. And its ranks were divided on the church-state issue.
To the President this situation seemed too difficult to cope with,
or, at any rate, he made no effort to cope with it. The momentum of the White House Conference was therefore lost, and the
debate in the House went through its fore-ordained course without significant action by Eisenhower. In the end the forces
opposed to aiding parochial schools and the forces "favoring"
the Powell amendment joined in unholy alliance to defeat the
bill.

When Eisenhower told his press conference of August 8, 1956,
that the Democrats "not only killed my bill . . . but helped to
kill their own," he was correct. But he omitted the fact that in
the final vote—194 for and 224 against—enough Republicans
had sided with Southern Democrats to make the difference. The
truth was that the bill was not simply a partisan measure but a
more widely and deeply divisive one. The fact that the President's party had only a minority in Congress need not have been
decisive. The possibility, at least, existed for the President to
rally and lead a coalition across party lines that would have been
large enough to win. He chose not to try. Had he made the
attempt, he might have failed. He had no mandate to secure
federal aid to the public schools, only the personal confidence of
a great majority of the people. Even if he had succeeded, he
would certainly have lost major segments of his popular support,
and his re-election in 1956 might well have been by a smaller
margin.

It is idle to speculate on the role that Eisenhower's personal
conception of presidential leadership may have played in the
failure of his education program, because that conception was in
any case personal and not a recurring factor in the continuing
political equation. What is more important is to observe that a
coalition that means to include everybody, or nearly everybody,

is an unlikely base upon which to make and carry out policy that appeals only to some. Unpartisan popularity is not a currency capable of being spent in divisive controversies or converted into action when agreement can not be achieved on the horizontal plane but only on the vertical. If Eisenhower, whom Marquis Childs once spoke of as a "captive hero," was something less than a heroic leader of his country on the domestic issues of his administration, this was in large part because he was a captive of his own popularity.

The evidence appears to underline the notion that a President whose popular following is a frankly partisan majority is likely to be effective in realizing his program, almost regardless of the merits of the program. If the popular majority identifies itself not only with a President but with his plans and proposals, it is less likely to disintegrate under the pressures and tensions of controversial decision-making. The President can more or less count upon it. Indeed, if he does not make use of it, he is likely to lose it. On the other hand, even very great unpartisan popularity is nearly useless when a President is faced by seriously divisive issues. If tested it seems likely by its nature to disintegrate; to be maintained it must not be tested.

But the relation between various kinds of popularity and presidential leadership on domestic issues may not hold so consistently when it is a matter of leadership in foreign affairs. On examination the experience of the more popular Presidents as leaders in foreign policy turns out to have been, in fact, somewhat different.

# V

## *Presidential Popularity and Foreign Policy*

1. *Leadership in foreign affairs of a different order from leadership in domestic matters. Partisanship less useful; unpartisanship more available* ੭ In the last third of the twentieth century foreign affairs consumes so great a portion of the President's time that it may be instructive to give some attention to times when this was not so. When crises were not so imminent —if only because communication was slow—Presidents could and did deal much more deliberately with problems of foreign policy than they possibly could today. Jefferson, for example, studied for months the problem posed by the British attack on the *Chesapeake* in 1807 before reaching his decision to try an embargo. But John Kennedy, in 1962, had to decide in a matter of days, even hours, how the United States should react to the discovery of long-range Soviet missiles aimed at the United States from Cuba. Both were popular Presidents; both could rally public opinion to support their decisions. But Jefferson had time to consider what effect his decision would have on his partisans and on his political enemies. This consideration might have modified his judgment; indeed, some of his friends advised him against the course he chose precisely because it would alienate some of his supporters. Kennedy, on the other hand, had to act, assuming that public opinion would back him, not calculating whether or not it would.

The case with partisanship in foreign policy is not the same as in domestic matters. The more successful American foreign policies have often been unpartisan or bipartisan, and unpartisan

Presidents have been much more likely to give successful leadership in foreign than in domestic affairs. Jefferson's policy was a failure, albeit an heroic one. But Monroe's was successful. Polk's Mexican policy won a war and a vast territory but cost his country dearly and permanently in moral standing. His partisan policy on Oregon, however, was a different matter, as we shall presently observe. Eisenhower's unpartisan strivings for international peace in his "open skies" and "atoms for peace" proposals were the high moments of his administration, and his decision not to intervene in Vietnam in 1954 cannot be held responsible for the failure of the Indo-China settlement thereafter. Theodore Roosevelt left a bitter legacy of suspicion and fear in the wake of his successful partisan policy on Panama, while Lyndon Johnson, if he could not settle the endemic miseries of Vietnam in the 1960's, was at least able to devise a policy that accented agreement in his own country and won respect from the free world. The evidence suggests, in short, that partisan Presidents have their best success in foreign policy by modulating their partisanship to a lower key, while the least partisan Presidents are likely to find that their policy of "national unity," which stultifies action on domestic matters, gets better results in the foreign field. But the emerging principle nevertheless holds that popular Presidents who make full use of their popular support are the effective leaders of the nation, while those who so fear to divide their following that any vigorous policy seems to them dangerous are likely to be weak and ineffective.

## 2. *Success in foreign policy: Polk settles the Oregon dispute with Great Britain—and with his own Secretary of State!* ঽ৯

If James Knox Polk is an example of the popularity of presidential policy rather than presidential personality, his is also an important example of leadership in foreign affairs strengthened and, indeed, sustained by confidence in his partisan backing. His Mexican policy and his skillful administration of the wartime government have been studied by many scholars—and by many Presidents. That issue was drawn largely by himself, insisted upon with growing popular support, and brought, despite such frustrating political obstacles as the presidential candidacies of both of his principal generals, to a successful conclusion. Whether the consequences of that success were also successful is surely still debatable. But the leadership of the President, as displayed in such other matters as the tariff fight and the establishment of the independent treasury, is not. Perhaps even more instructive is Polk's handling of the Oregon question, another issue that he himself largely defined, insisted upon, appealed to the people, and successfully brought to a conclusion.

At any rate, issues, not political stature, brought Polk the Democratic nomination in 1844. In the early spring of that year it was very nearly a foregone conclusion that ex-President Martin Van Buren would be the Democratic nominee. His only serious rival appeared to be John C. Calhoun, but Calhoun's political base was by then too narrow to afford him much chance. There was little enthusiasm for Van Buren, but he could muster some support in most sections, while Calhoun could only appear as a Southern sectional candidate. In short, it was not a promising year for the Democrats. The Whigs, dropping President John Tyler as a "Trojan horse" Democrat, were well settled on Henry Clay, and all indications were that he would, at last, achieve his ambition.

But President Tyler, forcing the issue on Texas with a vigorous annexation policy, decisively upset these dull advance calculations. Clay, of course, was opposed to annexation as a threat both to the peace and to the uneasy balance between slave and free states. He was confident that fear of war and of internal friction would direct the attention of the majority of the voters to his American System. The Whigs generally would follow Clay's line, and it seemed likely that much of the North and West would accept him, regardless of party. For Van Buren the issue was not so simple. On the one hand, he needed the support of pro-Texas Democrats who predominated in the South; on the other, if he favored annexation, he risked loss of major support in his own state of New York as well as in other areas of the North. In the end he chose to announce his opposition to annexation in the hope that, by siding with his opponent, the issue could be eliminated from the campaign. Accordingly he issued a statement, in the form of a letter to his political supporters, asserting the right of the United States to annex Texas, recalling his efforts as Secretary of State under Jackson to purchase the territory from Mexico, but concluding that at the moment he feared annexation would bring war with Mexico. In such a war, he said, the United States could not "hope to stand perfectly justified in the eyes of mankind." This was written on April 20, 1844. The Texas Treaty, negotiated by Calhoun, had been signed on April 12, and it was submitted to the Senate on April 22, six days before Van Buren's statement was published in Washington. Clay, for his part, had sent his views to the *National Intelligencer,* dated April 17, without the "smallest apprehension," as he wrote a political friend, that he would harm his chances by stating them.[1]

With the two probable candidates thus agreed in their opposition to the treaty, President Tyler presently torpedoed his own policy by underlining the advantages annexation would have to Southern slaveholders in shoring up their "peculiar institution." Secretary Calhoun, endeavoring to keep Great Britain out of the Mexico-Texas-United States controversy, also spoke hotly about preserving slavery, thus giving some credence to the anti-Texas line that annexation was a slaveholders' plot. In the Senate the treaty failed of ratification by a vote of 35 to 16.

But the failure of the treaty evidently did not please the public, at least the majority of the Democratic public, and President Tyler refused to give up his fight. Instead he proposed that Congress annex Texas by joint resolution, without consulting Mexico. This resolution, though it did not come to a vote before Congress adjourned on June 17, guaranteed that Texas would be a major issue in the approaching election. Debate on it was raging when the Democratic Convention met in Baltimore on May 27.

In the interval, political medicine was being brewed at the "Hermitage," Andrew Jackson's seat of alleged retirement from which he sought often, and often successfully, to arrange matters in the Democratic Party to suit his views. Jackson favored Van Buren and worked for him until the latter's Texas letter appeared. Thereafter, the old General was persuaded Van Buren could not win if nominated, so that his nomination would amount to conceding the election to Clay—an alternative, in Jackson's mind, too dreadful to contemplate. There was no obvious substitute for Van Buren. Calhoun would never be acceptable to the North, or to Jacksonians anywhere. Lewis Cass was eager but without sufficient national following. Levi Woodbury was not even acceptable to his native New England. James Buchanan would get the backing of Pennsylvania but lacked the strength of personality to have decisive appeal to the country— or to Jackson.

Under these circumstances the Tennessee group began to talk about "Governor" Polk. Speaker of the House in Jackson's time and a former governor of Tennessee, Polk was not only thoroughly trusted by the Jacksonians but had been the personal favorite of Old Hickory for many years. Polk was as dedicated a disciple of Jackson—and of Jefferson—as could be found in the country. He was, at the moment, an available candidate—perhaps the leading candidate—for Vice-President, but because he was not personally well known in the country and had never advanced himself, he had not been seriously considered for the Presidency itself. After Van Buren's disqualification Jackson seems to have realized that his young friend (Polk was 49) might not only be nominated but might win the election, precisely because he was not well known and had not advanced himself. In a deadlocked convention he might unite the party; in a tough campaign his appeal might be broader than Clay's.

Polk was urgently invited to go to the Hermitage for conferences on the whole matter. After a lengthy canvass of the various possibilities, two decisions were taken. First, Jackson would extricate himself from his commitment to Van Buren. Second, Polk would make known his availability to politicians like Cave Johnson who were to be active at the convention, suggesting that he had Jackson's approval. On May 14, Polk wrote Johnson that he had "stood by" Van Buren, would still stand by him, but "I now despair of his election—even if he is nominated." He reiterated his own frequent statements that he was interested only in the Vice-Presidency. But the next day he wrote Johnson again in less guarded language:

[Jackson] thinks the candidate for the Presidency should be an annexation man and reside in the Southwest, and he openly expresses (what I assure you I had never for a moment contemplated) the opinion that I would be the most available man; taking the Vice-Presidential candidate from the North.

Thus quietly did the future eleventh President enter the contest. But once in, despite continuing disclaimers, he took personal charge of his campaign. And he showed his political mettle in so doing.[2]

To Johnson, who now became Polk's informal campaign manager, he wrote careful instructions in the form of suggestions on how to "save the party." The idea was to appeal to the grass-roots delegates over the heads of the leaders of the various factions. When the delegates arrived at Baltimore, Johnson, or someone designated by him, was to seek one man from each state to meet privately, indeed secretly, to determine who would be the best candidate to unite the party. In this way, Polk believed, the delegates could "take the matter into their own hands, to control and overrule their leaders." "If you will quietly and without announcing to the public what you are at, undertake this with energy and prosecute it with vigor," he wrote, "the plan is feasible and I think will succeed." After the preliminary meeting the selected delegates were to go back to their delegations and carry the agreed message, reporting "at an adjourned meeting the result." Johnson accepted the assignment and, apparently, entrusted Gideon Pillow with a share in the enterprise. Other leaders, including Andrew Jackson Donelson, the ex-President's son-in-law, presently joined in the Polk movement.[3]

But in the first stages of the convention they worked very quietly, allowing the leading candidates to have their moments of glory. In order to stop Van Buren it was necessary first to beat down an attempt by Van Buren men to amend the rules in order to nominate by simple majority. The Polk men assisted in this maneuver, favoring the established two-thirds rule, but otherwise stuck with Van Buren until his cause was hopeless. After seven ballots it became clear, indeed, that none of the announced candidates could come close to nomination. At this stage Pillow and Johnson arranged with George Bancroft of Massachusetts to have Polk's name brought forward. With help from Pennsylvania as well as the Southwest, Polk entered the competition with forty-four votes on the eighth ballot. At this point the Van Buren men reluctantly and bitterly, but loyal to Jackson, swung to Polk, as did some of the Cass men and the small group for Buchanan. On the ninth ballot Polk was nominated, and the action was declared unanimous. George Dallas of Pennsylvania was chosen as Polk's running mate.

Although the Democratic Party was split to some degree in the campaign of 1844, it managed to gloss over its differences long enough to produce its full vote at the polls. This was enough to win, since the Democrats, when united, were clearly the majority party in the country. Polk carried New York and Pennsylvania as well as the South, thus restoring the ancient Jefferson-Jackson coalition. His defeat in his home state was galling but not crucial. With 170 electoral votes to Clay's 105, Polk had a solid majority of the popular vote, a vote that crossed party lines on issues rather than personalities. Annexation of Texas was, of course, the most popular issue, but Oregon, with the slogan "54-40 or fight," excited the West and swung votes to Polk.

Even before he was brought into the race for the Democratic nomination, Polk had formulated, and his friends had circulated, his stand on Texas and Oregon:

Let Texas be re-annexed and the authority and laws of the United States be established and maintained within her limits, as also the Oregon Territory, and let the fixed policy of our government be not to permit Great Britain or any other foreign power to plant a colony or hold dominion over any portion of the people or territory of either.

These were fighting words, sharply contrasting with Clay's customary search for conciliation. And they were popular words, exciting to ordinary people in a sense that Clay's "American system" formulations could never be. If the Democratic candidate was subject to ridicule—"Who is James K. Polk?"—his platform could not be dismissed either by thoughtful analysis or humorous thrust. A no doubt apocryphal story circulated in the campaign well illustrates the point. Clay's son was said to have brought to his father the news of Polk's unexpected nomination. " 'Well, my son, who is nominated?' 'Guess, father.' 'Why Mattey, of course.' 'No, father, guess again.' 'Cass?' 'No.' 'Buchanan?' 'No.' 'Then who the devil have they nominated?' 'James K. Polk.' " Wherewith Clay is said to have risen from his chair and strode angrily across the room shouting, "Beat again, by God!" Clay was right, and for the right reasons.[4]

Polk thus entered upon his term with well-defined public expectations that he would proceed vigorously to resolve the long-standing Oregon question. And the public was not disappointed. Between his election and his inauguration Polk chose a Cabinet of able and experienced men, with Buchanan at their head as Secretary of State, but he allowed no one to suppose that he would be content merely to preside over them, as some earlier Presidents had done. His Cabinet, he said, would have the "existing administration and the good of the country more at heart than the question who shall succeed me, and . . . in any event I intend to be *myself* President of the United States." As it turned out, the only serious opposition to his Oregon policy did in fact come from within his official family, and before the matter was finally settled, it did involve the politics of the future of the Presidency.[5]

In his Inaugural Address Polk asserted his Oregon policy without equivocation. It would be, he said, his "duty to assert and maintain by all constitutional means the right of the United States to that portion of our territory which lies beyond the Rocky Mountains." "Our title to the country of Oregon," he continued, "is clear and unquestionable, and already are our people preparing to perfect that title by occupying it with their wives and children." The title was, of course, questionable and being effectively questioned by Great Britain. And many Americans were not anxious to press the claim of the United States in the face of possible war with Britain, especially at a time when a war with Mexico seemed a "possible probability." Polk well understood that his views on Oregon and other matters were divisive and took pains to leave no doubt in the minds of his fellow citizens of the conception he held of the President as the agent of policy:

> Although in our country the Chief Magistrate must almost of necessity be chosen by a party and stand pledged to its principles and measures, yet in his official action he should not be the President of a part only, but of the whole people of the United States. While he executes the laws with an impartial hand, shrinks from no proper responsibility, and faithfully carries out in the executive department of

the Government the principles and policy of those who have chosen him, he should not be unmindful that our fellow-citizens who have differed with him in opinion are entitled to the full and free exercise of their opinions and judgments, and that the rights of all are entitled to respect and regard.[6]

When applied to the Oregon question this meant that Polk would take whatever measures he could to secure the whole territory for the United States; failing that, which he seems never to have seriously expected to accomplish, he would settle for no less than the territory south of the 49th parallel and full jurisdiction over the Columbia River. But he felt himself in honor bound to respect the offer made by his predecessor, which asked only for division at the 49th parallel. Accordingly, he authorized Buchanan to submit the proposal to Richard Pakenham, the British Minister, who summarily rejected it without even the courtesy of referring it to London. Buchanan was alarmed, seeing in the British position a willingness to go to war should the United States press its claims vigorously. But Polk was evidently delighted, since his hands were now freed to construct his own policy and develop his own strategy.

It was his running disagreements with Buchanan over Oregon that, fortunately for American presidential history, determined Polk to keep a diary. He wished, he said, to have an accurate record both for himself and for posterity of what transpired in his many conversations with the Secretary of State. The *Diary*, commenced on August 26, 1845, enables a student of the Presidency to follow every in and out of the formulation and application of Polk's Oregon policy from its inception to its ultimate success, to estimate his leadership capacity, to see him in action with his Cabinet, to gauge his political astuteness, to see how he handled the Senate, and, above all, to see how he made use of the partisan majority he knew was behind him on the issue.

After his Inaugural, which the London *Times* called a "grotesque exhibition of national vanity," Polk took his time in deciding what overture he would make to the British. There was much speculation as to the possibility of war with Britain, should he go ahead with a claim to the whole territory, and a national division on this issue found Polk's supporters prepared to follow him regardless of the consequences. Thus the Washington *Union:*

. . . we venture to predict that it is not Mr. Polk's wish to plunge his country into war, and still less to sacrifice her rights and her honor. He will never abandon either; and without meaning to bluster or to brave the British ministers, we undertake to say that this is the general and enthusiastic sentiment of the American nation. The President will carry out the wishes of the people . . . "Young Hickory will make good his title."[7]

Polk set out to do so when Pakenham rejected the compromise. The *Diary* now begins. Buchanan wished to reply to Pakenham in a conciliatory way, indicating American willingness to listen to a counterproposition, in fact inviting one. Polk flatly rejected such an approach to the matter. "Now if we withdraw our proposition," he wrote, "as it is agreed we shall, and at the same time give a formal invitation to the British Minister to make a proposition on his part, assuring him at the same time that when made it shall be deliberately considered, what will be the inevitable and irresistible inference?" The question answered itself, Polk told the Cabinet. "Why, that we are prepared to accept terms less favourable to the U.S. than the 49°, for it cannot be expected under such an invitation, that terms less favourable to Great Britain than 49° which she has already rejected will be proposed by the British Minister."[8]

Polk was not only taking charge of foreign policy, but, despite a complete lack of experience, he was taking a substantially more sophisticated approach to it than did Buchanan, who had years of diplomacy behind him. It is worth emphasizing that Polk's schooling in politics, in the art of guessing how much ground to give or take and how the other fellow will react, immediately turned out to be directly transferable to the conduct of foreign policy. But it was political skill as practiced by a man of firm conviction and courage, as the ensuing exchange with Buchanan illustrates. Polk admitted frankly that he "did not regret that the American proposal had been rejected by the British." His decision was to withdraw the proposal entirely and leave it up to the British to react to the claim, announced in the Inaugural, that the whole of Oregon belonged to the United States. If the British had any proposal to make, they would make it; if not, then not.

Mr. Buchanan then intimated that if the President's views were carried out, we would have war. To which the President replied, if we do have war it will not be our fault. Mr. Buchanan said that war would probably be the result ultimately, but he expressed the opinion that the people of the U. S. would not be willing to sustain a war for the country North of 49°, and that if we were to have war he would like for it to be for some better cause. . . .

Polk records his reply drily:

The President differed with Mr. B. as to the popular sentiment, and he thought we had the strongest evidence that was to be anywhere seen that the people would be prompt and ready to sustain the Government in the course which he proposed to pursue.

Buchanan was not easily put down. First he suggested that the reply to Pakenham be postponed until it could be known whether there would be war with Mexico. Polk dismissed this objection by asserting that there was "no necessary connection between the two questions," a view that seemed to outsiders like bravado but which was no less than a matter of conviction. Polk seems never to have feared a two-front war, perhaps because he never thought it would happen. Next Buchanan proposed delaying the reply to Pakenham until late in September, apparently hoping that some different British attitude would be expressed in later mails, but Polk would not wait. To delay, he said, would "carry the idea to Great Britain as well as to our own people, of hesitancy and indecision on our part." So far as the President was concerned, he added, digging hard at Buchanan, this "would be an erroneous inference." In the end, the President simply ordered Buchanan to prepare a reply to Pakenham containing a direct expression of the President's views.[9]

Thus at the outset Polk made full use of the popularity of the Oregon issue as it had been displayed in the election. To Buchanan, whose politics were then and later usually conducted on the basis of internal party relations with fellow Democratic leaders, Polk's behavior was rash and likely to have dangerous consequences. A few days later he reported to the President, "Well, the deed is done." But he could not resist again saying that he thought it should not have been. The President said "he was glad it was delivered, that it was right in itself and he saw no

Presidential Popularity and Foreign Policy193

reason for delaying it because of our relations with Mexico." And so the matter rested until the fall when, with Congress about to convene, Polk began to prepare his State of the Union message.[10]

Polk personally drafted the paragraphs on Oregon for his first message to Congress. On October 20th he gave the draft to Buchanan for his opinion. But work on the message was delayed by the arrival from London of a dispatch from the American Minister, Louis McLane, indicating that Lord Aberdeen, British Foreign Minister, had apologized for Pakenham's rejection of the compromise offer and stated a willingness to bargain on a settlement at the 49th parallel. He wished to know whether the United States would reopen negotiations. This turn of events did not suit Polk at all. He wanted the whole of Oregon, as did his supporters in the Northwest and elsewhere, or, at the worst, a settlement at the 49th parallel with complete control over the Columbia River. He doubted whether the British would offer an acceptable proposition. Buchanan, of course, saw the matter quite differently. Expecting a visit from Pakenham, he asked Polk to agree that he should tell Pakenham the United States would be interested in receiving a new proposal. Further, he expected Pakenham to ask what "modification of the American proposition would be accepted by us." How, Buchanan wished to know, should he reply to such an overture? Polk stuck to his hard line: "If the British Minister . . . called on Mr. Buchanan . . . all that could be said to him was, that if he had any further proposition to make on his part, it would be received and considered." Polk was adamant that "no intimation should be given to him of what the views or intentions of the administration were."

Buchanan was alarmed. "If we stopped the negotiation where it was," he told the President, "it would inevitably lead to war." The President was unperturbed. He was "well satisfied with the ground we occupied on the subject." But he nevertheless now moved an important step forward in his strategy for settling the issue. He told Buchanan once again that he was "sure" that the British would make no "new proposition which we could accept." However, when a proposition was received, "he would either reject it, or submit it to the Senate for their advice before he acted on it, according to its character." Buchanan seized upon this possibility of pleasing Pakenham. Could he, he asked the President, tell Pakenham that a new proposal would be submitted to the Senate? The answer, as he might have anticipated, was a flat *no*. "That would be improper," Polk said. The "British Minister had no right to know our councils or intentions. It was enough to let him understand . . . that *we* had not closed the door to a continuance of the negotiation." Once more Buchanan expressed his fear that Polk's line would lead to war. Once more Polk replied that he was "satisfied with the state of the negotiation as it stood." The President terminated the conversation by telling the Secretary of State that he "would maintain all our rights, would take bold and strong ground, and reaffirm Mr. Monroe's ground against permitting any European power to plant or establish any new colony on the North American continent." What he did not say was that if he should have to compromise on Oregon, as he well knew he would have to do, he would do it on the "advice" of the Senate, not the initiative of the President.[11]

Presently Polk made an opportunity to line up a powerful ally. Senator Thomas Hart Benton had not been enthusiastic about Polk's nomination; indeed he had been at odds with the other Jacksonians for a considerable period. But he was a redoubtable "old Republican" and the leading advocate of the West in the Senate. Polk told Buchanan to show Benton the correspondence with the British on the Oregon question, hoping that Benton would respond by making an overture to the White House. He did so almost immediately. On October 24th he called on Polk, and the two men had a long and, to Polk, very satisfactory conversation. "His manner and conversation," Polk noted, "were altogether pleasant and friendly, and such as they had always been in former years when I was in Congress with him." They reviewed the whole series of events. Polk stressed the fact that he had proposed the 49th parallel to Pakenham only because his predecessors had done so. He reaffirmed his own policy, following the British rejection, and spelled out his proposed course of action:

1st. That the 12 months notice for the abrogation of the Convention of 1827 should be given.

2nd. That our laws & jurisdiction should be extended over our citizens in Oregon, to the same extent that the British laws had been extended over British subjects by the act of Parliament of 1821.

3d. That block-houses or stockade forts should be erected on the route from U.S. to Oregon, and that two or three Regiments of mounted riflemen should be raised, for the protection of emigrants on their route to Oregon.

4th. That our Indian policy should be extended to Oregon.

To all this Benton fully agreed, as he did to Polk's reassertion of the Monroe Doctrine. He told the President he was ready to accept settlement at the 49th parallel, but Polk thought he was less clear as to jurisdiction over the Columbia. The conversation, at any rate, "closed pleasantly." Polk noted in his diary that he had before him on his desk the rough draft of his message to Congress which he used as notes for the statement of his position, but he did not allow Benton to see it. Evidently he preferred to let the Senator assume, when he read the final message, that the conversation had helped the President to determine the substance of the paragraphs on Oregon.

The next day, October 25th, Buchanan received a note from the British Minister that said, in effect, that the British government was interested in renewing negotiations and invited the United States to resubmit the proposal that had been rejected earlier. Polk had no wish to reopen the matter on such terms; indeed, to have done so would have been contrary to his whole strategy, since such an act would presume that the proposal was negotiable—that, in short, the United States might consider relinquishing its claim to sole control and proprietorship of the Columbia. Buchanan, of course, differed. He drafted a note that Polk thought "conciliatory . . . and conceded too much." The President, as in previous episodes, refused to accept Buchanan's approach, repeating his own emphatic desire to force the British to initiate any proposal that might serve to reopen the negotiation. Polk revised Buchanan's draft and asked and received the support of the whole Cabinet on the revised language. Buchanan confessed that he was unhappy, but agreed to go along.

At the next Cabinet meeting, however, Buchanan suggested a new method of ingratiating himself and, presumably, the President with Pakenham. Would Polk allow him to *read* the United States reply aloud to the British Minister? By this device Pakenham would have an option to withdraw his own note as unofficial, thus forestalling what Buchanan believed would be a dangerous impasse. He told the President that Pakenham had, in fact, intimated in conversation that his note might "be regarded as official or not." Polk, of course, would have none of this kind of diplomatic playing of cat and mouse. Pakenham, he said, must make up his mind "whether his note was to be regarded as official or not, before he could see our answer or know its contents." Buchanan was insistent but only succeeded in drawing the President to stronger expressions of his fixed position. "I had been considering [the note] official," he told the Secretary, "as I supposed we all had, at two Cabinet meetings in which we had been preparing the answer." He told Buchanan "with earnestness and emphasis" that he would not permit "our views as contained in the answer to be read to Mr. P. or the substance in any way made known to him, unless he first decided that his note of the 25th was official and was to go on the files of the Department." The President then formally instructed the Secretary as to how he was to proceed. "He would inform Pakenham distinctly that he must decide whether he wished his note of the 25th to be official or not; if he decided it was official then [Buchanan] would deliver the answer to him; but that if he said it was unofficial that he would inform him that I had no answer to give or any information to impart to him on the subject." Buchanan, Polk recorded, said "he would follow my directions." But he did so "most reluctantly, as was manifest from his manner & the objections he urged to such a course."

On the same day Buchanan had the expected conversation with Pakenham and immediately afterward reported it in detail to the President. He had done, he said, exactly as Polk had directed. "Mr. Pakenham . . . seemed to be in doubt what to do," said the Secretary, "and made some remark of his anxiety to see some way to continue the negotiation." Buchanan observed to Pakenham that "he could not expect us to abandon the ground we had taken in the negotiation." Pakenham's reaction was to withdraw his note, whereupon the conversation ended. "I said to Mr. Buchanan," noted the President, "it was his remark that had induced him [Pakenham] to take that course, and that it would have been better if he had said nothing and left him to decide for himself."

There is no way of knowing whether the Secretary of State intended to warn Pakenham, thereby subverting the President's plan. But Polk was skeptical, at least, if not suspicious. As he meditated on the transaction afterward, he noted that "it was manifest to me in the whole discussion in Cabinet on yesterday & today, that Mr. Buchanan disapproved the course which he saw I inclined to take. . . . Indeed he said . . . that he differed with all the Cabinet . . . but that if I was resolved to accept nothing less than what had been offered by us and rejected, that ended the matter." But in fact it did not end the matter at all, for in his interview with Pakenham the Secretary had let the President's "settled decision" be known. This, wrote Polk, was "unfortunate." "The result is that after two Cabinet meetings and much anxious discussion the matter ended where it began."[12]

After this unfortunate episode, Polk returned to the business of writing his annual message. More than ever resolved to take the hard line, he stated the American claim categorically and asked Congress forthwith to authorize him to give the British the required one-year's notice that the Convention of 1827 was to be terminated. Once this was done, the United States could move in to protect the American settlers, establish posts, and declare the application of American law. That this would bring sharp British reaction could not be doubted. That it would bring war Polk did not believe. In his view a favorable settlement was much the more likely outcome. At any rate he was prepared to take the risk, confident that the popular majority was with him and that Congress would provide whatever backing in law and money the Executive might need.

Buchanan, still hopeful that he could change the President's mind, submitted a draft "modifying and softening" the tone of Polk's draft. "I prefer the bold ground which I have taken in my draft," the President said, but he would "further examine the subject." Meanwhile he took pains to get the chairman of the Senate Committee on Foreign Affairs on his side. William Allen of Ohio was a "54-40 or fight" man, young and somewhat opinionated. He was an ideal lead horse for the President. The Senate majority had to be under constant pressure to accept no compromise on Oregon, lest by indicating in advance that they would approve something less they hopelessly weaken the President's position. Allen fully approved the strong ground Polk proposed to take in his message. "He was in fine spirits," Polk noted, "and will, I have no doubt, give an ardent support to the administration." His confidence was well placed.

On November 29th Buchanan made one final effort to dissuade his chief from taking an uncompromising position on Oregon. He told Polk that "from what he had heard from members of Congress who had spoken to him, that they would be favourable to a settlement of the question on the parallel of 49° of North Latitude." Confident of the support of men like Benton and Allen, the President replied that "his channels were very different from mine; that there was not one in ten of the members whom I had seen who were not roused on the Oregon question and were going the whole length." Buchanan countered by expressing the opinion "with some earnestness that the country would not justify a war for the country North of 49°, and that my greatest danger would be that I would be attacked for holding a warlike tone. I told him," said the President, "that I would be attacked for having yielded to what had been done by my predecessors and in deference alone, as he knew, to their acts and commitments." Polk repeated his view that he had done his "duty" by offering the compromise originally but that he "did not regret that it had been rejected by the British Minister." Indeed, he told Buchanan he thought that if the proposition had been accepted, his Administration would have been in serious trouble with the people. "As we came in on Texas the probability was we would have gone out on Oregon." For the moment this was the end of the matter. Three days later Polk sent his message up to Congress, firmly claiming Oregon and asking that the Convention of 1827 be abrogated according to the treaty:

All attempts at compromise having failed, it becomes the duty of Congress to consider what measures it may be proper to adopt for the security and protection of our citizens now inhabiting or who may hereafter inhabit Oregon, and for the maintenance of our just title to that Territory.

For the record, Polk urged Congress to observe carefully the provisions of the Convention of 1827. "The faith of treaties, in their letter and spirit, has ever been, and, I trust, will ever be, scrupulously observed by the United States."

. . . A year's notice is required to be given by either party to the other before the joint occupancy shall terminate and before either can rightfully assert or exercise exclusive jurisdiction over any portion of the territory. This notice it would, in my judgment, be proper to give, and I recommend that provision be made by law for giving it accordingly. . . .

The implication of giving such notice would be, Polk told the Congress, that at the end of the year "we shall have reached a period when the national rights in Oregon must either be abandoned or firmly maintained. That they cannot be abandoned without a sacrifice of both national honor and interest is too clear to admit of doubt."[13]

In the days following the appearance of the message, Polk received many callers. "All who spoke on the subject," he noted, "highly approved my message." Even a Virginia Whig expressed his "gratification" at the Oregon section of the message and said he believed he was "half a Polk-man." Benton called to offer his approval and support. "Well! You have sent us the message," he said. "I think we can all go it as we understand it." Polk reminded Benton that the phrase "as we understand it" had been used by Jackson with regard to the Constitution, so that Benton had "very high authority."

Soon Buchanan was again asking what he should say if and when Pakenham inquired how the British were to interpret the message. Polk told him that the message spoke for itself. "But," Buchanan insisted, "suppose Mr. Pakenham inquires whether any further proposition which the British Government might make would be received, what shall I say to him?" Polk answered that Pakenham had no right to ask such a question or reason to expect an answer. The United States would not "invite him to take any step whatever." However, if he chose to do so, "it would be time enough for me to consider what disposition should be made of it." Again he said he was satisfied that Pakenham would make no proposition that was acceptable. Buchanan wanted to know whether if Pakenham offered to settle for 49°, Polk would submit the proposal to the Senate before acting on it, and "whether he was authorized to say so to Pakenham." At this stage it is hard to resist the impression that Buchanan was either obtuse or disloyal. To make the same objections to Polk's line on every occasion and to propose repeatedly to tip the President's hand to the British Minister suggests either that Buchanan's diplomatic abilities were minimal or that he was attempting, by less than loyal means, to pursue his own policy. At any rate, the President once more told him that he could not give Pakenham any such information. "The British Minister should not know anything of any consultation with the Senate, even if I determined to ask the advice of that body, which I had not." Again the conversation terminated with Buchanan muttering about avoiding war, while Polk insisted that though he "did not desire war . . . at all hazards we must maintain our just rights."[14]

A similar interchange took place later in December when Buchanan was drafting a letter of instructions to McLane in London. The President, said the draft, would "feel strongly inclined to submit a proposal to settle on the 49th parallel to the Senate for their advice." Polk, of course, struck out the passage. In its place he wrote that the "President would judge of the character of any new proposition when made, and if in his opinion it was such as to justify it, would feel inclined to submit it to the Senate for their previous advice before he would take any action on it." He added that because his decision could mean peace or war, he felt a duty to consult his "constitutional advisers before a final decision." Buchanan persisted, declaring that if the dispatch were not sent as he had written it, "we had better prepare for war." Polk was blunt. "I told Mr. Buchanan . . . that I intended to hold the whole subject in my own hands, and to judge of such a proposition, if made, when I saw it and knew what it was." There was further discussion, Polk noted, but the matter was closed "by having the amendment made which I had directed." George Bancroft, he added, after Buchanan had left the room, "remarked to me that he thought I was right."[15]

So, too, did John Quincy Adams. Polk, looking for useful allies, conveyed through Bancroft an invitation to Adams to dine at the White House. The old man had been on opposite political sides from Polk in the House and had never, of course, been a friend of the Jacksonians, but he commanded respect on the Whig side and could be helpful when the House considered any measures on the Oregon question Polk might need to bring before it. Adams declined the invitation on the ground that he had declined a similar invitation from Jackson, but he authorized Bancroft to remind the President that their personal relations "had never been disturbed" despite political differences. Further, Polk noted, "he expressed his determination to support my administration on the Oregon question, and that he would take an early occasion to make known his views in the House."[16]

Among the other leading men, Calhoun called on the President to express his fear that "the greatest danger of disturbing the peace between the two countries would grow out of the hasty action of Congress and the debates which would arise," as the result of Polk's message. He urged Polk to advise the Congress to postpone action and "restrain them from taking warlike measures." Polk concluded that he would get no support from the Calhoun wing of the party, nor would Calhoun's Whig friends, Webster and Clay, do anything but oppose. Polk, of course, expected nothing from any of these men and did not bother to see Clay or Webster. But he was willing to talk over the whole issue privately with any member of the Senate.[17]

Meanwhile, despite his confidence that Britain would not actually go to war over Oregon, Polk thought it prudent to put the country into "a state of defence without delay." On this, at least, he and the Secretary of State were agreed. He ordered Bancroft, Secretary of the Navy, and William Marcy, Secretary of War, to consult with the chairmen of the military and naval committees of the two Houses of Congress, "communicate the administration's views to them, and aid them in drafting the proper bills." When, in the same meeting of the Cabinet, Buchanan once more asked whether the President would submit a compromise proposal of the 49th parallel to the Senate, the President varied his reply by saying that if the British offered the 49th parallel plus "free ports North of 49° on the sea and the Straits of Fuca," he would "consult confidentially three or four Senators from different parts of the Union, and might submit it to the Senate for their previous advice." This suggestion must have been small solace to Buchanan, since both men knew well enough that no such proposal would be made.[18]

What in fact the President expected, and what he got, was a proposal to arbitrate. Pakenham, at the end of December, proposed that the question "not of title but to divide the Oregon Territory" be referred "to the arbitrament of some friendly power." "I instantly said it must be rejected," wrote Polk, "in which decision Mr. Buchanan and Mr. Bancroft both agreed." For once there was no haggling over the language of the American reply. Categorical rejection, however, only produced from Pakenham on January 16, 1846, a second proposal to arbitrate. This time Buchanan seems to have become alarmed again and, though he concurred in rejecting the new proposal, wished to do so in conciliatory terms, even stating that "direct negotiation between the parties" was preferable to arbitration. Polk "directed" that all the conciliatory parts of Buchanan's draft be removed, and again a categorical rejection was dispatched to the British Minister.[19]

Shortly after the first of the year the Senate began to consider Polk's recommendation that notice of termination of the 1827 Convention should be given. The debate was lengthy and tense. Polk held numerous quiet private conversations with Allen and other Senators on whom he could count and some, like Speight of Mississippi and Colquitt of Georgia, who were undecided. That the President's wishes would prevail in the end was never really in doubt.

But as he waited impatiently for action, Polk had abundant opportunity to observe the stultifying effect of ambition upon the legislative process. On one occasion he made a lengthy entry in his diary analyzing the relation between presidential ambitions and the position of Senators on the question of serving notice to the British. There was, for example, Calhoun, perennial candidate for President, striving to make a comeback after his fatal blunder on nullification. Polk thought he had probably believed "he would best advance his views upon the Presidency, by placing himself at the head of the peace party in the country." "Now he finds his mistake," said Polk, "and is struggling to extricate himself from his embarrassment." As the majority sentiment in favor of the notice makes itself known, Calhoun "finds that he will not be sustained by either party in the country." There were as many as "16 Democrats in Va. & So. C. in the House," Polk thought, who were induced by loyalty to Calhoun to oppose the notice; Calhoun could not let them down. Yet to oppose the notice would be suicidal; thus was Calhoun politically immobilized. "Mr. Allen, on the other hand, will hear to no compromise under any circumstances, and would probably prefer war to peace, because it might subserve his ambitious views." The same view, Polk concluded, was held by Cass "as probably his best chance of reaching the Presidency," though he is "not so ultra or ardent." The redoubtable Benton was seeking, by firmness on Oregon, to redeem himself with the Texas Democrats among whom he had "lost caste." But he was unhappy in his position and not as reliable an ally as he ought to have been. In short, Polk feared that he was left "without any certain or reliable support in Congress, & especially in the Senate." Under these circumstances, he told himself, he was fortunate not to be a candidate for re-election. He could and would "appeal to the people for support." And so he did, on every occasion of meeting with members of Congress. He simply made the notice to Britain on Oregon an issue between the President and the people, on the one hand, and the Congress, on the other. Congress was unlikely, in the face of the popularity of Polk's position, to decide against him in the end.[20]

But before the Congress acted, Polk had to pull a good many political strings. When one Senator, a friend of Polk, argued in a speech for compromise, another friend claimed foul play. The President was forced to make plain to both that neither spoke for the Administration. But men like Allen were very "excited" and seemed more concerned to "strike down their political enemies" than to advance the measures of the President. "My fear," Polk confided to his diary, "is that these factions looking to the election of my successor in 1848, will so divide and weaken the Democratic Party by their feuds as to defeat my measures and render my administration unsuccessful and useless."[21]

Presently, to the surprise of his Cabinet colleagues, but not to Polk, Buchanan began to show signs of changing his mind. As it became evident that the majority in the Senate was going to support Polk and that the country was with him, Buchanan sensed that he himself was slipping. His eminence in the party and the country, on which he counted for his chance at the Presidency, might be fatally undermined if he were politically wrong on Oregon. He had wrestled with himself as to whether he wished an appointment to the Supreme Court—somewhat to Polk's disgust—and decided against it. Evidently he could be satisfied with nothing less than the Presidency. If his chances for that office required a change of heart on Oregon, he was apparently capable of making the switch. On March 22, 1846, for example, Polk noted that "Mr. Buchanan seemed wholly to have changed the tone he had held during the whole of last year on the Oregon question. . . . His dread of War & anxiety to avoid it by a compromise has been often expressed to me, in and out of the Cabinet." Buchanan had, even in recent weeks, told the President of his belief that "Gen'l Cass . . . was making political capital by insisting on our extreme rights on the question, and by his course in favour of warlike preparations." In view of this attitude, Polk thought it evident from Buchanan's own changed view that he was now considering himself in competition with Cass. He had, said Polk, "manifested a decided change of his position, and a disposition to be warlike. . . . It is a great misfortune," he concluded, "that a member of the Cabinet should be an aspirant for the Presidency, because I cannot rely upon his honest and disinterested advice."[22]

However, in the Senate, Benton, Allen, and other friends of the President closed ranks. By the second week in April Benton was taking leadership. A strongly-worded message from the President on the need for military preparations (March 24) brought matters in the Senate to a head. Benton offered to make a speech for the Administration favoring Polk's insistence on outright ownership of the Columbia if the 49th parallel were accepted. Polk advised him to do so only in an executive session. "I told him," said the President, "that I thought the great error of the whole debate in both Houses had been that whatever had been said was spoken not only to our own people but to the British Government; that we thereby exposed our hand while our adversary kept hers concealed." Benton "concurred in this view."

As the day for a vote in the Senate neared, Polk adopted a somewhat fatalistic posture. It was not "54°-40′ or 49° which had divided the Democratic majority, so much as '48," he wrote. "I will however do my duty whatever may happen. I will rise above the interested factions in Congress, and appeal confidently to the people for support."[23]

From the perspective of the mid-twentieth century it may be difficult to see how Polk expected to apply popular support against Congressional politicians when he had excluded himself from future political consideration. The common objection to the two-term limitation on the Presidency had been that in a President's second term he would lose his influence over Congress and over his party generally. Even so cautious a man as Eisenhower expressed doubt that it was wise to take from the President his power to go to the people as a candidate for a third term. But Polk had announced that he would serve only one term, no matter what might happen. He was a lame duck, presumably, from the outset. How could he have been so successful in driving through Congress all of the major measures of his program—annexation of Texas and the Southwest, low tariffs, the independent treasury, and the acquisition of Oregon? His own view was that he could rely on the people. Members of Congress had to run for re-election; he did not. Therefore he was free to take extreme positions, regardless of offense to the feelings and wishes of the minority. If his views did in fact reflect those of the majority, it was the Congress that would have to conform, on pain of defeat at the polls. If his views did not fairly represent the wishes of the country, they ought not to prevail in any case.

It was a "democratic" position, as well as a Democratic one. It worked because the President's views were in fact the views of the majority. If "Young Hickory" was a somewhat forced sobriquet, the President's program was a well-formulated expression of the will of the majority, as he had himself suggested in his Inaugural Address. He succeeded because he was partisan. Had he been nonpartisan or unpartisan, he would certainly have floundered. Surrounded, as Monroe had been in his second term, by presidential candidates without loyalty to the President, and uncertain as to what course he should pursue, he could not have driven his Oregon policy through the Senate; indeed, he could not have had an Oregon policy at all. Only by accepting as regrettable but inevitable the opposition of those who wished to settle with the British by arbitration or by what seemed to him a weak compromise could Polk reach a point where he could dominate the issue.

He reached that point on April 23, 1846, when the Senate voted his request for notice by 42 to 10 and the House concurred, 142 to 46. The sequel was exciting to the nation and satisfying to Polk, but it was anticlimax. As Polk had wisely assumed, the British had no stomach for a war at the furthest reaches from home base and no desire to settle a negotiable matter by the sword. In six weeks' time they had offered Polk all that he had ever expected to get: the 49th parallel as the permanent boundary, the Hudson's Bay Company people south of the parallel to hold their properties but subject to the laws of the United States, and the United States to have full title to the Columbia River. The Hudson's Bay Company, as the British asked, should be allowed free navigation during the life of their charter. Polk thought this latter point a minor compromise since the Company's charter would lapse in thirteen years.

The matter was not yet quite settled to Polk's satisfaction. Mindful of the "54-40 or fight" people who had provided him with the enthusiastic backing that had enabled him to bring the Congress into line—and keep Buchanan in bounds—he would not take personal responsibility for the "compromise," even though it was not so much a compromise as a clear-cut victory. On June 10 he sent the proposition to the Senate for their "prior advice," *without* his recommendation. In private talks with his Senate friends he let it be well understood that he would sign the treaty if advised to do so, thus assuring a favorable vote. But when the Senate did indeed "advise and consent" two days later, it was the Senate's responsibility, not the President's, if anyone was still unhappy! As for the partisan President, in the eyes of the great majority who approved, his leadership was sustained and vindicated.

3. *Failure in foreign policy: Jefferson gets an embargo but cannot enforce it and has to admit defeat. When a policy, short of war, is too injurious to too many people, even a Jefferson cannot sustain it* &ঙ If Polk's leadership on the Oregon question illustrates how a partisan President with no great personal popularity can nevertheless effectively carry out a popular parti-

san policy, Thomas Jefferson's unhappy experience with the embargo of 1808 reveals how even the most beloved of partisan Presidents, with solid majorities in Congress, can fail with an unpopular policy. It may be argued that success or failure in foreign policy sometimes, perhaps commonly, depends upon circumstances beyond the control of the President. Thus Oregon would not have been settled according to Polk's wishes had Britain preferred war; Jefferson's embargo may have been defeated as much by the circumstances of the European war as by the opposition at home. But such complicating circumstances, once recognized, ought not to obscure the processes of political leadership nor the relation between that leadership and the popular backing of a President.

When Jefferson was faced, in the fall of 1807, with the accumulated American grievances against the British—impressment, the unprovoked attack upon the U. S. frigate *Chesapeake,* and finally, the Orders in Council forbidding neutral trade with any enemy port—he had three options. He could ask for a declaration of war; he could merely continue to protest, hoping that in time the British would alter their policy; or he could take some sort of drastic measure short of war that might persuade the British to change their policy. War, to Jefferson, was the last and most hated recourse for a people who put their faith in reason. If war was not to be avoided at all costs, it was nevertheless to be avoided at whatever costs could be afforded without loss of national honor and safety. To continue to add protest upon protest was evidently a fatuous policy, since the British had been led to their depredations upon American commerce by what they judged to be their own national interest under the circumstances of their war with Napoleon. They would not alter such a policy simply because the United States objected. Thus some sort of economic sanctions seemed to Jefferson the only sensible alternative. If the behavior of the United States, in matters of vital concern to England, were to alter the circumstances under which England had to conduct the war, she might reconsider her American policy.

To this end Congress had authorized the President (1806) to forbid imports from Britain. This was not done, however, until November, 1807, because it seemed a worse punishment to the United States than to England. In any case, it was not her export trade upon which England depended in wartime, but her

imports. To cut off her American sources of cotton, flour, and
naval stores might hurt enough to cause a change of mind. At
the same time the cost of war in lives and treasure would be
avoided. Such a policy would likewise be effective against the
French, whose American policy, if less important, was hardly
more friendly. In a letter to a friend Jefferson thus summed up
the situation he had to resolve:

> The sum of these mutual enterprises on our national rights is that
> France, and her allies, reserving for further consideration the pro-
> hibiting our carrying anything to the British territories, have vir-
> tually done it, by restraining our bringing a return cargo from them;
> and Great Britain, after prohibiting a great portion of our commerce
> with France and her allies, is now believed to have prohibited the
> whole. The whole world is thus laid under interdict by these two na-
> tions, and our vessels, their cargoes and crews, are to be taken by the
> one or the other, for whatever place they may be destined, out of our
> own limits. If, therefore, on leaving our harbors we are certainly to
> lose them, is it not better, as to vessels, cargoes, and seamen, to keep
> them at home?[24]

In the election of 1804 Jefferson had been returned to office by
a great margin—162 electoral votes to 14—carrying even all of
formerly Federalist New England except Connecticut. No records
were kept of popular votes, but all accounts agree that Jefferson's
plurality was, proportionately, one of the greatest in American
history. His program of acquiring Louisiana, abolishing excise
taxes, reducing government expenditures, and steering a perilous
neutral course as between England and France could hardly have
been more emphatically endorsed. But his immense personal
popularity and the general satisfaction with his record nevertheless gave him no mandate in 1807 to place an embargo on
commerce. Indeed, one reason for the satisfaction of New England merchants and shippers had been the success of the small
United States Mediterranean fleet in ending the Barbary piracy
to the greater safety of American ships. Thus, as Jefferson contemplated asking Congress to enact an embargo, he knew that he
would have to rely, in the first instance, on party loyalty in the
Congress and, secondly, on his ability to rally popular support
for a measure that was bound to be unpopular with many people.
   Having decided what he would do, he laid the groundwork in

his annual message, calling Congress into session earlier than usual to suggest the urgency of the situation, both to the members and to the public. No one ever questioned Jefferson's mastery over his political family, but the differences between himself and Albert Gallatin, his Secretary of the Treasury and closer to him politically than anyone else excepting only Madison, evidence the fact that the policy he was about to undertake was his own, not the product of a collective leadership.

The President's state of mind as he set to work to draft his message is indicated in a letter to Attorney-General Caesar Rodney: "Everything we see & hear leads in my opinion to war; we have therefore much to consult and determine on, preparatory to that event." The consultation was chiefly with Gallatin. In mid-October he sent him his first draft, a strongly-worded document containing no suggestion of possible accommodation with England. Before reviewing the events that had taken place since the last session, Jefferson proposed to tell Congress:

. . . the moment seems approaching when we may owe it to mankind as well as to ourselves to restrain wrong by resistance and to assist in maintaining among nations the authority of . . . right by defeating all interests calculated on a violation of it. . . .

Gallatin was shocked. Unlike Jefferson's July proclamation denying British warships access to American harbors, the message appeared to the Secretary of the Treasury "to be rather in the shape of a manifesto issued against Great Britain on the eve of a war, than such as the existing undecided state of affairs seems to require." He could not, he said, really make any suitable suggestions for revising the draft, because his "objections [were] less to details than to its general spirit." He reviewed the recent course of relations with Britain, suggesting at each point that the President was taking too narrow or too partial a view. On one or two points of fact he differed categorically. But the thrust of Gallatin's criticism was for a moderate tone, firm but leaving the door open for negotiations:

In every view of the subject, I feel strongly impressed with the propriety of preparing to the utmost for a war & carrying it with vigor if it cannot honorably be avoided; but in the meanwhile of persevering in that caution of language & sanction which may give us some more time, and is best calculated to preserve the remaining chance of peace & most consistent with the general system of your administration.

Gallatin's preoccupation with what the British would think led him to ignore entirely what the American public might think. That Jefferson was more concerned about the latter is displayed in the message as delivered to Congress on October 27. Although he made some changes reflecting his respect for Gallatin's judgment, he nevertheless put the matter in terms so strong that both the British government and the American people could expect drastic action by the United States. Americans, aroused by the nationalistic tone of the message, might be expected to welcome it:

That love of peace so much cherished in the bosoms of our citizens, which has so long guided the proceedings of their public councils, and induced forbearance under so many wrongs, may not ensure our continuance in the quiet pursuits of industry, and the moment seems approaching when we may owe it to mankind, as well as to ourselves to restrain wrong by resistance, and to defeat those calculations of which justice is not the basis.

Gallatin had proposed to strike out this whole passage, but Jefferson saw fit to make only one significant change—what the Americans would "defeat" became "calculations" instead of "interests." Thus the message was not a "manifesto on the eve of war," but on the eve of a major change in policy.[25]

Nor did Gallatin like the new policy, even though it was short of war. In fact, somewhat inconsistently, he preferred war to embargo, or at least to a continuing embargo. On the very day that Jefferson's special message was dispatched to Congress, Gallatin was pressing for modifications in the draft resolution that was going around in the Administration. "An embargo for a limited time," he told the President, "will at this moment be preferable in itself [to an indefinite embargo] and less objectionable to Congress." He went on to make his feelings quite clear:

In every point of view, privations, sufferings, revenue, effect on the enemy, politics at home, &c., I prefer war to a permanent embargo.

Despite their many years of agreement on practical matters, Gallatin's social values were in one respect, at least, fundamentally different from Jefferson's, as the next paragraph revealed:

Governmental prohibitions do always more mischief than had been calculated; and it is not without much hesitation that a statesman should hazard to regulate the concerns of individuals as if he could do it better than themselves.

There were, of course, innumerable matters in which Jefferson would have accepted this sententious pronouncement. But when it was a matter of war or peace, reason or surrender to passion, the President was not afraid to embark upon "governmental prohibitions."

Nevertheless he invited Gallatin to the White House to talk about it before the message was sent to Congress—"but come here before half after ten, and let us be together before the message goes out of our hands." He was even willing to make one concession: as Gallatin had suggested, foreign vessels in American ports at the time the embargo was declared would be permitted to sail "in ballast, or with such cargoes as they may have on board at the moment." But though Jefferson himself did not anticipate a long-enduring embargo, he was not willing to ask Congress to place a limit upon it. And so the message was sent:

> The communications now made [indicating that the British Orders in Council had been put into effect] showing the great and increasing dangers with which our vessels, our seamen, and merchandise, are threatened on the high seas and elsewhere, from the belligerent powers of Europe, and it being of great importance to keep in safety these essential resources, I deem it my duty to recommend the subject to the consideration of Congress, who will doubtless perceive all the advantages which may be expected from an inhibition of the departure of our vessels from the ports of the United States.
>
> Their wisdom will also see the necessity of making every preparation for whatever events may grow out of the present crisis.[26]

The President had laid the groundwork well. The Republican leaders in the Senate were ("doubtless") prepared with a bill based on Jefferson's own draft resolution. Samuel Smith, of Maryland, brother of the Secretary of the Navy, was entrusted with putting the bill through. On the same day as the message was received, Smith's committee, which included Federalist Senator John Quincy Adams, reported the measure out, and the Senate passed it by 22 to 6. Adams, joined by veteran Federalist William Plumer of New Hampshire, crossed the aisle to support Jefferson's

measure—and thereby guaranteed the loss of his seat in the
Senate while taking a long stride toward the Presidency. Adams
was disturbed at the haste with which the Senate wished to act,
but he was satisfied by Senator Smith's assurance that the President was anxious to avoid a delay that would alert the merchants
and enable some of them, at least, to rush out their ships before
the deadline. This, Smith pointed out, would mean that some
American ships would be out of the country for the best part of
a year, to the advantage of their owners, while other merchants
were losing money by compliance. Another advantage in quick
action was that the measure would be of value to Secretary of
State Madison in his negotiations with a special British envoy,
expected momentarily, to settle the *Chesapeake* affair.

To his father Adams wrote, "We have now, at the express call
of the President, an unlimited embargo. To this measure . . . as
merely precautionary and defensive, I gave my assent and vote."
To his diary he confided a few days later, "On most of the great
national questions now under discussion, my sense of duty leads
me to support the Administration, and I find myself of course in
opposition to the Federalists in general . . ." He silently implored
"that Spirit from whom every good and perfect gift descends"
that he might "never be governed in my public conduct by any
consideration other than that of my duty." Up in Braintree old
John Adams, despite his bitterness toward Jefferson, believed
that his son had done right. On the same day as the embargo was
enacted, Plumer put his thoughts into writing in a note to
Adams: "In times like these we ought to feel as Americans, rise
superior to the interest of party, & decide on men and measures
by their merits, not their names."[27]

The patriotism of these Federalists was only reluctantly
matched by some of Jefferson's own party associates. Governor
James Sullivan, for example, holding office precariously—on Jefferson's coattails—in Federalist Massachusetts, could hardly have
been less happy. He wrote to the President that while he supported the Administration, he did not believe the embargo was
enforceable. What he meant was no doubt that with an election
coming up in April, *he* did not wish to enforce it. Lieutenant
Governor Levi Lincoln, to the contrary, wrote Jefferson that "the
great body of the people, all the republicans & many of the fed-

eralists believe in the necessity and utility of the measure." At any rate the Republicans won the election in Massachusetts with, as Lincoln was able to report, greater margins than before. This was more than four months after the embargo had gone into effect. However, the outgoing legislature elected John Quincy Adam's Federalist opponent, James Lloyd, by 246 to 213.[28]

Between December, 1807, and July, 1808, Jefferson was almost wholly preoccupied with problems of enforcing the embargo. The merchants of the New England states were more and more bitterly opposed and rebellious. If a Southern state like South Carolina displayed an unexpected patriotism, electing Republicans for the first time in many years, and other Southern states faithfully supported the President, dissension in New York and Pennsylvania brought a balancing loss of commitment to the President. Gallatin, to whom fell the administration of the law, reported increasing difficulties in making the embargo effective. Coastal commerce had to be permitted, since much of the Northern area was dependent on the South for food and fiber, while the South needed the manufactures of the North. But even the strictest licensing system could not prevent shippers from having their ships "forced off course by storms," so that they found themselves inadvertently in the West Indies, or from falsifying papers so that they could sail with no serious purpose of calling at American ports. Jefferson, intent upon succeeding with his experiment, met the problem by asking for more authority to enforce the law.

By an act of January 9, 1808, coastwise vessels were put under bond not to proceed to any foreign port, and fishing and whaling ships were put under similar bond and required to land their catch only at American ports. An act of March 12, 1808—a Congressional response to the pressure of the merchants—contrary to the President's wishes, authorized the President to license vessels "in ballast" to sail for foreign ports to bring back goods belonging to American citizens. The first of two so-called "enforcement acts" (April 22, 1808) gave authority to commanders of revenue cutters and naval vessels to stop a vessel on suspicion, even on the high seas; to collectors to detain a vessel on suspicion, with release granted only by the specific direction of the President; and to collectors, again, to take into custody unusual deposits of goods adjacent to foreign territory.[29]

Jefferson laid it down to Gallatin that he wished these immense and unprecedented powers freely used:

In the outset of the business of detention, I think it impossible to form precise rules. After a number of cases shall have arisen they may probably be thrown into groups and subjected to rules. The great leading object of the Legislature was, and ours in execution of it ought to be, to give complete effect to the embargo laws. They have bidden agriculture, commerce, navigation, to bow before that object, to be nothing when in competition with that. Finding all their endeavors at general rules to be evaded, they finally gave us the power of detention as the panacea, and I am clear we ought to use it freely that we may, by a fair experiment, know the power of this great weapon, the embargo.

The President never lost an opportunity to direct the Secretary's attention to the underlying principle of his policy. For example:

. . . I place immense value in the experiment being fully made, how far an embargo may be an effectual weapon in future as well as on this occasion.

Contrary to the opinion of his enemies, he was prepared to lose popularity in order to see the thing succeed. "I do not wish a single citizen in any of the States," he told Gallatin, "to be deprived of a meal of bread, but I set down the exercise of commerce, merely for profit, as nothing when it carries with it the danger of defeating the objects of the embargo." This was in May, 1808. In July he stated the position even more emphatically:

My principle is that the conveniences of our citizens shall yield reasonably, and their taste generally to the importance of giving the present experiment so fair a trial that on future occasions our legislators may know with certainty how far they may count on it as an engine for national purposes.

As he wrote, Jefferson was well aware of the hardships the embargo was in fact causing. He knew that some merchants, at least, were risking any punishment of the law to send out their vessels, making so great a profit that they could afford to lose half their ships either to depredations or to the United States Treasury. It was the longshoremen on the wharves of Boston, New York, Philadelphia, Baltimore, Charleston, and New Orleans—all Republican strongholds—as well as shipyard workers, who were hardest hit. To them embargo was an embargo on livelihood. Republican politicians kept reminding Jefferson that these people would be disaffected; the Republican cause would go down with the embargo.[30]

But the principle of economic sanctions as the more reasonable alternative to war meant more to Jefferson than even the Republican cause—or his own popularity. Ironically, it was at this juncture that his presumed overweening self-esteem was being offered to an English envoy by the President's somewhat less than loyal associate, Navy Secretary Robert Smith, as reason for making concessions to the United States. In January George Rose had arrived as a special envoy to settle the *Chesapeake* affair. But because he was not empowered to agree to reparations until Jefferson's proclamation against British warships had been withdrawn, negotiations were at stalemate. Madison, who was conducting the conversations, found it useful to have someone else unofficially sound out Rose as to what reparations or other concessions might be forthcoming if the proclamation were to be withdrawn. Smith, with Jefferson's concurrence, was entrusted with the mission. According to Rose's report to London, Smith made Jefferson look like a vainglorious fool. "I must be aware," wrote Rose, "how dear to Mr. Jefferson his popularity must be, and most especially so at the close of his political career . . . and he [Smith] pressed me earnestly to take such steps as would conciliate the President's wish to give His Majesty satisfaction on the point in question and yet to maintain the possession of what was pre-eminently valuable to him." Thus the President of the United States would negotiate, not to serve his country but to preserve his own popularity! The Federalists could hardly have invented a more damaging story. Unaccountably, Smith was believed by many early historians. That Rose reported accurately is beyond question. But, as Irving Brant acidly observes, "Smith would have been bastinadoed had it been known that he talked as he did." Indeed, even had his words in fact represented the President's position, that position, for obvious reasons, would not have been revealed to Smith!

At any rate, the Rose-Madison negotiations failed. Jefferson neither withdrew his proclamation nor gave up hope of succeeding with the embargo—and both his own popularity and that of his policy declined. Because the embargo ultimately depended on public support, its failure was proportionate to the falling-off of the President's popularity. Under the circumstances Jefferson's persistence may seem to have been somewhat quixotic. Yet as late as June and July, 1808, he was buoyed up by reports from England that the embargo was having the desired effect:

From what I observed when in England & from the best information I was able to procure [wrote James Bowdoin to Jefferson in June] I think myself founded in supposing, that the British cabinet will soon be constrained to modify or recall them [the Orders in Council] in order to recover the advantages of our commerce: her critical situation with respect to the continental powers, the distressed state of her manufacturers at home, added to that of her West India colonies must throw so many embarrassments in the way of her continuing the war without a better understanding with the United States that I expect not only a repeal of the orders of council, but the most conciliatory overtures to place the commerce of the two countries upon a better footing than it has hitherto stood.

A month later Bowdoin repeated this view. "Considering the present posture of affairs," he wrote the President, "no measure could be better devised than the Embargo." This, of course, was precisely what Jefferson wished to hear. If the report were true, then the unrest and even the sacrifices at home with their bitter political consequences for Jefferson, were worth the trouble. If not, then war remained the only honorable alternative. And, though Jefferson could not know it, the British Minister in Washington, too, for many months believed that the embargo was both enforceable and popular. If at least one of the powers did not withdraw its orders, Erskine wrote to Canning, the President's policy would "certainly continue to be approved by a large majority of the people."[31]

But Gallatin, struggling hopelessly with enforcement, could see only still greater application of unprecedented authority—and political disaster—ahead. He, not Jefferson, was right. On July 29 he told the President he was satisfied "that if the embargo must be persisted in any longer, two principles must necessarily be adopted in order to make it efficient: 1st, that not a single vessel shall be permitted to move without the special permission of the Executive; 2nd, that the collectors be invested with the general power of seizing property anywhere, and taking the rudders or otherwise effectually preventing the departure of any vessel in harbor . . . and that without being liable to personal suits." Such powers, comparable only to those that have occasionally been granted in wartime, yet directed not against enemies but against Americans, seemed to make a mockery of Jeffersonian liberal democracy. In Gallatin's view the people were already "altogether against the law." Jefferson, replying from Monticello, agreed that "Congress must legalize all *means* which may be necessary to obtain its [the embargo] *end.*" That a continuance of the embargo would be preferred to war, he said, was the "universal sentiment" in Virginia.[32]

As the time for Congress to reconvene drew near, Jefferson was as firm as ever that the embargo should be continued. To Madison he sent a succinct statement of policy for the Secretary of State's guidance:

> If the British government repeal their orders, we must repeal our embargo. If they make satisfaction for the *Chesapeake,* we must revoke our proclamation, and generalize its operation by a law. If they keep up impressments, we must adhere to nonintercourse, manufactures and a navigation act.[33]

The President's clarity and determination were the more remarkable in view of the venomous attacks of the Federalist press, the growing threat of secession in New England, and even the badgering he was receiving personally. One Beatty, for example, stopped Jefferson as he was taking his daily ride and thrust a license application upon him. The President wearily listened and then agreed to send the paper on to Gallatin for decision. One example of the press attacks will suffice. The *New England Palladium* for October 14 had this to say, under the head "Mr. Jefferson Disgraced":

Happily for the country, it will soon be well understood by the world that THE PEOPLE of *America* do not support Mr. Jefferson in his gallic attachments.—Next to the direful effects of the Embargo Laws, (dictated by Mr. Jefferson to pacify Bonaparte), the indecent manner in which the government papers have treated the cause of the Spanish patriots, has tended to wean the people of this country from their attachments to this hypocritical mock-Philosopher. etc. etc.

As for New England, Senator Timothy Pickering had led the forces of disunion from the arrival of Rose, with whom he undertook to deal directly on behalf of the disaffected, through the whole year of embargo. Sullivan and Lincoln frequently reported secessionist tendencies in Massachusetts, and the newspapers on both sides contained endless threats and counterthreats. Jefferson's attitude toward this danger is well illustrated in a letter to Secretary of War Dearborn:

The Tories of Boston openly threaten insurrection if their importation of flour is stopped. The next post will stop it.[34]

Jefferson faced the preparation of his last annual message with little zest for the exercise. About the only consolation he had was the easy election of Madison as his hand-picked successor. A flurry of opposition early in the summer, led by John Randolph and making James Monroe an uncomfortable candidate, had quickly died out. Madison won the Democratic-Republican nomination by a great margin in the Congressional party caucus and was elected over C. C. Pinckney by 122 to 47 electoral votes. There were small Federalist gains in the House of Representatives, but the Republican majority remained firm. The election was certainly a tribute to Jefferson's continuing hold over the majority of the American people. But it was no subject for gloating in a State of the Union message, and, in any case, it could hardly be interpreted as an enthusiastic endorsement of the embargo. The other news was all bad. Neither England nor France showed serious signs of breaking under the strain of the American embargo, and both retained in force their decrees denying the Americans freedom of the seas. Worst of all, the *Chesapeake* affair remained unsettled, with no apology or restitution by the British.

Under these circumstances Jefferson told Congress, in effect, that he expected the embargo to be continued, though he was prepared at any moment to invoke his power to suspend it should either of the European belligerents revoke its decrees. Adopting a draft prepared by Madison, this time with scant heed to Gallatin's suggested revisions, the President defended the embargo policy vigorously:

We have the satisfaction, . . . to reflect, that in return for the privations by the measure, and which our fellow citizens in general have borne with patriotism, it has had the important effects of saving our mariners and our vast merchantile property, as well as of affording time for prosecuting the defensive and provisional measures called for by the occasion. It has demonstrated to foreign nations the moderation and firmness which govern our councils, and to our citizens the necessity of uniting in support of the laws and rights of their country, and has thus long frustrated those usurpations and spoliations which, if resisted, involve war; if submitted to, sacrificed a vital principle of our national independence.

And he was still confident of popular support:

. . . it will rest with Congress to decide on the course best adapted to such a state of things; and bringing with them, as they do, from every part of the Union, the sentiments of our constituents, my confidence is strengthened that in forming this decision they will, with an unerring regard to the essential rights and interests of the nation weigh and compare the painful alternatives . . .[35]

Jefferson had himself, of course, already compared the painful alternatives. Anticipating a move by the Federalists to repeal the embargo, he had thoroughly briefed Senator William Giles, the Administration's floor leader, and held private talks with all the key Republicans. Giles was able to quote from the respected *Liverpool Prices Current* for September to show that England was really suffering—inflated prices, "good sweet American flour" unavailable, and the cotton supply cut in half. Such evidence, coupled with party loyalty, was sufficient to give the Administration a resounding victory. The embargo was sustained in the Senate by 22 to 6.

In full control of the Congress still, Jefferson pressed for an all-out enforcement bill. Again behind Giles' leadership in the Senate, with able assistance from John Jackson in the House, the big Republican majorities gave the President what he sought. On January 9 he signed into law a bill that gave the Treasury and the President almost all the powers Gallatin had called for in the previous summer. Collectors could seize property on suspicion, either on ships or "on carts, wagons, sleighs or in any manner apparently on their way towards the territories of a foreign nation, or the vicinity thereof." The collectors could be sued, but they could plead in their defense both the new statute and the directions of the President. The President, for his part, was empowered, "or such other person as he shall have empowered for the purpose . . . to employ such part of the land or naval forces or militia of the United States . . . as may be judged necessary" to enforce the embargo laws. This was probably the zenith of Jefferson's power. But it was in a lost cause, and he knew it. At the very moment the new enforcement bill was being enacted, he was conferring with Gallatin, Madison, Giles, and other colleagues on terms for ending the embargo and substituting nonintercourse with France and England in its stead.[36]

On January 2, 1809, Jefferson wrote a full account of his changing views to T. M. Randolph, his son-in-law. He would call for an end to the embargo as of June 1, he said, with a new nonintercourse law to go into effect on that date. By permitting trade with other neutrals American suffering would be alleviated to some extent. Though some ships would no doubt get their cargoes to the belligerents, the number might not be greater than it was already. Further,

. . . it is possible that England may be wrought upon, (1) by the documents published at the meeting of Congress which prove our fair conduct toward both countries which she had affected not to believe; (2) by the determination of the Presidential election; (3) by the failure so far of expected insurrection in Massachusetts; (4) by the course of affairs in Spain, where there can be little doubt that Joseph is re-enthroned . . . Parts of the country will hold out for awhile, but the ultimate issue must very soon be visible. If these things have the effect they ought to have on a rational government they will prevent a war with us. The nonintercourse law will be past. This is a summary view of our present political situation.[37]

In a few weeks the new legislation was ready, again put forward by Giles. Jefferson's bill called for extending the embargo until June 1, but the Senate chose to end it with the beginning of nonintercourse. The bill was passed by the Senate on February 21 and by the House on the 28th and signed into law by the President on March 1, three days before he left office.

Although the President had, at last, certainly begun to be seriously concerned about the possibility of a secession movement in New England and had all along been distressed by the hardship embargo brought to many Americans, his leading reason for bringing an end to his great experiment in economic sanctions was undoubtedly the wish to have Madison take over the presidency unencumbered by so serious a handicap. Embargo, despite Madison's earnest and loyal support, was Jefferson's policy. It was the work of his Administration, and it had failed of its purpose. The new Administration should have its opportunity to try its own experiments.

It is idle but tempting to speculate on what might have happened if the embargo had been rigorously enforced over another six months or so. Looking back upon it in 1815, as the War of 1812 came to an end, Jefferson thought even two more months would have allowed the embargo to succeed. Minister William Pinkney in London always believed it would have worked if given a better chance. It was, he said, "a noble and magnificent effort, suited to the extraordinary occasion by which it was suggested. . . . Any other measure . . . would have been madness or cowardice." Impressive statistics indicate that it was having relentless effect on the British economy—perhaps deadly effect.[38]

But its effect on Americans turned out to be worse. Jefferson discovered, to his unrequited sorrow, that even the most devoted partisan following tends to prefer economic goods to sacrifices for principle. If war must be, as all Presidents, popular or unpopular, have found, the people will make any sacrifice. But short of war, belt-tightening is so distasteful, and there are always so many who are unwilling to submit to its discipline, that policy based on it is almost certainly doomed in advance. A partisan foreign policy, even when conducted as a means to avoid war and by the most popular of partisan Presidents, must, apparently, appeal

more directly to self-interest than did Jefferson's conviction that
with obedience and patriotism the British would eventually
change their ways.

4. *Successful failure: Theodore Roosevelt "takes Panama."
The power of the President, as chief executive and as commander-in-chief, brought to bear in a popular cause, gets the
desired results but not desirable consequences* 〰 When,
after the most serious of many threatened ruptures over the years,
Presidents Kennedy and Johnson struggled in the 1960's to restore good relations with Panama, they were caught in the consequences of what another popular, partisan President called his
"most important action . . . in foreign affairs." Theodore Roosevelt's handling of relations with Colombia and Panama in 1903
was proclaimed by him an unqualified success. And it was certainly ratified at the polls in 1904, despite half-hearted criticism
by Alton B. Parker and other more forthright Democrats, as well
as denunciation by independents like William James. In retrospect the Panama affair seems so little like the achievement of
which Roosevelt boasted that it is worth studying, principally as
an example of how not to conduct the Presidency, with or without partisan popularity. Indeed, Roosevelt's leadership in 1903,
contrasting with his leadership in the coal strike of 1902 in every
respect except temperamental love of "action," was of a sort the
complexities of contemporary government—and problems—have
made quite impossible. If Lyndon Johnson could, and did in
important ways, emulate his dynamic predecessor in settling in
the public interest a long and bitter labor dispute, he could only
look upon the same predecessor's Panama policy with frustrating
regret. Indeed, Johnson's intervention in San Domingo in 1965,
which had to be defended before the United Nations Security
Council and approved by the Organization of American States,
brought with it a renewed chorus against "Yankee imperialism"
of the very sort Roosevelt had stimulated sixty-odd years before.

In his autobiography Roosevelt wrote that "at different stages
of the [Panama] affair believers in a do-nothing policy denounced
me as having 'usurped authority'—which meant, that when nobody else could or would exercise efficient authority, I exercised

it." This must deserve a place among the more audacious passages in the endless literature of self-esteem. The facts were that in June, 1902, Congress had passed and Roosevelt had signed the Spooner Act, authorizing the building of a canal across the Isthmus of Panama if a suitable treaty could be worked out with Colombia; if not, then through Nicaragua. Secretary of State John Hay carefully negotiated the necessary treaties with Nicaragua and Costa Rica and, after much bargaining with interested Senators, concluded a treaty with Colombia. The latter was signed by the United States and ratified by the Senate in March, 1903; but despite the most extreme pressure from Roosevelt, via Hay, the Colombian government in August rejected the treaty. Roosevelt then prepared to go ahead and build the canal in Panama anyway, defying the sovereignty of Colombia. He was saved the need for such drastic "action," however, by a convenient uprising in the State of Panama which declared its independence of Colombia and promptly signed the appropriate treaty with the United States. Thus there was never a time when "nobody else could or would exercise efficient authority." Roosevelt's feat consisted simply in extending recognition to the new government of Panama and "protecting lives and property" in the isthmus during the uprising, that is, backing up the rebels. The rebels, for their part, needed no backing, since they easily bought off the only Colombian soldiers around. By 1911 T.R. was saying categorically, "I took Panama." Panamanians of a later day have often been inclined to believe him—to the sorrow of later Presidents trying to conduct Latin-American policy on the basis of mutual respect.[39]

Elsewhere in his autobiography Roosevelt says, "I took Panama without consulting the Cabinet." What merit he intended to claim by this declaration it is difficult to see. Perhaps the statement serves to disarm the reader who might wonder whom he did consult, if anyone. At any rate, he did not lack for advisors, and there is some value in following the transaction briefly in order to see what kinds of advice a President may get—and take—if he is already headstrong.[40]

As late as April, 1902, Roosevelt had no firm opinion as to where the canal should be built. He was simply determined to build one. The Nicaraguan possibility was inviting, both because that country was agreeable to the proposed American terms and because it would obviate United States involvement in the affairs of the bankrupt French Panama Canal Company, through which de Lesseps, builder of Suez, had tried and failed in Panama. A canal in Nicaragua would cost a good deal more because it would be longer, but there would be no pay-off to the French company. It was on this point that Roosevelt got his most effective advice —from the ex-chief engineer of the French company, Philippe Bunau-Varilla, and its American counsel, William Nelson Cromwell. These two men, whose personal stake in the American decision was both immense and obvious, were the principal influences both in the United States and in Colombia, and when the Colombian government balked, it was Bunau-Varilla more than anyone else who brought off the revolution in Panama. John Hay let Roosevelt know that he preferred Nicaragua; so did Senator John T. Morgan, chairman of the Senate subcommittee on the proposed canal. But Cromwell and Bunau-Varilla were indefatigable in their lobbying, both in the Senate and in the White House. Aided powerfully and for somewhat obscure reasons by Senator Mark Hanna, they made their cause prevail. Indeed, it would be no great stretch of the truth to say that Cromwell and Bunau-Varilla acted while Roosevelt acquiesced.

Both Cromwell and Bunau-Varilla had access to the most influential people in the government. The former was a partner in an eminent Wall Street law firm so well connected with high finance that no Republican President—or perhaps Democratic, for that matter—could afford to ignore him. In any case, he was the legal agent for the company that owned the isthmian railroad and the rights to build a Panama canal. If there were to be negotiations with the company, they would be with Cromwell. And Cromwell was accommodating: when a presidential commission examined the properties in Panama and placed their value at $40 million, Cromwell hastily reduced earlier demands to fit this estimate. In the end this was the sum actually paid by the United States; Cromwell's fee was $800,000. As for the Frenchman, Bunau-Varilla, he seems to have been a remarkable combination of sincere idealist, plunger, and practical businessman. As a young subordinate engineer under de Lesseps, he conceived a vision of the East and the West opened to each other by the two great canals his superior would build—Suez, already built, and Panama. When the company failed, Bunau-Varilla, who had been promoted to chief engineer, determined that he would somehow take over the project and make it succeed. And presently he became the company's and the canal's leading propagandist. In the end he fomented the Panamanian revolution—and became first Panamanian Minister to the United States!

The terms of Hay's treaty with Colombia were not only originally suggested by Cromwell and Bunau-Varilla in a series of conferences with Secretary Hay in the summer of 1902, but the first draft was actually written by Cromwell. The Colombian Minister, Concha, anxious to please the President, was apparently prepared to agree to anything. But when, uninvited, the United States landed some marines in Panama to keep the isthmian railroad open during a short-lived insurrection, Concha was angered and refused to go ahead with the treaty. Nothing further could be done until a new envoy, sent at Hay's urgent request, took over.

Minister Herran was also accommodating. The treaty provided for American control in perpetuity over what was later to become the Canal Zone, though Colombian sovereignty was formally recognized, and the United States agreed to pay $10 million plus $250,000 a year. These figures were suggested by Bunau-Varilla. In a separate transaction, the United States would pay the $40 million to the Panama Canal Company.

This treaty entirely satisfied the President and was sent to the Senate, where, despite opposition from Morgan, it was ratified on March 17, 1903. Thereafter ensued a long period of waiting to see what the government of Colombia would do. The country at that time was under the dictatorial control of President Marroquin. This gentleman, apparently annoyed that his government was not to get a share of the payment to the canal company, decided not to act on his own but to convene a Congress for the purpose. His government was able to make sure that the Congress would reject the treaty as unacceptable to a "sovereign nation," confident that the United States would raise the bid.

Roosevelt, already impatient, and learning from Hay the procedure in Colombia would probably produce a negative response, was enraged. When the United States Minister in Colombia reported that the press in Bogota was bitterly against "the attempt of a stronger nation to take advantage of Colombia," the President began to talk of "those contemptible little creatures in Bogota." They had no right to reject a treaty already signed in good faith! Not long before he had asserted categorically, in connection with the Hay-Pauncefote Treaty, that the United States was never bound by a treaty until ratified by the Senate. Colombia, it now appeared, was not entitled to invoke this principle. T.R. instructed Hay to bring every pressure on Colombia. As he wrote to Hanna, he would "warn these cat-rabbits that great though our patience has been, it can be exhausted." Hay, following the instruction of the President, ordered the United States Minister to say to the Colombian government that rejection of the treaty might cause Congress to take action "next winter which every friend of Colombia would regret."[41]

Meanwhile Roosevelt received an interesting memorandum from Professor John Bassett Moore of Columbia University, a former Assistant Secretary of State, that argued that under the treaty of 1846 with New Granada, the predecessor state to Colombia, the United States might well be justified in building the canal in Panama without a new treaty. Moore quoted Secretary of State Lewis Cass in 1858 as an authoritative interpreter of the 1846 treaty and of established United States policy:

Sovereignty has its duties as well as its rights, and none of these local governments, even if administered with more regard to the just demands of other nations than they have been, would be permitted, in a spirit of Eastern isolation, to close the gates of intercourse of the great highways of the world, and justify the act by the pretension that these avenues of trade and travel belong to them and that they choose to shut them, or, what is almost equivalent, to encumber them with such unjust relations as would prevent their general use.

If, under the law of nations as well as under the 1846 treaty, the United States could maintain rights of passage, Moore argued, it could build a canal as well as defend a railroad. Roosevelt ever afterwards cited the Cass pronouncement and the Moore memorandum in justification of what he expected to do, but never in fact did—send Congress a message asking authority to go ahead with the canal despite Colombian rejection of the treaty. For example, he wrote to Hanna, "I feel we are certainly justified in morals, and therefore justified in law, under the treaty of 1846, in interfering summarily and saying that the canal is to be built and that they must not stop it." In this view Roosevelt was strongly encouraged by his advisors. Bunau-Varilla, pressing the President through Moore, warned that a year's delay (requested by Colombia) would put Roosevelt in the position of campaigning "before the people without a solution of the canal problem." Cromwell, for his part, wrote the President, "Your virile and masterful policy will prove the solution of this great problem." The policy was embodied in the proposed message:

. . . The interest of international commerce generally and the interests of this country generally demands that the canal should be begun with no needless delay. The refusal of Colombia properly to respond to our sincere and earnest efforts to come to an agreement, or to pay heed to the many concessions we have made, renders it in my judgment necessary that the United States should take immediate action on one of two lines: either we should drop the Panama Canal project and immediately begin work on the Nicaraguan Canal, or else we should purchase all the rights of the French company, and, without any further parley with Colombia, enter upon the completion of the canal which the French company has begun. I feel that the latter course is the one demanded by the interests of this Nation. . . .[42]

But Bunau-Varilla, now become a Panamanian activist, evidently believed that a treaty with an independent Panama was greater security for his beloved canal than even the swagger of the American President. Making common cause with an old Panamanian rebel, Manuel Amador, and relying on Roosevelt's determination to keep the isthmus open to international transit, Bunau-Varilla arranged for an insurrection. Though Bogota had advance notice that there would be an uprising, the soldiers dispatched to deal with it were either neutralized or bribed to join it, and on November 3, without bloodshed, the Republic of Panama was proclaimed.

When Roosevelt received the news from American naval officers who were "protecting" the isthmus, he immediately told Hay to recognize the rebel government. In the Cabinet, the President facetiously observed, "I simply lifted my foot." "Oh Mr. President," responded Attorney-General Philander Knox, "do not let so great an achievement suffer from any taint of legality." Though Roosevelt and Hay certainly knew that the insurrection

228 *The American Presidency*

was coming, there is in fact no good evidence of American complicity.[43]

Amador became President of Panama. Apparently after some hesitation, he appointed Bunau-Varilla as Panamanian Minister to the United States. The new Minister presented his credentials to the President on November 13. His principal service as negotiator for the new republic was to revise Hay's draft of a treaty to make sure that all of the $40 million indemnity went to the Panama Canal Company, instead of permitting his new country to have a share, as Hay proposed. On November 18, fifteen days after the Revolution, the treaty was signed. Roosevelt had his way.

That the Panama Treaty was popular, that Roosevelt's partisans applauded his vigor in forwarding the canal project, cannot be questioned. In the campaign of 1904 Roosevelt made his Panama policy a major issue. To the committee notifying him of his nomination by the Republican National Convention he sounded his theme:

We conducted the negotiation for its [the canal's] construction with the nicest and most scrupulous honor, and in a spirit of the largest generosity toward those through whose territory it was to run. Every sinister effort which could be devised by the spirit of faction or the spirit of self-interest was made in order to defeat the treaty with Panama and thereby prevent the consummation of this work. The construction of the Canal is now an assured fact; but most certainly it is unwise to intrust the carrying out of so momentous a policy to those who have endeavored to defeat the whole undertaking.

Later in the campaign he began the practice of questioning the honesty of any who were doubtful about his "generosity" to either Colombia or Panama and, indeed, any who ventured to criticize his Panama policy at all. His opponents, he said, "attack [his policies or acts] only when they have first misrepresented them; for a truthful recital would leave no room for adverse comment." In his autobiography Roosevelt demeaned himself, perhaps, more than his critics by still more intemperate language. "Criticism," he said, ". . . can come only from misinformation, or else from a sentimentality which represents both mental weakness and a moral twist."

Roosevelt's victory in 1904 was clear-cut. In part no doubt he

benefitted from a deep split in the Democratic Party and the ineffective campaign of Judge Parker. But there was nevertheless
certainly a strong endorsement of T.R.'s policies, including Panama. Partisan popularity enabled the President to put through
his program despite doubts in Congress among members of his
own party, penetrating criticism from anti-imperialist liberals,
and the acute discomfort of his own Secretary of State. A remarkable letter to Hay from N. T. Bacon reveals how unhappy the
Secretary must have been throughout the proceedings his office
required him to conduct. In November or December of 1903,
Bacon recalled, he had spent an evening alone with Hay talking
about Panama and related matters. In that private conversation
Hay told Bacon that "the Nicaraguan route was preferable" and
that, in fact, "his personal sentiment was against the construction
of either canal." Bacon wished to publish his letter during the
campaign of 1904 so that Hay would be removed from the political firing line. Hay, as a loyal servant of Roosevelt, of course declined the favor.

But Roosevelt's vindication at the polls is no demonstration of
his wisdom. Indeed, one of the discouraging lessons to be learned
from the study of presidential leadership is that while partisan
popularity is certainly the most effective tool in a President's kit,
it is only a tool, only a means for getting something done. Popular support of the President is no guarantee of either popular or
presidential wisdom. The line between popular partisanship and
demagoguery is a fine one, and neither Roosevelt nor any of the
other great partisans always perfectly identified it. As recent Presidents would no doubt agree, the wisest contemporaneous comment on T.R.'s Panama "success" was Hay's frank statement to
the President that the treaty was "vastly advantageous to the
United States, and we must confess, with what face we can
muster, not so advantageous to Panama."[44]

5. *Unpartisan Presidents in action on foreign affairs: Monroe's patience and persistence succeed in Latin America and
acquire Florida* ᘒᕍ The bland character of Monroe's administration, viewed in terms of domestic achievement, is heavily
compensated, of course, by his sponsorship of the nearly permanent

United States foreign policy that bears his name—and contrasts sharply and happily with T.R.'s on Panama. The Monroe Doctrine, on which the American people were as united as they had been on the President's candidacy for a second term, grew out of complex circumstances that have often been studied and chronicled. For the present purpose it is enough to notice that, even though British backing was assured, it was a bold pronouncement for a young nation to make and it displayed the firmness with which a popular but unpartisan President can act when his course is not divisive. To establish such a policy required the support of the nation, which he had, and, though he sought the advice of elder statesmen Jefferson and Madison, he did not hesitate. Thus Monroe found the foreign field quite different from the domestic. The nearly universal respect and acceptance which persuaded him to avoid domestic action that might set section against section or class against class gave him the confidence to act, even against strong political opposition, when it was a question of the nation as against the rest of the world. And the popularity of the Monroe Doctrine—become in later years a kind of mystic shibboleth—has served many Presidents, from Polk to Truman, Eisenhower, Kennedy, and Johnson, as an indispensable foundation upon which to build policies for their own times.

But Monroe's policy in regard to the revolutionary governments of Latin America, a policy that led to the peaceful acquisition of Florida and to the Monroe Doctrine itself, is a more instructive—and less-often noticed—instance of presidential leadership in foreign affairs than the historic doctrine upon which his fame rests. The problems involved were complex, and the pressures great. The country was not unified on the issue, and there was an articulate opposition with a potent and popular leader—Henry Clay. Principles and self-interest seemed to be at odds.

As set forth in 1816 by President Madison and Secretary of State Monroe, United States policy regarding the uprisings in Latin America was to maintain strict neutrality. A few days after his own inauguration President Monroe wrote to Richard Rush in London that the "disposition of the United States" was "to maintain impartial neutrality between the contending parties, & of a friendly disposition to Spain." There were two solid reasons for this disposition: (1) the United States was always anxious to avoid involvement in European wars or in the wars of European powers, and (2) the prospects of acquiring Florida by peaceful negotiation were good but would certainly be jeopardized by official American preference for the rebellious colonies of Spain. On the other hand, Monroe had himself had a bitter experience with the practices of delay and hypocrisy which the Spanish government normally followed. His failure, as Minister to Spain under Jefferson, to acquire Florida, or even to make a treaty that would pacify the Spanish-United States borders, was one of the more rankling of his numerous diplomatic frustrations. He intended, as President, to succeed.[45]

John Quincy Adams, Monroe's Secretary of State and a veteran diplomat, was a powerful ally in making and conducting the policy of neutrality and in handling the problem of recognition. Adams was seriously skeptical of the ability of the rebelling South American states to govern themselves. He favored independence as a matter of principle, and he was as anxious as anyone to get Spain out of the Western Hemisphere. But he was in no hurry. The independent governments being set up throughout the continent seemed to him little better than the Spanish colonial regimes had been. Thus his definition of neutrality in the revolutionary struggles was scrupulously correct according to the ancient precedents of the law of nations. "By the usual principles of international law," he wrote to Gallatin in Paris, "the state of *neutrality* recognizes the cause of both parties to the contest to be *just*—that is, avoids all consideration of the *merits* of the contest."[46]

President Monroe was more responsive to the cause of the rebels, both because as the elected chief executive he had perforce to listen to public opinion, which was enthusiastically for the rebels, and because his own lifelong revolutionary principles had been invoked in the Latin-American uprisings.

Monroe formally opened the question of recognition of the rebel states in a Cabinet meeting in October, 1817, putting to his colleagues a series of questions for their advice: (1) Did the President have power to acknowledge the independence of new states when the parent country does not and while civil war is going on?

(2) Does sending a minister constitute recognition? (3) Would it be "expedient" for the United States to recognize one or more of the rebel states? (4) What ought to be United States policy toward Spain, in view of her unwillingness to settle outstanding claims and disputes? (5) Ought the United States to "break up the Amelia Island establishment"? (6) Ought the President to send a commission to South America to study the progress of the revolution and report on its prospects, country by country? The decisions taken on these questions were to postpone recognition, send no ministers, continue negotiations with Spain, take over Amelia Island (a pirate nest pretending to be under rebel governments), and send the commissioners. The decision on Amelia Island was difficult, as it was well known to be a station for privateers assisting the South American rebels; but it was also a base for depredations against American commerce. The President's decision was certain to provoke the indignation of the friends in Congress of immediate recognition—Speaker Henry Clay and his band of oppositionists.[47]

And so it did, as did the decision to send commissioners to investigate. Clay, as an ardent friend of the South American revolution, had been sought out by Aguirre, agent for the Buenos Aires rebel government and spokesman in Washington for South American independence, and the two men constituted a high-level lobby in Congress and the State Department. Clay objected to the commission because it seemed to undercut Aguirre, and he opposed the Amelia Island operation as giving aid and comfort to Spain. In March, in a speech in the House, Clay delivered himself of a characteristic piece of impassioned oratory, signalling the kind of emotional response he sought to stir up against the President's policy:

Mr. Clay said he was no propagandist. He would not seek to force upon other nations our principles and our liberty, if they did not want them. He would not disturb the repose even of a detestable despotism. But if an abused and oppressed people willed their freedom; if they sought to establish it, we had a right, as a sovereign power, to notice the fact, and to act as circumstances and our interest required. He would say, in the language of the venerated father of his country, "Born in a land of liberty, my anxious recollections, my sympathetic feelings, and my best wishes, are irresistibly excited, whensoever, in any country, I see an oppressed nation unfurl the banners of freedom." For his own part, Mr. C. said, that whenever he thought of Spanish America, the image irresistibly forced itself upon his mind of an elder brother, whose education had been neglected, whose person had been abused and maltreated, and who had been disinherited by the unkindness of an unnatural parent. And, when he contemplated the glorious struggle which that country was now making, he thought he beheld that brother rising, by the power and energy of his fine native genius, to the manly rank which nature, and nature's God intended for him.

Clay's course thereafter was to make just this sort of propaganda whenever a likely occasion presented itself and to tack amendments onto Administration bills that would embarrass the President and, if carried, force his hand on recognition. But the President's backing in Congress, and in the nation, was too strong, and Clay's measures were consistently defeated by substantial margins.[48]

The President himself was probably at least as devoted a supporter of South American independence as was Clay. On one occasion he even suggested in the Cabinet that ways might be found to supply arms to the rebels by unofficial government action. Adams recorded the episode in his diary:

The President proposed for consideration the question, upon the proposal of Manuel Torres [a rebel agent] that the Government should sell upon credit to the Republic of Colombia, any number short of twenty thousand stand of arms, to enable them to extend the South American Revolution into Peru and Mexico. By one of those backstair proceedings which I often feel without seeing, a report has been made from the Ordnance Department to the Secretary of War, just at the critical moment, that there are some thousand stand of English arms which might with advantage to the public service be sold.

It is unlikely that Monroe himself was privy to the arrangement Adams suspected—backstair transactions were the last in which Monroe was likely to be found. But he thought well enough of the idea to pose it for the advice of the Cabinet. Adams argued that such a decision would be a flagrant violation of neutrality and give mortal offense to Spain. He was certainly right on the latter point, if not on the former, and in any case Monroe decided against the plan. But the incident reveals the conflict in his mind, like many a President after him, between adherence to his life-long revolutionary anticolonial principles and the immediate interests of the United States. The President must have envied Clay, who could speak so freely without being held accountable. Monroe, however, could and did take consolation in the fact that his countrymen, in private and illegal transactions, were supplying most of the rebel arms. Indeed, this illicit traffic was an important part of his policy.[49]

The arms-selling incident in the Cabinet took place in 1820, but Monroe had had to discipline himself from the beginning to make sure that his principles did not break out of the control his policy required. In a remarkable confidential letter to his son-in-law George Hay, in September, 1818, Monroe discussed his recognition policy as he intended to state it in his forthcoming annual message:

Should it [the decision about to be taken] be against an immediate recognition, under the apprehension that it may produce war & sacrifice our commerce & revenue, & risk even our government, without a prospect of rendering any service to the Colonies, I shall, as I presume, take an attitude the most friendly to the Colonies, by speaking as well of their means as the report [of the U. S. Commissioners to South America] will justify; of the utter incompetency of Spain to subdue them; of the injury which the continuance of the controversy does to the commerce of all nations, & add, in a tone of interrogation, how long will other powers bear the continuance of a contest fraught with so much annoyance & loss to them.

Adams, of course, opposed the use of such strong language. But Monroe finally decided against it for a different reason—word from the conference of the European powers at Aix-la-Chapelle that an attempt would be made to mediate between Spain and her colonies and that no force would be applied to bring about a settlement. In the message as he sent it to Congress, Monroe limited himself to reporting the extent to which the South American rebels had established independent governments and underlining his "satisfaction" with the news from Europe "because it is a course more consistent with justice." He restated his policy with calculated ambiguity:

From the view taken of this subject, founded on all the information that we have been able to obtain, there is good cause to be satisfied with the course heretofore pursued by the United States in regard to this contest, and to conclude that it is proper to adhere to it, especially in the present state of affairs.[50]

Henry Clay could not have agreed less. Adhering to established policy meant not only neutrality but nonrecognition, pending a settlement with Spain. That Monroe made no effort to stop the substantial illegal arms traffic between the United States and South America—preferring not to be informed on the subject—was much too little for Clay. He presently took up the cause of Aguirre's successor in Washington, an adventurer named David Charles DeForest who had gone out from Connecticut to make a fortune in running arms and outfitting privateers for the rebel governments of South America. In the winter of 1818–1819 he was representing the government of Buenos Aires. With Clay's warm endorsement, DeForest pressed for recognition as consul-general for that embryonic Latin American republic.

Clay's influence was sufficient to get a resolution through the House in January, 1819, asking the President whether any independent government in South America had asked for recognition of a minister or consul-general, and if so, requesting that the papers in the matter be submitted for inspection. Secretary Adams complied with the request. DeForest had applied, Adams reported, and had been refused, since recognizing him as consul-general would imply recognition of his government. Similarly, the President had refused to recognize one Clemente from Venezuela. Clay and his friends professed indignation at the "news." For his part, Adams noted in his diary quite correctly that "the call is made for the purpose of baiting the Administration." The Secretary, as he often did, mistakenly took the matter personally. The Clay group, he told himself, were "especially" anxious to fasten "upon the Secretary of State the odium of refusing to receive South American Ministers and Consuls-General."

But if Adams was overly preoccupied with self-defense, he certainly knew how to handle DeForest, much to Clay's disgust. Calling in the would-be South American diplomat, Adams pointed out that as a citizen of Connecticut, DeForest was liable to prosecution for violation of the neutrality laws of the United States. DeForest did not even ask what evidence there was against him. Instead he immediately changed his position, announcing that the Administration was correct in its policy of nonrecognition coupled with informal friendship. He even told Adams that Clay's opposition had done the cause of the rebelling governments more harm than good! Thus ended the DeForest episode.

And in a few days the Clay opposition also ended, or should have ended, because the Monroe policy paid off in the long-awaited deal with Spain. A treaty was concluded in which Spain ceded Florida and settled the frontier from the Gulf of Mexico to the Pacific.[51]

But Spain refused to ratify the treaty, chiefly because it contained no guarantee that the United States would not recognize the rebel governments. And so Clay was in business again. He denounced the President's policy as weak because it sought, as would be said in the twentieth century, to "appease" the Spanish monarchy instead of standing forthrightly with the Spanish republicans in South America. Adams, too, was unhappy with Monroe, for the opposite reason. The treaty, he felt, had been refused in Madrid because the President was too friendly to the rebels.

The reaction of the President, confirmed rather than suggested by consultation with Adams and others in his Cabinet and with his friends, Jefferson and Madison, was to ask Congress in his annual message (December 7, 1819) for authority to settle the matter according to the terms of the treaty whether Spain liked it or not—in short, to take over Florida by force. The treaty itself, Monroe asserted, ought to have been ratified by the Spanish government, since it had been negotiated in accord with the Spanish Minister's instructions. "A treaty concluded in conformity with instructions," he said, "is obligatory, in good faith, in all its stipulations." In rejecting the Florida treaty, he continued, "the Government of Spain has rendered to the United States a new and very serious injury." Under the circumstances, direct action was fully justified:

. . . It is submitted to the consideration of Congress whether it will not be proper for the United States to carry the conditions of the treaty into effect in the same manner as if it had been ratified by Spain

. . . By pursuing this course we shall rest on the sacred ground of right. . . .

If there is a certain parallel between this response to Spain's calculated vacillation looking to greater advantage from the United States, and Theodore Roosevelt's threatened treatment of Colombia some eighty years later, it is a parallel that ends abruptly. There was no convenient revolution to overthrow the power which would not accept the terms of the United States, such as enabled Roosevelt to put his policy into effect, and Spain, in any case, was a colonial power, not an independent republic. Nor did Monroe in fact change his policy of negotiation. When Spain sent a new envoy to try for better terms, the Congressional authorization for Monroe to occupy Florida was a powerful influence on the outcome. It never had to be used: Spain ratified a new treaty, and on February 22, 1821, the treaty was ratified by the Senate with only four negative votes. Adams made this amusing entry in his diary:

[The four who voted negatively were] Brown of Louisiana, who married a sister of Clay's wife; Richard M. Johnson of Kentucky, against his own better judgement, from mere political subserviency to Clay; Williams of Tennessee, from party impulses, connected with hatred of General Jackson; and Trimble of Ohio, from some maggot in the brain, the cause of which I do not yet perfectly know.[52]

In the wake of the treaty Monroe had only to grant recognition to the various governments of South America when he was convinced of their stability and when he believed that recognition would serve a useful purpose. The popularity of the settlement with Spain was so great that Clay's opposition forthwith melted into an innocuous resolution that Congress would "give its constitutional support to the President of the United States, whenever he may deem it expedient to recognize the sovereignty and independence of any of the South American republics."[53]

The President "deemed it expedient" in March, 1822. By this time rebellions were clearly successful in at least five states, stable governments were in power, and the danger of a resurgence of Spanish political influence or military strength was past. In a special message to Congress, Monroe briefly reviewed the history of the rebellions, pointing out that "through the whole of this

contest the United States have remained neutral, and have fulfilled with the utmost inpartiality all the obligations incident to
that character." He did not, of course, remind the Congress of
what it well knew—that the United States government had been
informally cordial and encouraging to the rebels from the beginning and that it had pursued a policy of lax enforcement of those
provisions of the neutrality laws that would seriously have
slowed down the flow of arms to the rebels. Now that independence was assured, it was time to admit these new states to the
family of nations. "When the result of such a contest is manifestly
settled," said the President, "the new governments have a claim
to recognition by other powers which ought not to be resisted."
The Congress concurred by 167 to 1 in the House and 39 to 3 in
the Senate. And Colombia, Peru, Mexico, Chile, and Buenos
Aires were forthwith recognized.[54]

The President's unpopular means of carrying out popular
policy thus brought the results for which he had hoped and, in
another year, made possible the Monroe Doctrine. It took five
years, many irritating political battles at home, and long, patient,
and frustrating negotiations by Adams and United States Ministers. But Monroe's opposition never was able to place enough
pressure on the President to force him to modify his course. The
public generally trusted the old man in the White House, and
the President relied on their trust.

In domestic matters, at the very moment of the triumph of his
South American policy, Monroe's administration was almost a
shambles, as we have previously noted. The cutthroat competition among members of his Cabinet—and Speaker Clay—for the
right to succeed Monroe as President made governing almost
impossible. His popularity, like that of Eisenhower in another
era, was safe only so long as he kept aloof. He knew it well, and
did so. If he had some small preference for Crawford over the
others, he was careful not to let it be known outside the "family"
of Jefferson, Madison, and a few other intimates. Nothing he said
could have been usefully quoted except, perhaps, his evident
opposition to Clay. Even Jackson, whose conduct in Florida had
greatly embarrassed the Administration, had no reason to doubt
the President's good will; Monroe, in fact, appointed him first
Governor of Florida. The President fumed in private about the

self-serving of his colleagues; in public he maintained his posture of impartiality and backed off further and further from the divisive issues.

But in foreign affairs it was a different matter. Secretary Adams was loyal and skillful. Public opinion was clear as to what the national objectives should be: (1) acquire Florida, (2) encourage and recognize the new states of South America, and (3) avoid getting into war. And so Monroe was able to act with firmness and persistence and to maintain a consistent policy without serious concern for his opposition. The decline of Spain in Europe weakened her in the Western Hemisphere, and American might had grown to a level the Spanish knew they could not resist. In the end, therefore, all of the American objectives were achieved. There had been some sentiment, it should be noted, for forcing Spain and Mexico to relinquish Texas to the United States. But the pressure at this time was not great, and Monroe, in any case, was opposed to it. He saw in such an acquisition only an exacerbation of the slavery problem that was boiling up over Missouri, and he had no desire to test the strength of the Union again so soon, if ever. If his policy was less forceful—less boastful, perhaps—than Polk's Mexican policy was to be a generation later, and no more successfully carried out, it may nevertheless have been wiser.

6. *Eisenhower retreats on free trade but advances on atomic energy* ⮡ The difficulties to be encountered by a popular, unpartisan President in making partisan foreign policy decisions were discovered by Dwight Eisenhower, the most popular of Monroe's unpartisan successors, almost immediately upon his taking the oath of office.

One of the convictions Eisenhower brought with him to the White House was that "free trade" was good for American business and good for the world. He was committed to urging renewal of the Reciprocal Trade Agreements Act and anxious that his Administration should do what it could to cut tariffs and otherwise encourage free international competition. The issue, of course, was sharply divisive, since segments of both business and labor still demanded protection. Emmet Hughes, a White House

assistant, kept notes of a series of Cabinet meetings in the spring
of 1953 that illustrate how ineffective was the President's leadership, in foreign as in domestic policy, when a problem, even if it
involved a principle to which he was committed, could not be
readily resolved by persuasion. Defense Secretary Charles Wilson
brought to the President's attention (March 6) the fact that a
British firm was low bidder, by a substantial percentage, on the
generators for the Chief Joseph Dam. Since American industry
very much wanted the contracts, Wilson wondered what the
President's views were. "Well, just shooting from the hip," said
the President, "I'd say to give the order to the British."

But the British did not get the contract. A week later the Cabinet considered the matter of raising the tariff on Italian briar
pipes. The small American pipe industry was putting what pressure it could on the government for protection against its Italian
competitors. Eisenhower acted on this matter without hesitation.
"Can't be done," he said, "at least not with Italian elections
soon." There was no mention of generators. But two weeks later
Wilson stated flatly that he would give that contract to an American firm. Under-Secretary of State Bedell Smith reacted strongly,
pointing out that the British were "watching this episode as a
serious test of whether Eisenhower means what he says about
freer trade." Wilson rejoined that he was under great pressure
from Senators on behalf of Westinghouse. "But I thought they
had just about all the business they could handle, no?" asked the
President. "Yeah," Wilson answered, "but they wouldn't mind at
all having this too." At the end of the meeting Wilson said he
"thinks" the verdict is for Westinghouse, and the President said
nothing.

The next week Secretary of State Dulles was present and spoke
out against snubbing the British. "If the *Executive* doesn't show
a strong lead in these trade questions, how in the world can you
expect Congress to go along with knocking down trade barriers?"
To this Wilson replied that many Senators were pressing him so
hard on this matter that he feared they would punish the Administration for an adverse decision on it by voting against the
Trade Agreements Bill. Hughes observed that though Vice-
President Nixon at this point sided with Dulles, the President
remained silent. Finally, Wilson said he would "double-check

the specifications to be sure the British will produce the same quality as the Americans."

At the meeting of April 10 Secretary Wilson produced a "solution" to the problem of the generators—he would start all over again with a new call for bids. From Dulles this announcement brought a blunt reaction. "I have an increasingly strong suspicion," he said, leaning across the President to face Wilson, "that the British are never going to get this contract." Wilson muttered something about "engineering complexity," but the President, Hughes recorded, seemed to acquiesce. "Well, all right Charley," he said, "but let's be sure the new specifications are really on the level—and not drawn so that *only* an American firm can meet them." Somewhat surprisingly, as Hughes notes, Presidential Assistant Sherman Adams interrupted to point out that "this all looks like a rather diabolical way of getting foreign bidders to tip their hands and letting American companies have a second chance to undercut them." Eisenhower, however, said nothing more. And, of course, the contracts went in the end to the Americans.[55]

This listless episode does not, fortunately, tell the whole story of Eisenhower's leadership on free trade. Years later, as he approached the end of his second term, and when the Congress was solidly Democratic, he appointed the Randall Commission and gave to its report—calling for tariff reductions and other devices to stimulate international trade—his full backing. On that occasion he called members of Congress personally and spoke frequently of the matter in his press conferences. But his refusal to act on the British bid for the Chief Joseph generators was in the earlier, more characteristic Eisenhower style.

Yet even in the early years of his administration Eisenhower could and did act decisively when he knew the nation was behind him. When the nation was divided on foreign policy, he avoided issues if he could. But because the people were nearly unanimous in the quest for peace, containing communism, and controlling nuclear weapons, Eisenhower sometimes felt a freedom to act in foreign policy that sharply contrasted with the constraint he felt in domestic matters. His "atoms for peace" proposal in 1953, perhaps the most enduring achievement of his administration, is a fair example of his nonpartisan leadership in the international field.

At the outset of his administration, Eisenhower was deeply anxious to find some way of breaking down the walls of prejudice and hate that marked the Cold War and made international peace seem like a utopian dream. As an old soldier he had seen enough of war to know that its horrors never really resolve the human problems that cause them. More than anything else he wished to make a place in history as a peacemaker. Hughes tells of a poignant conversation with the President only a few weeks after his inauguration. The occasion was the need to rethink American policy in the light of Stalin's death. "Look," said Eisenhower, "I am tired—and I think everyone is tired—of just plain indictments of the Soviet regime. I think it would be wrong —in fact, asinine—for me to get up before the world now to make another one of those indictments." Instead, he told Hughes, he wished to offer the Soviet Union, and the whole world, an opportunity to make a fresh start:

*Here* is what I would like to say.

The jet plane that roars over your head cost three quarters of a million dollars. That is more money than a man earning ten thousand dollars every year is going to make in his lifetime. What world can afford this sort of thing for long? We are in an armaments race. Where will it lead us? At worst, to atomic warfare. At best, to robbing every people and nation on earth of the fruits of their own toil. . . .

Now, there could be another road before us—the road of disarmament. What does it mean? It means for everybody in the world: bread, butter, clothes, homes, hospitals, schools—all the good and necessary things for decent living.

So let *this* be the choice we offer.

The President went on to say that he wished to do away with "double talk" and "sophisticated political formulas" and "slick propaganda devices." The "past," he said, "speaks for itself. I am interested in the future." Both the Soviet Union and the United States, he pointed out, had new governments. "The slate is clean. Now let us begin talking to each other. *And let us say what we've got to say so that every person on earth can understand it.*" Finally, he told Hughes, "this is what I want to say. And if we don't really have anything to offer, I'm not going to make a speech about it." When it was called to his attention that Secretary Dulles took a quite different view, Eisenhower was nevertheless insistent. "Now we either cut out all this fooling around and make a serious bid for peace," he said, "or we forget the whole thing." As the session ended, the President said, "You know it is *so* difficult. You come up to face these terrible issues, and you know that what is in almost everyone's heart is a wish for peace, and you want so much to do *something*. And then you wonder . . . if there really *is* anything you can do . . . by words and promises. . . . You wonder and you wonder." In those words Eisenhower spoke out of the loneliness of all American Presidents.

If the "slate" was not in fact "clean" as Eisenhower began his administration, he was at least so confident that the yearning for peace was nearly universal that he persisted in his purpose despite the opposition of his Secretary of State. And Dulles did object at every stage in the preparation of the speech the President decided to deliver. The burden of his comment was that Eisenhower was "falling in with the Soviet scheme of things"—a view presently—and noisily—shared by Senator Joseph R. McCarthy! One of the President's memorable responses on being told of Dulles' views was "Well, I know how he feels, but sometimes Foster is just too worried about being accused of sounding like Truman and Acheson. I think he worries too much about it."[56]

On April 16, 1953, before the American Society of Newspaper Editors, Eisenhower delivered his address, known afterwards as "Toward a Golden Age of Peace." It was a clear and forceful restatement of United States desire to work for a world rule of law. The President, starting with the wartime alliance of the West and the Soviet Union, traced the paths of divergence and regretted them. Then, stressing the willingness of the West always to "welcome sincerely any genuine evidence of peaceful purpose enabling all peoples again to resume their common quest for peace," he made the plea for disarmament that it had been his purpose from the beginning to make. The language, indeed, was similar to the impromptu address he had made to his assistant a month before.

Of his five proposals—limitation of the size of forces, limitation on production of strategic materials, international control of atomic energy, limitation of other categories of weapons, and United Nations inspection—the third was to bulk largest in the

President's mind. But at the moment he had no specific proposal
to offer on atomic energy. It took seven months to move from
the generalizations of the April speech to an international atomic
energy program.[57]

The President assigned a special assistant, C. D. Jackson, to
study the problem and draft a speech on it, giving him authority
to consult anyone and everyone. Jackson and his colleagues "produced draft after draft," Eisenhower recalls in his memoirs. "But
when they had finished, Jackson and I agreed that the exposition
left the listener with only a new terror, not a new hope." According to Sherman Adams, Jackson "found his service in Washington
a frustrating experience generally." Not the least of these frustrations were those he encountered in talking to people, in many
agencies, about the atomic energy problem. Nothing, in fact,
ever did come of his efforts, except the skilled phrasing of a great
speech.[58]

For it was the President himself who hit upon "atoms for
peace." Sherman Adams suggests that it was the Russian explo-
sion of a hydrogen bomb that stimulated the President to develop
his policy. Eisenhower himself recalls that he began to think
about it when he realized that nothing creative was emerging
from the efforts of his staff. "One day I hit upon the idea of
actual physical donations of isotopes from our then-unequalled
nuclear stockpile, to a common fund for peaceful purposes." By
September he had formulated a program and determined to make
a speech on it before the United Nations. On September 10 he
took up the idea with Robert Cutler, Special Assistant for National Security Affairs, and issued instructions for staff work on
the speech. "Within minutes after [Cutler] left my office," Eisenhower writes, "he was writing to Lewis Strauss [Chairman of the
Atomic Energy Commission]: 'The President suggested that you
might consider the following proposal which he did not think
anyone had yet thought of. . . . Suppose the United States and
the Soviets were to turn over to the United Nations, for peaceful
uses, X kilograms of fissionable matter. . . .' "

With this idea Cutler, Strauss, and Jackson set to work, and
Ambassador Henry Cabot Lodge was directed to make arrange-
ments for the President to address the General Assembly of the
United Nations in December. But the speech did not grow easily.

Jackson, who was in charge of the project, found many of the same difficulties Hughes had found earlier in the year in preparing the address to the newspaper editors: Dulles feared the President would play into the hands of the Soviets; Strauss was doubtful about giving up nuclear materials, and some members of the Republican Congressional leadership thought Eisenhower was going too far. Before he had satisfied everybody and delivered the semifinal version to the President, Jackson had done thirty-three versions of the speech. The President himself then took it up and produced the text that he actually gave. The last stage was hectic; in fact the text was still being revised as the President flew from Washington to New York to deliver it. As he finished each sheet, he passed it to Dulles, Strauss, and Jackson, in turn, and the last man gave it to the stenographer to type. The stencils were then mimeographed for distribution to the press when the plane arrived at New York. They did not quite make their deadline, and the pilot had to circle for fifteen minutes to give the President and his staff time to finish the job, "only minutes before delivery of the speech," Eisenhower recalled.

In his memoirs Eisenhower gives the core of the speech:

To hasten the day when fear of the atom will begin to disappear from the minds of the people . . . there are certain steps that can be taken now.

I therefore make the following proposals:

The governments principally involved, to the extent permitted by elementary prudence, to begin now and continue to make joint contributions from their stockpiles of normal uranium and fissionable materials to an International Atomic Energy Agency. We would expect that such an agency would be set up under the aegis of the United Nations. . . .

Undoubtedly initial and early contributions to this plan would be small in quantity. However, the proposal has the great virtue that it can be undertaken without the irritations and mutual suspicions incident to any attempt to set up a completely acceptable system of world-wide inspection and control.

The [World] Atomic Energy Agency could be made responsible for the impounding, storage, and protection of the contributed fissionable and other materials. The ingenuity of our scientists will provide special safe conditions under which such a bank of fissionable material can be made essentially immune to surprise seizure.

The more important responsibility of this Atomic Energy Agency would be to devise methods whereby this fissionable material would be allocated to serve the peaceful pursuits of mankind. Experts would be mobilized to apply atomic energy to the needs of agriculture, medicine, and other peaceful activities. A special purpose would be to provide abundant electrical energy in the power-starved areas of the world. Thus the contributing powers would be dedicating some of their strength to serve the needs rather than the fears of mankind.[59]

Eisenhower knew in advance that his proposals would be well received by the British, since he had spoken of his plan at the Bermuda conference with Churchill and Eden only a short while before. But he was not, perhaps, fully prepared for the worldwide chorus of approval that followed the ovation accorded him at the United Nations. Even the Soviet Union was no more than skeptical in its initial reaction, and the smaller nations, the neutrals, and the Western allies were uniformly enthusiastic.

But more important, of course, than reaction was the action that followed. The General Assembly, at its session in 1954, adopted a resolution favoring the creation of such an agency as Eisenhower had proposed and established an international committee to plan it. In October, 1956, the plan of the committee was unanimously approved by an eighty-one-nation conference, and in July, 1957, the International Atomic Energy Agency came into being. With headquarters in Vienna, the IAEA had received (as of 1965) several hundred tons of uranium and other nuclear materials and a number of research reactors (estimated to be worth some $100 million), awarded fellowships, and published learned papers on topics ranging from safety measures in handling fissionable materials to medicinal uses. Measured against the potentials of nuclear energy for the service of mankind, the achievement of the early years of the agency was, of course, small. But measured against the nearly endless frustrations and failures of international relations in the mid-twentieth century, its achievement—and Eisenhower's—was immense.

And there can be no doubt that it was Eisenhower's achievement. Although the United States under President Truman had offered to share its nuclear monopoly with the United Nations (the Baruch Plan of 1947), conditions in the intervening years had entirely altered. The Baruch plan had been rejected by the

Russians precisely because they wished to break the American monopoly. Their success, as well as the success of the British, had created the deadly nuclear arms race Eisenhower hoped to impede. Partisan politics interfered, in 1956, with efforts to reach an agreement to ban nuclear testing. But the test-ban treaty finally approved by President Kennedy in 1963—despite divided public opinion—first became a possibility when President Eisenhower made his "atoms for peace" offer ten years before.

Eisenhower's response to the world's yearning for relief from nuclear terror was both creative and sustained. In developing and projecting his international nuclear energy policy he was buoyed by his confidence in the unity of the American people, not hesitant because they were divided. The issue was unpartisan and nonpartisan so that his action could be wholly consonant with his public image—indeed, it was in a way necessary to the maintenance of that image. His experience poses once more a fundamental question all popular Presidents must face: how far is it desirable—or feasible—to press domestic policies and programs that are divisive in view of the imperative need for "national unity" in the continuing international crises of the modern era? Eisenhower believed that "unity" should be the overriding concern of the President. Over and over again he abandoned, or modified into inconsequence, policies and proposals to which he had had some degree of attachment or commitment, when it appeared that his image as the unifying figure of the country would be diminished by persistence. Even in foreign affairs, when decisive action would have had divisive effects at home, he vacillated or simply stepped aside, leaving the decision to others. Whether he could have taken positive positions on such issues, alienating some while winning the partisan support of others, and yet led the nation and the world in the effort to control the atom cannot, of course, be known for certain. But a comment of Walter Lippmann—not on Eisenhower but on Lyndon Johnson —seems remarkably appropriate:

When [Johnson] tells his visitors that the "ice is very thin," although the polls show that he has overwhelming popular support [on the Vietnam problem] the skepticism does not arise because he has a silly yearning to have everybody agree with him. The President's skepticism arises because he is wise in the ways of politics. Once the shooting starts, any and every President can count on a big majority. "My country right or wrong."

Dwight Eisenhower was not, on his own testimony at any rate, "wise in the ways of politics"—partisan or not. It may be instructive, at the conclusion of these studies, to examine an instance of leadership in foreign policy by a President at once popular and partisan, grasping the thorniest nettle of danger in the world of the 1960's.

7. *Lyndon Johnson cloaks a controversial policy in Vietnam in a soothing politics of consensus to add a new dimension to the process of presidential leadership* ஜ In the same article Walter Lippmann went on to say:

What matters to the President is the indisputable fact that in the big majority who support him in the polls today, there is deep doubt and anxiety about the course we are taking. This is why he knows the ice is very thin.

Johnson, one can hardly escape observing, did not hesitate to skate on the thin ice when there was no other way to cross the pond. He inherited the Vietnam crisis along with the Presidency when John Kennedy was assassinated on November 22, 1963; Kennedy, for his part, had inherited the involvement of the United States in South Vietnam affairs from his predecessor, Dwight Eisenhower.

In the winter of 1953–1954 President Eisenhower decided, with some misgiving, against going directly to the aid of the French in their struggle with the Indo-Chinese Communists. Pressed by his Secretary of State, the Vice-President, the Chairman of the Joint Chiefs of Staff and many others, Eisenhower nevertheless decided against American participation. He feared it was already too late when the French asked for help. Because the French were unwilling to give unconditional guarantees of Indo-Chinese independence once the fighting had stopped, Eisenhower also was strongly opposed to involving the United States on the side of empire in what thus seemed to be a colonial rebellion. But after the Geneva settlement establishing North and South Vietnam,

Cambodia, and Laos as separate nations, Eisenhower quickly offered American assistance to South Vietnam, an infant non-Communist and pro-Western country. From 1954 to 1959 United States aid was chiefly economic, though American military experts trained a South Vietnamese army to maintain the nation's security. Despite early successes in stabilizing the government and improving economic conditions, South Vietnam had by 1959 to face resurgence of Communist guerrilla warfare. By 1961 the situation was serious.

At this juncture President Kennedy took the decision to send substantial American military equipment to South Vietnam and to provide advisers to accompany Vietnamese troops in the field. The Communist Viet Cong nevertheless continued to make bloody progress and gradually gained control, with direct and indirect help from North Vietnam, of great areas of rural South Vietnam.

When Lyndon Johnson assumed responsibility for American policy in Southeast Asia, the options had agonizingly narrowed. To most observers it appeared that the Viet Cong was slowly but surely winning the war. The Communist world—except perhaps for the Soviet Union—was enthusiastically backing the guerrillas. The Chinese, in particular, were conducting a massive propaganda campaign in favor of the "National Liberation Front" and against the American "imperialists." Many, indeed most, of the new nations of Africa and Asia shared the Chinese view at least to some degree. In the West no one was happy. The French gave the United States no support, calling instead for "neutralization" of the whole of Southeast Asia, while other allies, like Great Britain, were uneasy and lukewarm in their endorsement of United States policy. Only Thailand, fearing it would be next on the Chinese agenda, the Philippines, Australia, New Zealand, and Malaysia were emphatically in favor of the American Intervention to support South Vietnam. At home the new President was made uncomfortably aware of a growing sentiment for getting out of the area, or at least offering to negotiate some kind of settlement that would facilitate withdrawal. Among the more articulate critics of American policy were some prominent members of the President's own party in the Senate, including Mike Mansfield, the Majority Leader, and William Fulbright, Chair-

man of the Foreign Relations Committee. On the other hand,
there was also a chorus calling for a greater American effort, even
an escalation of the war that might lead to a "confrontation"
with China.

Thus the new President was presented with a kind of either/or
proposition: get out or get much farther in. Unwilling to accept
so irrational a set of alternatives, Johnson for months postponed
making a new decision. Better, his steady build-up of support for
the South Vietnam government was itself a kind of decision—a
decision not, in any event, to withdraw. As if the military situation were not grave enough, Johnson had also to reckon with
unbelievable instability in the government of South Vietnam.
Coup followed coup as military cliques and Buddhist leaders
fought each other more effectively than either fought the Communists. It is hard to recall any comparable episode in which an
American President had to maintain a wartime alliance—and
his own patience—with a government so unreliable.

And Johnson had also to conduct an election campaign. His
opponent, Senator Barry Goldwater, made Vietnam a major
issue, calling in every speech for stronger measures—even suggesting the use of nuclear weapons. Recognizing it as both
inescapable and divisive, the President dealt with the issue with
characteristic caution. Without shirking his responsibility to explain the Administration's course in Vietnam, but frequently
allowing the news of United States actions to speak instead of
words, Johnson based his campaign on his vision of a "Great
Society," a campaign in which domestic issues and policies predominated. In the end he succeeded in building a massive coalition, much like that led by Franklin D. Roosevelt in the 1930's,
which rejected Goldwater's excited approach to Vietnam while
endorsing limited involvement under Johnson's leadership. But
the coalition was certainly more interested in the President's
domestic program—and more confident of it.

Johnson, in the months following his election, appeared to
read the returns as reflecting a popular conviction, like his own,
that the United States should continue the fight against Communism, a conviction accompanied by equally popular confusion
and uncertainty as to how it should be done, or even whether it
could be done successfully. In short, he had no mandate to pur-

sue a decisive course. Whatever he decided to do would certainly sharpen the division of American opinion. There was no way, had he wished to find one, of escaping the burden of decision and so maintaining his popularity intact. The popularity he had he would have to risk.

That the President would persist in South Vietnam was never in doubt. The degree to which he would press was revealed in February, 1965, when, in retaliation for strikes on an American base and terrorist bombing of the American embassy in Saigon, Johnson ordered air attacks on the North Vietnam source of Viet Cong strength. The bombings produced precisely the expected developments in American and world opinion: the lines hardened. The Soviet Union, until then uncomfortably trying to sit out the crisis, joined its voice to the Chinese propaganda campaign and pledged all kinds of support to North Vietnam and the Viet Cong. The neutrals expressed shock and dismay. The allies were still more greatly disconcerted. One segment of American opinion deplored the "escalation" and demanded that the President withdraw as quickly as possible, while another segment cheered because action was at last being taken against the "real enemy." Students marched, demonstrated, and demanded in many parts of the world, including the United States. At the diplomatic level, seventeen neutral nations appealed to the contending powers to negotiate a settlement.

A third voice was more and more heard in this period, in the press and in government councils, regretting with greater or lesser emphasis the apparent lack of a clear objective in United States policy. Although stopping aggression was a grand principle, and unexceptionable, it gave no "signal" either to the Communist enemy or to the friends of the United States as to what, in positive terms, the President wished to achieve. This third voice caught the President's ear, or perhaps expressed his own concern. At any rate, this questioning voice was what the President answered when he had reached the point of decision.

In the latter part of March the White House let it be known that Johnson would make a major address on Vietnam at the Johns Hopkins University in Baltimore on April 7. Television time was arranged on all networks, as well as radio facilities for worldwide broadcast. Meanwhile the President went to work on

his critics. On April 2 he invited some twenty-three members of
the liberal pressure group, Americans for Democratic Action, to
the White House to discuss Vietnam policy with him. A.D.A.
had repeatedly criticized Johnson for failing to articulate a
"positive" policy. The "discussion" turned out to be a reading
by the President of the draft of his Baltimore speech. When he
had concluded, this hypercritical group spontaneously applauded.
On the morning of Wednesday, April 7, Johnson invited a group
of Senators, notorious for their opposition to escalating the war
and their pressure for negotiations, to study advance copies of the
speech. For more than an hour, after they had read the text, the
President "reasoned together" with them. If they did not ap-
plaud, they were at least friendly to what the President proposed
to say. It goes without saying that the President's military advisers, already long on record as favoring a hard line in Vietnam,
were consulted during the preparation of the speech.[60]

What some 60 million Americans and uncountable millions
around the world heard was a peculiarly Johnsonian mixture of
something old and something new. There was something old: to
display American commitment to the continuing effort to stop
aggression and build a world of law. There was something new:
to display the President's commitment to the future of Southeast
Asia. There was something for the critics who wished to withdraw, or at least to negotiate at once. There was something for
the critics who wished to carry the war more aggressively against
the Communist enemy. There was, in short, a full-scale appeal to
that "consensus" Johnson often said he wished to build in support of his Administration. But the speech was no grab bag. It
was, on the contrary, a carefully articulated state paper as well
as a moving and politically effective address.

The President began by answering in both general and specific
terms the question: "Why are we in South Vietnam?" "We fight,"
he said, "because we must fight if we are to live in a world where
every country can shape its own destiny. And only in such a
world will our own freedom be finally secure." Such a world, the
President conceded, "will never be built by bombs and bullets.
Yet the infirmities of men are such that force must often precede
reason—and the waste of war, the works of peace." More specifically, the United States was fighting in Vietnam because "over

many years, we have made a national pledge to help South Vietnam defend its independence. I intend," said Johnson, "to keep our promise." The alternative of withdrawal had to be rejected, because "to leave Vietnam to its fate would shake the confidence of . . . people [from Berlin to Thailand] in the value of American commitment. The result would be increased unrest and instability, or even war." The final reason the President offered was his conviction that if the struggle were given up, "the battle would be renewed in one country and then another. The central lesson of our time," he said, "is that the appetite of aggression is never satisfied." If it is argued, he went on, that "China's power is such it is bound to dominate all Southeast Asia . . . there is no end to that argument until all the nations of Asia are swallowed up."

Turning to the bitterly debated issue of American bombing in North Vietnam, the President spelled out his policy and underlined it:

> In recent months, attacks on South Vietnam were stepped up. Thus it became necessary to increase our response and make attacks by air. This is not a change of purpose. It is a change in what we believe that purpose requires.
>
> We do this in order to slow down aggression.
>
> We do this to increase the confidence of the brave people of South Vietnam who have bravely borne this brutal battle for so many years and with so many casualties.
>
> And we do this to convince the leaders of North Vietnam—and all who seek to share their conquest—of a simple fact:
>
> We will not be defeated.
>
> We will not grow tired.
>
> We will not withdraw, either openly or under the cloak of a meaningless agreement.

If this message was clear, Johnson said, "it should also be clear that the only path for reasonable men is the path of peaceful settlement." The conditions for peace would be "an independent South Vietnam—securely guaranteed and able to shape its own relationships to all others—free from outside interference—tied to no alliance—a military base for no other country." The United States, Johnson added, "will never be second in the search for such a peaceful settlement." He was prepared to negotiate immediately and discussions would be "unconditional." If the Communists could—and did—seize upon this word and quote the President's own words to disprove it, they would only be asking the United States to surrender its objective as the price for negotiating about it.

While the United States, and the world, waited for discussions to begin, the President pledged that he would "try to keep the conflict from spreading." "We will use our power with restraint, and with all the wisdom we can command," he said, "but we will use it."

But the fact of war need not blur the purposes of peace. And the President proceeded to outline, in practical terms, his hopes for the modernization of all Southeast Asia.

> Stability and peace do not come easily in such a land. Neither independence nor human dignity will be won by arms alone. It also requires the works of peace. . . .
> The first step is for the countries of Southeast Asia to associate themselves in a greatly expanded cooperative effort for development. We would hope that North Vietnam will take its place in the common effort just as soon as peaceful cooperation is possible.

The United States would bolster the effort of the nations in the area through the United Nations. "And I would hope tonight," the President continued, "that the Secretary General of the United Nations could use the prestige of his great office—and his deep knowledge of Asia—to initiate, as soon as possible, with the countries of the area, a plan for cooperation in increased development." As for the United States, Johnson pledged that he would "ask the Congress to join in a billion dollar investment in this effort when it is underway." He hoped, he said, that "all other industrialized countries—including the Soviet Union—will join in this effort to replace despair with hope, and terror with progress."

Johnson went on to specify what he meant by development:

> The vast Mekong River can provide food and water and power on a scale to dwarf even our own TVA. The wonders of modern medicine can be spread through villages where thousands die for lack of care.

Schools can be established to train people in the skills needed to manage the process of development. . . .

I also intend to expand and speed up a program to make available our farm surplus to assist in feeding and clothing the needy in Asia. . . .

He would, he said, "name a special team of patriotic and distinguished Americans to inaugurate our participation in these programs." And he was not talking of what would be done after peace had been secured; "we cannot wait for peace to begin the job."

In the end Johnson restated some ancient wisdom that has never been popular. "I know this will not be easy," he said. "I know how difficult it is for reason to guide passion and love to master hate. The complexities of this world do not bow easily to pure and consistent answers." He was not impressed by the "guns and bombs, the rockets and warships . . . all symbols of human failure." They are "witness to human folly." But they "protect what we cherish" and may be necessary in order to achieve what is truly impressive: a dam, electric power, a rich harvest, healthy children in a school room. Finally, he said, "we will choose life. And so doing we will prevail over the enemies within man, and over the natural enemies of all mankind."[61]

It was notable that the President said no scathing word about the evils of communism or the Communists. There was no belligerence in the speech, only firmness. But there was firmness in abundance to reassure both South Vietnam and those in the United States and elsewhere who believed in the necessity of the fight. There was no "appeasement." But there was a forthright statement of willingness to end the war, well short of the anti-Communist objectives desired by the so-called "hawks." There would be no withdrawing, but "unconditional discussions" could start immediately. Above all, there was a clear statement of a program for the future. No one could thereafter fairly say that the United States was not clear as to its intentions in Vietnam.

The next day the President replied to the seventeen neutrals in the same terms. Johnson thus gave leadership both to his country and to the cause of freedom and independence and progress in Southeast Asia. The kind of leadership he offered was, of course, divisive, because it could not satisfy those at home or abroad who were opposed to the war. Nor could it satisfy entirely those who feared that bombing in the North would impede negotiations, nor those who favored still more drastic military measures. But within the limits imposed upon him by his conviction that the war was just and necessary, the President skillfully worked to build the consensus, which was his unspoken purpose. How well he succeeded was presently measured by world reaction and by opinion polls at home.

The critical French welcomed the President's address "with reservations." They doubted, said the Foreign Office, "whether China will permit North Vietnam to negotiate the end of a war that sustains Peking's political and propaganda position in Asia." If their judgment was sound, as it proved to be, it is hard to see how President DeGaulle's repeated call for negotiated "neutralization" in Southeast Asia made any sense. The British, for their part, called the speech "statesmanlike and imaginative," while in other Western capitals there was a chorus of approval. In the Pacific and Asia the response was similar. The Australian government, for example, welcomed especially the "very imaginative and constructive" financial inducement to North Vietnam. The Japanese government re-emphasized its solid backing of Johnson's efforts in Vietnam. In Manila there was approval mixed with caution about "pressing negotiations where Communists are concerned."

As the French foretold, and the President no doubt anticipated, the Chinese violently and the North Vietnamese flatly rejected the offer to negotiate. The Russians, in more restrained language, repeated their view that negotiations would be impossible until the United States had withdrawn from the area.

But immediate negotiations were certainly not the outcome Johnson expected from his decisive statement of policy. The other side was still winning; it could not reasonably be expected to yield its momentum to the advantage of the United States and South Vietnam. It was for this reason that the President had so firmly underlined the American intention to stay and to fight. If and when the tide of battle turned, the talk of peace could be formalized. Meanwhile the two sides would continue to exchange signals—and the American signal now sent out by President Johnson was not to be misunderstood by anybody.

But the transcendent purpose of the speech had been to give a "signal" to the American people and to win their support so far as could be. And this the President accomplished. Perhaps the most critical national organization in the field of foreign policy—The National Committee for a Sane Nuclear Policy (SANE)—greeted Johnson's statement enthusiastically. They doubted whether China was playing so great a role in Vietnam as the President said it was, but they nevertheless called the speech "the first major step by the United States toward a peaceful settlement." Editorial comment, from all sides, was favorable if not uniformly uncritical. Public men, including even such Republican stalwarts as Goldwater and Richard Nixon, gave their approval. Congressional approval crossed party lines.[62]

But the issues remained divisive. No speech and no policy on Vietnam could have produced the kind of near unanimity that Presidents Monroe or Eisenhower required before they were prepared to act. The first opinion samples taken after the Baltimore speech showed that Johnson's Vietnam policy was less popular than his stand on any other question. While on domestic issues involved in his program to build a "Great Society" the polls at this time showed 65 to 77 per cent supporting the President, the percentage dropped to 57 on Vietnam. Interviews by opinion analyst Samuel Lubell indicated that Johnson's proposal for a billion-dollar development program had less support than the military measures he was taking, suffering apparently from a general concern that foreign aid over the years had not been effective. Johnson nevertheless continued to press hard on precisely this point. In May, for example, he proposed that the United States push for and support financially an Asian Development Bank. At the same time he called once more "on every industrialized country, including the Soviet Union, to create a better life for the people of Southeast Asia. Surely the works of peace can bring men together in a common effort to abandon forever the ways of war." And he underlined his sincerity by suspending the bombing of North Vietnam for many days. When no answering "signal" was given, he ordered the bombing resumed.[63]

Johnson persisted in his efforts to build support for his policy. Although the nation was treated to widely publicized "teach-ins" by some professors who had been supporters of Kennedy, vigorously and sometimes inaccurately denouncing the United States position in Vietnam, it was worth observing that not one of Kennedy's principal foreign policy advisers, all of whom had been retained by Johnson, thought fit to disagree with the policy or to resign. Indeed, McGeorge Bundy, Kennedy's and Johnson's White House national security adviser, carried the load for the Administration in the "teach-ins," invoking his credentials as a former Dean of Harvard College. But the President himself led the forces of his Administration in speech after speech and in press conferences of all sizes and degrees of formality. Some of his critics thought he spoke too much. However, the people did not appear to think so. Between April and July their support for the President's Vietnam policy, in the face of organized opposition and despite rising American casualties in the war, steadily increased. Over-all support, according to the Harris survey, rose from 57 to 65 per cent. Though 73 per cent favored unconditional negotiations, as did the President, 79 per cent believed that the United States must stand firm to save all of Southeast Asia from going Communist. In domestic terms, at least, Johnson's policy was a success.

From the point of view of understanding presidential leadership the point, of course, is not whether Johnson's policy was correct or would, in the end, be successful. Rather, the point is that he was taking decisive action on a deeply divisive issue by means of unifying tactics. What he said was conciliatory, not only to the Communist enemy but to the various kinds of opposition in his own constituency. His appeal for consensus, his repeated assertion that he would always seek to unify the people, not divide them, was a masterful politics for action, though it had been a politics for inaction as employed by other Presidents. If it could not produce unanimous backing for the hard course he was taking, it nevertheless held nearly intact the consensus he had built in the election campaign, while it made sharp criticism so difficult as to be largely ineffective. With a firm majority supporting his leadership and with criticism thus blunted, the Congress was not likely to place obstacles in the way of the President's conduct of the war or his efforts for peace. When, for example, Johnson asked Congress for $700 million in a special appropriation for the Vietnam war, it was voted in a few days almost unanimously. If the ice was thin, at least there was ice!

8. *Partisanship, thus, makes for effective leadership in foreign affairs* ἓ In the crucial field of foreign affairs it thus appears that the popularity of an unpartisan President is more available to his use as a means to leadership than is the case in domestic affairs. A Monroe could conduct a Latin American policy persistently opposed by some politicians without seriously testing his own popular support, because the objectives of the policy were nearly unanimously approved. An Eisenhower could move the world a short step toward freedom from nuclear terror, because not only his own country but the whole world approved his purposes.

But the President whose popularity is partisan retains nevertheless in many matters an advantage. The frustration of Eisenhower's efforts for a freer trade policy contrasts sharply with the decisive leadership of Polk in dealing with the Oregon question. The one President could not act effectively without alienating important friends; the other could act effectively because he had never expected to make friends on the other side of the issue. The case of Theodore Roosevelt and the Panama Canal may serve as a reminder, however, that vigorous action by the President, with the enthusiastic backing of his partisans, is no warrant that action taken will be wise or prudent, or even in the national interest.

Lyndon Johnson's leadership, finally, like Jefferson's on the embargo, displays tenacity in holding to a divisive course because the President believes that course is in the best interest of the nation he serves. Accepting the obligation to lead, both men accepted also the political consequences of pursuing a controversial policy because they thought it necessary. But Johnson's politics improved upon Jefferson's because it was a politics of conciliation. Johnson seemed to have learned from the un-partisan Presidents the usefulness of promoting an "era of good feeling." His experiment in the politics of consensus, glossing over but never obviating the divisions his commitments required him to sustain, added a new dimension to presidential leadership that would continue to be tested not only by himself but no doubt also by his successors.

# Notes and References

ABBREVIATIONS

L C—Library of Congress
H S P—Historical Society of Pennsylvania
P U L—Princeton University Library
T S A—Tennessee State Archives

## I INTRODUCTION

1. See Richard Neustadt, *Presidential Power: The Politics of Leadership,* 1960, pp. 86–107. Although such other writers as Harold Laski, Clinton Rossiter, Edward S. Corwin, Sidney Hyman, Wilfred E. Binkley, and Louis Koenig all deal with the popularity of American Presidents, only Neustadt tackles the relation between power and popularity directly.

## II THE POLITICS OF PRESIDENTIAL POPULARITY

1. Adlai E. Stevenson, *Major Campaign Speeches,* 1953, p. 9.
2. Monroe to Jefferson, July 27, 1817 (*Writings,* ed. S. Hamilton, VI, 26–29, hereafter cited as *Writings*); Monroe to Madison, July 27, 1817 (Rives Collection, LC).
3. Monroe to Richard Rush, July 20, 1817 (Gratz Collection, HSP); *Daily National Intelligencer,* July 28, 1817.
4. Monroe to Madison, *op. cit.;* Monroe to Jefferson, *ibid.*
5. *Narrative of a Tour of Observation Made During the Summer of 1817,* Philadelphia: A. Mitchell and M. Ames, 1818 (University of Pennsylvania Library).
6. Speech at Louisville, Ky., 1819 (Gratz Collection).
7. John Sherman to W. T. Sherman, November 1, 1867 (Sherman, *Recollections,* 1895, I, 415).
8. Gideon Welles, *Diary,* ed. 1960, II, 477–478.
9. In a series of increasingly disillusioned articles in the *North American Review* (1869–1870) Adams pointed to Grant's failures, despite his great popularity, to give effective leadership, or any leadership at all. He had, Adams said, "recoiled from the task" (October, 1869); James G. Blaine, *Twenty Years of Congress,* 1893, II, 386.

10. The Grant-Eisenhower parallel is richly documented in Russell Farnen's unpublished dissertation, *Grant: The Soldier as Politician,* 1963 (Syracuse University Library).

11. See Harry S. Truman, *Memoirs,* 1956, and Dwight D. Eisenhower, *Crusade in Europe,* 1948.

12. Acceptance Address, Republican National Convention, 1952.

13. See Angus Campbell, Warren Miller, *et al., The Voter Decides,* 1954.

14. *A Summary View of the Rights of British America,* 1775; Virginia Statutes Revised, 1777–1781.

15. Jackson to John Overton, January 22, 1798 (Overton Papers, TSA); also Jackson to Overton, February 23, March 6, 1798; Jackson to Monroe, November 12, 1816 (*Correspondence of Andrew Jackson,* ed. J. S. Bassett, 1926, **II,** 263, hereafter cited as *Correspondence*).

16. A. C. McLaughlin, *Lewis Cass,* 1891, pp. 149–150; J. Q. Adams, *Memoirs,* 1874, **VIII,** 546.

17. Jackson to R. B. Taney, October 13, 1836 (*Correspondence,* **V,** 429–430).

18. See John Jay Chapman, *Causes and Consequences,* 1898, and Amos Pinchot, *History of the Progressive Party,* 1958.

19. *Letters of Theodore Roosevelt,* ed. Elting Morison, 1951, **II,** 1054, hereafter cited as *Letters; ibid.,* 1190.

20. Roosevelt to Charles E. S. Wood, October 23, 1899 (*Letters,* **VII,** 1087–1088).

21. Roosevelt to Henry Cabot Lodge (*Letters,* **II,** 1023, 1166).

22. Roosevelt to Paul de Constant, September 1, 1903 (*Letters,* **III,** 583); Roosevelt to Lemuel Clarke Davis, October 5, 1903 *(Letters,* **III,** 618–619).

23. Roosevelt to Kermit Roosevelt, June 21, 1904 (*Letters,* **IV,** 840).

24. Roosevelt to Lodge, July 19, 1908 (*Letters,* **VI,** 1135).

25. Sara Delano Roosevelt to Franklin D. Roosevelt, October, 1917 (*Personal Letters of Franklin D. Roosevelt,* ed. Elliott Roosevelt, 1948, **II,** 274–275, hereafter cited as *Letters*).

26. *Public Papers and Addresses of Franklin D. Roosevelt,* ed. S. Rosenman, 1938–1945, **II,** 216–217, hereafter cited as *Papers.*

27. See Rexford G. Tugwell, *The Democratic Roosevelt,* 1957, and "The Preparation of a President," *Western Political Quarterly* (June, 1948).

28. Roosevelt to Ray Stannard Baker, *Letters,* **III,** 466–467.

29. See Archie Robertson, "From 'Bully' to 'Vigah,' " *Horizon,* **V,** No. 8 (November, 1963), pp. 68–71.

30. According to a study by Paul B. Sheatsley and Jacob J. Feldman, the rise of Kennedy's partisan following can be measured by the

fact that in July, 1963, 59 per cent of a national sample said that they had voted for Kennedy in 1960, and after his death in 1964, 65 per cent said they had voted for him. The actual vote in 1960 gave Kennedy fractionally less than 50 per cent of the total vote and fractionally more than 50 per cent of the two-party vote. "The Assassination of President Kennedy, A Preliminary Report on Public Reactions and Behavior," *Public Opinion Quarterly* (Summer, 1964).

## III PRESIDENTIAL POPULARITY AND CONSTITUTIONAL ISSUES

1. Jefferson to Mazzei, April 24, 1796 (*Jefferson's Works,* ed. P. L. Ford, **VIII**, 235–241, hereafter cited as *Works*).
2. *Works,* **X**, 36.
3. *Works.* **X**, 3–12.
4. *Works,* **X**, 29.
5. Monroe to Madison, April 18, 1818 (*Writings,* **VI**, 32).
6. See *Niles' Register,* 14, p. 63; Monroe to Madison, April 28, 1818 (*Writings,* **VI**, 49–51).
7. Clay, *Works,* ed. C. Colton, 1904, **I**, 469–470.
8. *Messages and Papers of the President,* 1789–1902, ed. J. Richardson, 1902, **II**, 142–143.
9. *Ibid.,* 173.
10. Monroe to Madison, February 5, 19, 1820 (Rives Papers, LC).
11. *Congressional Globe,* 30th Congress, First Session, Appendix, 67. Senator Westcott, in 1848, inserted into the debate on Oregon a nearly complete set of Monroe's papers dealing with Missouri.
12. Hay to Monroe, November 16, 1820 (*Writings,* **VI**, 159–161).
13. *Congressional Globe, op. cit.,* 66; Richmond *Enquirer,* February 12, 1820.
14. Jackson to Hugh L. White, April 29, 1831 (*Correspondence,* **IV**, 271–272). It is worth noting that by 1835 Jackson was breaking with this once-trusted old friend because of White's opposition to Van Buren as Jackson's successor.
15. *Messages and Papers of the Presidents,* **II**, 451–452.
16. Jackson to Overton, October 22, 1829 (Overton Papers, TSA).
17. *Messages and Papers of the Presidents,* **II**, 483–493.
18. See Grundy to Jackson, October 22, 1829; Ingham to Jackson, November 26, 1829; Berrien to Jackson, November 27, 1829; and Hamilton to Jackson, January 4, 1830 (*Correspondence,* **IV**).
19. *Messages and Papers of the Presidents,* **II**, 462.

20. Jackson to Moses Dawson, July 17, 1830 (*Correspondence*, **IV**, 161–162).

21. Benton to Jackson, June, 1832 (*Correspondence*, **IV**, 445–446).

22. See *Correspondence*, **IV**, 458–459.

23. Quotations from the veto message are in *Messages and Papers of the Presidents*, **II**, 576–591.

24. Jackson to Robert Hayne, February 8, 1831 (*Correspondence*, **IV**, 241–243). See Adrienne Koch and Harry Ammon, "The Virginia and Kentucky Resolutions: An Episode in Jefferson's and Madison's Defense of Civil Liberties," *William and Mary Quarterly*, third series, **V** (April, 1948), 146ff. See also Calhoun's Address, March 4, 1850 (*Congressional Globe*).

25. Jackson to Van Buren, October 29, 1832 (*Correspondence*, **IV**, 483).

26. Draft is in *Correspondence*, **IV**, 489–490.

27. *Correspondence*, **V**, 25–28.

28. See Eisenhower, *Mandate for Change*, 1963.

29. Eisenhower, *Papers*, **II**, 491 (May 19, 1954).

30. *Ibid.*, 700.

31. Eisenhower, *Papers*, **IV**, 269–270.

32. *Ibid.*, 340.

33. See Stuart Gerry Brown, *Conscience in Politics: Adlai E. Stevenson in the 1950's*, 1961, p. 96. See also Eisenhower's Press Conference of March 14, 1956.

34. Eisenhower, *Papers*, **IV**, 668–669; *ibid.*, 737.

35. Eisenhower, *Papers*, **V**, 646.

36. *Ibid.*, 694.

37. Eisenhower, *Papers*, **VI**, 626, and **VII**, 123–124. See *Mandate for Change*, p. 230. "Although as President, I never expressed either approbation or disapproval of a Court decision, in this instance there can be no question that the judgment of the Court was right."

38. Roosevelt, *Letters*, **III**, 459–460.

39. See Roosevelt, *Public Papers and Addresses*, **VI**, 123–124.

40. Roosevelt to Charles Burlingham, February 23, 1937 (*Letters*, **III**, 661–662).

41. Roosevelt, *Papers*, **VI**, 129–130.

## IV   PRESIDENTIAL POPULARITY AND DOMESTIC POLICY

1–7. *Messages and Papers of the Presidents*, **II**, 8–9, 18, 60, 73–74, 91–92, 106–107, 191–192, 215.

8. *Correspondence*, **V**, 32–33.

9. Two unpublished letters in the archives of the State of Tennessee reveal that Kendall introduced himself by mail to Jackson on August 22, 1827. "Although I have never had the pleasure of a personal acquaintance with you, there are some circumstances of a peculiar nature which induce me now to address you. . . ." On August 27 Kendall followed up his discussion of the political situation in Kentucky with a formal invitation to Jackson to attend a dinner in his honor in Frankfort. Jackson did not attend, but some 4,000 Jacksonians did, in contrast to the 2,000 who turned out for Clay. See also *Correspondence*, III, 379.

10–15. *Correspondence*, V, 75–101 (McLane's paper), 102, 107–108, 111–112, 113–114, 115, 128, 129, 147–148.

16. The full report of the government directors is given in *Correspondence*, V, 160–165; Jackson to Polk, August 20, 1833 (*ibid.*, 168).

17. Jackson to Van Buren, August, 1833 (*ibid.*, 154, 159); Van Buren to Jackson, September 14, 1833 (*ibid.*, 185).

18. Kendall to Jackson, August 11, 1833 (*ibid.*, 152).

19. Jackson to Van Buren, September 19, 1833 (*ibid.*, 203).

20. Jackson to Van Buren, September 23, 1833 (*ibid.*, 206).

21. See E. A. McCormac, *James K. Polk*, 1922, p. 660.

22. *Messages and Papers of the Presidents*, IV, 406–408.

23. Polk, *Diary*, I, 367–371 (April, 1846).

24. *Messages and Papers of the Presidents*, VIII, 39.

25. Quoted in Henry F. Pringle, *Theodore Roosevelt*, 1931, p. 267.

26. Roosevelt, *Letters*, III, 349.

27. Roosevelt to Lodge, September 27, 1902 (*Letters*, III, 331).

28–30. Roosevelt to Lodge; to Mark Hanna; to Grover Cleveland; October, 1902 (*Letters*, III, 331, 337–338, 339).

31. See *Letters*, III, 362, and Roosevelt, *Autobiography*, 1913, p. 475.

32. Roosevelt, *Autobiography*, pp. 476ff.

33. *Letters*, IV, 806–807.

34. James Marlow, Associated Press News Analysis, April 27, 1964.

35. *Public Papers and Addresses*, IV, 47.

36. Rexford G. Tugwell, *The Democratic Roosevelt*, p. 375.

37. *Papers*, IV, 134–135.

38. *Ibid.*, 324–325.

39. *New York Times*, September 27, 1936. For a useful account of Landon's misfortunes with social security, see Arthur M. Schlesinger, Jr., *The Politics of Upheaval*, 1960, pp. 610ff. See also Harold F. Gosnell, *Champion Campaigner: Franklin D. Roosevelt*, 1952, pp. 155ff.

40. *Papers*, V, 392–393.

41. Quoted by Schlesinger, *op. cit.*, p. 635.

42–46. *Papers*, V, 529, 536, 548–549, 560–561, 568–569, 570.

47. Eisenhower, *Mandate for Change*, p. 193; *Papers*, I, 406–407.

48. *Mandate for Change,* p. 193.
49. Eisenhower's account of the Durkin episode is in *Mandate for Change,* pp. 195ff.
50. *Papers,* II, 51.
51. *Papers,* VII, 428 (June 3, 1959).


V  PRESIDENTIAL  POPULARITY
AND  FOREIGN  POLICY

1. *Washington Globe,* April 28, 1844; Clay to Crittenden, April 21, 1844 (Crittenden Papers, LC).
2. Polk to Johnson, May 13, 14, 1844 (Polk Papers, LC). Polk had directed his own campaign with similar caution and toughness when he ran for Governor in 1839, as an unpublished letter to Jackson shows: "I saw the President last night. He intends during the months of April and May to make a tour through the Southern and some of the Southwestern States, and will visit Tennessee or not as may be thought best by his friends. My settled opinion is, and I frankly so informed him, that his appearance in the State in the midst of our elections, would have a decidedly bad effect and would probably be followed by disastrous consequences. . . . Upon communicating these views to him, Mr. Van Buren at once said he would not place his friends in such a situation, and we separated with the understanding that after full conference with you and other friends upon my return home, I was to invite him to New Orleans, and he would be governed in his movements by our advice. . . ." (Polk to Jackson, February 7, 1839, TSA). Jackson, less subtle than Polk, wrote Van Buren that he saw no objection to the President's visit to Tennessee. If the Whigs, as Polk suggested, wished to cry "Dictator," let them. (See *Correspondence,* VI, 6). The point, of course, was that Polk could hardly tell Van Buren that the real reason for keeping him away from the state during the campaign was the President's massive unpopularity in the West.
3. Polk to Johnson, May 14, 1844 (Polk Papers, LC).
4. *Washington Globe,* May 6, October 29, 1844.
5. Polk to Johnson, December 21, 1844 (Polk Papers, LC).
6. *Messages and Papers of the Presidents,* IV, 381, 382.
7. *Washington Union,* May 12, 1845.
8–12. Polk, *Diary,* I, 3, 4–7 *passim,* 11–12, 62–65 *passim,* 76–83 *passim.*
13. *Ibid.,* 89–102 *passim; Messages and Papers,* IV, 395, 397.
14–22. Polk, *Diary,* I, 119–120, 122–123, 129, 131–132, 133–135, 148–149, 264–265, 280, 297.

23. *Messages and Papers, op. cit.*, 426–427; *Diary,* I, 325, 345.
24. Jefferson to General John Mason, 1807 (*Works,* ed. Lipscomb and Bergh, XI, 402).
25. Jefferson to Gallatin, October 8, 1807 (*Works,* ed. Ford, X, 503). Ford prints both the first and second drafts with the corrections and revisions made in each. The version cited here is as it appeared in the first draft without revision. Gallatin to Jefferson, October 21, 1807 (*Writings,* ed. Henry Adams, I, 358–361).
26. Gallatin, *Writings,* I, 367–369; Jefferson, *Works,* ed. Ford, X, 530–531.
27. J. Q. Adams, *Writings,* ed. C. F. Adams, III, 168; Adams, *Diary,* ed. A. Nevins, December 31, 1807; Plumer to J. Q. Adams, December 22, 1807 (Plumer Papers, LC).
28. See Louis M. Sears, *Jefferson and the Embargo,* 1927, pp. 68ff.
29. Leonard D. White, *The Jeffersonians,* 1961, gives an excellent history of embargo legislation and its administration.
30. Jefferson, *Works,* ed. Lipscomb and Bergh, XII, 56, 66, 83.
31. James Bowdoin to Jefferson, June 9 and July 18, 1808 (Jefferson Papers, LC).
32. See Gallatin, *Writings,* I, 398; and Jefferson, *Works,* ed. Lipscomb and Bergh, XII, 122.
33. Jefferson to Madison, September 6, 1808 (*Works,* ed. Lipscomb and Bergh, XII, 158).
34. *Ibid.,* 161.
35. Jefferson to Madison, August 9, 1808 (*Works,* ed. Lipscomb and Bergh, XII, 119). Passages from the message are in *Works,* ed. Ford, XI, 64–65. In one respect Jefferson did take Gallatin's advice. In the draft the President spoke enthusiastically about the development of domestic manufactures under the stress of the embargo. On a number of occasions, indeed, he had given encouragement to manufacturers to a point almost reversing his stand against Hamilton in the 1790's. But when Gallatin drew his attention to the apparent endorsement of a manufacturing economy not only above agriculture but above commerce, too, Jefferson toned down the language and dealt with the matter in low key, evidently not wishing to alienate any more of the "Old Republicans" than he had to. See Gallatin, *Writings,* I, 423–424, and Jefferson, *Works,* ed. Ford, XI, 69–70.
36. See the discussion of this law in White, *op. cit.,* pp. 463–464.
37. Jefferson to Thomas Mann Randolph, January 2, 1809 (Jefferson Papers, LC).
38. See Sears, *op. cit.,* Chs. IX, X; and White, *op. cit.,* p. 471.
39. Roosevelt, *Autobiography,* pp. 512, 548.

40. The principal sources on the Panama affair are: *Diplomatic History of the Panama Canal* (Senate Document 474, 63rd Congress, 2d session); *The Story of Panama* (Hearings before the House Committee on Foreign Affairs, Washington, 1913); Philippe Bunau-Varilla, *Panama: the Creation, Destruction, and Resurrection,* 1913; Henry F. Pringle, *Roosevelt,* Bk. II, Chs. 5–6; Tyler Dennett, *John Hay,* 1933, Ch. XXX.

41. Pringle, *op. cit.,* pp. 310–312.

42. Roosevelt, *Autobiography,* pp. 513–514; Roosevelt, *Letters,* III, 625; Pringle, *op. cit.,* p. 318; Roosevelt, *Autobiography,* pp. 530–531.

43–44. Dennett, *op. cit.,* pp. 381, 378–379, 382.

45. Monroe to Rush, March 13, 1817 (Rush Papers, PUL).

46. Adams to Gallatin, May 19, 1818 (*Writings,* VI, 317).

47. Memorandum dated October, 1817 (Monroe Papers, LC).

48. *Papers of Henry Clay,* ed. James Hopkins and Mary Hargraves, 1961, II, 517.

49. Adams, *Diary,* ed. Nevins, p. 236.

50. Monroe to Hay, May 19, 1818 (Hoes Collection, LC); *Messages and Papers of the Presidents,* II, 43–44.

51. Adams, *Memoirs,* IV, 223–225. See Samuel F. Bemis, *John Quincy Adams and the Foundations of American Foreign Policy,* 1949, pp. 347–349.

52. *Messages and Papers of the Presidents,* II, 57; Adams, *Memoirs,* V, 285–286.

53. *Annals of Congress,* 16th Congress, 2d session, pp. 1081–1092 *passim.*

54. *Messages and Papers of the Presidents,* II, 116–117.

55–56. Emmet John Hughes, *The Ordeal of Power: A Political Memoir of the Eisenhower Years,* 1963, pp. 140–142, 103–112 *passim.*

57. Eisenhower, *Peace with Justice,* 1961, pp. 34–44.

58. Sherman Adams, *Firsthand Report,* 1961, p. 110.

59. *Peace with Justice,* pp. 54–65; *Mandate for Change,* pp. 252–255; Adams, *op. cit.,* p. 112.

60. *ADA World,* April, 1965.

61. Citations from Johnson's address are taken from the text in the *New York Times,* April 8, 1965.

62. See *New York Times* for April 9, 1965, and succeeding days.

63. Speech to the Association of Political Cartoonists, May 13, 1965, as reported by the Associated Press.

# Index

National Guard, Alabama, 109
*National Intelligencer* (newspaper), 8, 185
National Labor Relations Act, 164
"National Liberation Front," 249
National Resources Committee, 114; *see also* Roosevelt, Franklin D.
National Youth Administration, 114, 164; *see also* Roosevelt, Franklin D.
NATO, *see* North Atlantic Treaty Organization
Neuberger, Richard, 107
Neustadt, Richard, 2
New Deal, 18–19, 46, 49, 51, 112 ff., 160 ff.
Second, 48, 114, 160; *see also* Roosevelt, Franklin D.
*New England Palladium* (newspaper), 217
*New Republic, The* (magazine), 2, 102
*Niles' Register*, 67
Nixon, Richard M., 24, 52, 110, 240, 257
Nobel Prize for peace, 41
North Atlantic Treaty Organization (NATO), 19, 20
Northern Securities Company, 40, 147
"Notes on Nullification" (Madison), 94
NRA, 48, 111, 112, 164; *see also* Roosevelt, Franklin D.
"Nullification Proclamation" (Jackson), 95

Old Hickory, *see* Jackson, Andrew
Organization of American States (OAS), 222
Overton, John, 82

Pakenham, Richard, 190, 202
Panama Canal Company, 224, 225, 228; *see also* Roosevelt, Theodore
Panama Treaty, 228

Panic of 1837, 143
Parker, Alton B., 40, 222, 229
Pickering, Timothy, 218
Pierce, Franklin, 1
Pillow, Gideon, 187
Pinckney, C. C., 218
Pinkney, William, 221
Platt, Thomas C., 34, 35, 36–37, 147
Plumber's Union, 173
Plumer, William, 211, 212
Polk, James K., 42, 87, 141–42, 186–207, 230
campaign of 1844, 188
"Constitutional Treasury," 143–46
*Diary*, 190–91
election of 1844, 144
first annual message, 144
first message to Congress (1845), 193
Inaugural Address, 189–91
Mexican policy, 183, 239
opposes Clay's American System, 144
Oregon dispute, 183–84, 188–206, 259
partisanship of, 206
popularity of, 144, 146
retires from Congress, 143
runs for Governor of Tennessee, 143
State of the Union message (1845), 193
Mexican policy, 183
Texas annexation, 188
Poore, Ben Perley, 14
Powell, Adam Clayton, 107, 179–80
*Profiles in Courage* (Kennedy), 54
Pullman strike of 1894, 147

Quay, Matt, 148, 149, 151, 152

Railroad Retirement Act, 112
Randall Commission, 241
Randolph, John, 27, 218
forms "Tertium Quids," 80
Randolph, T. M., 220
Rayburn, Sam, 178